Creativity and Advertising

Creativity and Advertising develops novel ways to theorise advertising and creativity. Arguing that combinatory accounts of advertising based on representation, textualism and reductionism are of limited value, Andrew McStay suggests that advertising and creativity are better recognised in terms of the 'event'. Drawing on a diverse set of philosophical influences including Scotus, Spinoza, Vico, Kant, Schiller, James, Dewey, Schopenhauer, Whitehead, Bataille, Heidegger and Deleuze, the book posits a sensational, process-based, transgressive, lived and embodied approach to thinking about media, aesthetics, creativity and our interaction with advertising.

Elaborating an affective account of creativity, McStay assesses creative advertising from Coke, Evian, Google, Sony, Uniqlo and Volkswagen among others, and articulates the ways in which award-winning creative advertising may increasingly be read in terms of co-production, playfulness, ecological conceptions of media, improvisation, and immersion in fields and processes of corporeal affect.

Philosophically wide-ranging yet grounded in robust understanding of industry practices, the book will also be of use to scholars with an interest in aesthetics, art, design, media, performance, philosophy and those with a general interest in creativity.

Andrew McStay lectures at Bangor University and is author of *Digital Advertising, The Mood of Information: A Critique of Online Behavioural Advertising* and *Deconstructing Privacy*, the latter forthcoming in 2014.

Creativity and Advertising
Affect, events and process

Andrew McStay

Routledge
Taylor & Francis Group

LONDON AND NEW YORK

First published 2013
by Routledge
2 Park Square, Milton Park, Abingdon, Oxon OX14 4RN

Simultaneously published in the USA and Canada
by Routledge
711 Third Avenue, New York, NY 10017

*Routledge is an imprint of the Taylor & Francis Group,
an informa business*

British Library Cataloguing in Publication Data
A catalogue record for this book is available from the British Library

Library of Congress Cataloging in Publication Data
McStay, Andrew, 1975–
Creativity and advertising : affect, events and process / Andrew McStay.
  pages cm
Includes bibliographical references.
1. Advertising. 2. Creative ability. I. Title.
HF5821.M37 2013
659.1–dc23   2012048477

ISBN: 978-0-415-51954-0 (hbk)
ISBN: 978-0-415-51955-7 (pbk)
ISBN: 978-0-203-49220-8 (ebk)

Typeset in Sabon
by Cenveo Publisher Services

Printed and bound in Great Britain by MPG Printgroup

Contents

1 Introducing the sensational world of creativity and advertising

The notion of creativity is at the very centre of contemporary advertising. Indeed, the inside cover of Andrew Cracknell's book *The Real Mad Men* (2011) reveals: 'Of all the places where people make money, advertising is one of the most exotic. People are paid to be crazy and applauded for being heretic. It's where commerce meets showbiz and where hard money meets artistic whimsy.' Creative output is an advertising agency's calling card and, given that agencies do not formally advertise their services, their creative capacity is judged by the advertising they produce. The centrality of creativity is not only the opinion of many within the advertising industry, but also clients who employ advertising agencies and come seeking magic so to better their intangible brand assets and fortunes, raise awareness of charitable causes, and persuade voters one way or another.

Without creativity, the world of advertising agencies would look utterly different. As a discourse that informs and comprises both boutiques and behemoths, the notion of creativity permeates all areas of the advertising business. It is literally the means by which many people in advertising define themselves and while one might doubt the existence of 'true' creativity in advertising, what is undeniable is the self-identification of the advertising business as a creative one. It also deeply affects the output of the industry and that which it valorises and rewards. Of course, from an outsider's point of view, the idea that advertising is creative might come as a surprise, particularly given that our reaction to the majority of advertising, at best, tends towards indifference. Too often advertising tends towards the pornographic in that frequently it lacks guile, is lurid, crass, leaves nothing to the imagination and is utterly lacking in seductive qualities. This low-grade advertising that permeates the vast gamut of our mediated experiences is not the focus of this book. Instead my interest is in that which wins awards and that which is experimental in its trials of newer forms of media, modes of representation or means of affecting us.

The advertising sector's intensity of feeling about the value of creativity is evidenced in industry blogs, publications such as the US-based *Advertising Age*, and the UK weekly industry periodical *Campaign*, which are awash with discussions of creative awards and creative excellence. Despite this, thought-out suggestions as to what the word might mean are not forthcoming. Even the ad world's most thoughtful commentators such as Jeremy Bullmore (2006) tend toward quite hackneyed accounts of creativity involving expressions such as the 'Mad Inventor' who challenges convention, makes novel connections and invents new analogies (this person is contrasted with 'Time-and-Motion Man'). Trade associations for the creative advertising industry such as D&AD (2012), originally British Design & Art Direction, are similarly hazy and brief on what creativity might signify. D&AD's website for example refers to creatives as curious, restless, bloody-minded, commercially savvy, weird, sometimes romantic and other times cynical. The judging criteria for the highly sought-after D&AD awards provides a little more detail. For example, in 2012 these were threefold where the work was to contain a highly original and inspiring idea; be exceptionally well executed; and be relevant to its context (D&AD, 2012a). Indeed, the role of the idea continues to be pre-eminent in creative advertising and people in advertising are obsessed with ideas – or the guiding thought that dictates what is to be said and the means by which this is best expressed.

However, as creativity contributes so much to the advertising industry and elsewhere, this is still an unsatisfying and unclear account for those seeking a more specific definition or deeper insights. The aim here is to interrogate that which goes unquestioned and assess, probe and better understand the relationship between creativity and advertising. We will not reach a final conclusion on what *it* is but rather the aim is to open up new borders, depths and dimensions in how we think about creativity, and its relationships with advertising.

The book then is not aimed at a specific audience but is for anyone with an interest in creativity, advertising, media, representation, developments in commercial persuasion and how we might account for these in the broadest possible terms. It will also be most enjoyed by those of a philosophical disposition. As will become clear the book is wide-ranging and encompasses many modes of thinking and approaches. While this is an academic monograph and jargon is to be expected, it is highly interdisciplinary and I have tried where possible to pare back the language around ideas for them to be as accessible as possible. (Apologies in advance for where I have not succeeded in this.)

In addressing creativity and advertising, I develop and explore two key propositions that appear in various guises throughout the book:

1 Creativity in advertising is not just representational but sensational;
2 Creativity involves acts of will in situations without clear determinates.

The first point has to do with the premise that longstanding approaches within cultural and media studies to understanding creativity and advertising are predicated on what will be accounted for as combinatory approaches to representation. These I argue are limited in their capacity to adequately characterise creative endeavour. Where advertising was once synonymous with frame-based visual representation (generally conceived in terms of posters, press and television) things have developed in light of newer forms of media, novel modes of engagement and also approaches that are less contingent on visual media. Where the professionalisation of advertising from the turn of the nineteenth into the twentieth century involved developments in representation, play with meaning and the building of sign value through knack and high proficiency with images and words, this version of advertising is no longer as assured as it used to be. Likewise, Saussurean-inspired semiotic critique of advertising is not as all-embracing as it once was. Identification of impotency in traditional approaches used to account for developments in advertising first appeared in my book *The Mood of Information* (McStay, 2011) that deals with feedback systems and political economy, and emerged in a very different guise in the writing of the book you are reading now. Both books however express dissatisfaction with the semiotic, representational and ideological enterprise to account for advertising. Where *The Mood of Information* examined online behavioural advertising, media and biocapitalist concerns, *Creativity and Advertising* is different in orientation. It shares, however, a common sentiment in that it recognises the dramatic shifts to have taken place in the practice of advertising and that the once assured indexical link between images, representation and advertising is no longer as firm as it was once thought to be.

In loose alliance with what has been dubbed 'the affective turn' (Clough, 2007) and its digressions from the pre-eminence of representation, the arguments presented here derive in part from the developing advertising and media environment, and the ways in which commercially harnessed creativity is adapting in light of this. Indeed, criticisms of representational accounts of media are emerging from many quarters. These revolve around the observation that representational or textual approaches are over-concerned with images and do not pay enough attention to place, time and the 'liveness', 'nowness' or 'vitality' that accompanies mediation (Kember and Zylinska, 2012). The origins of the affective turn are generally located in Spinoza (1996 [1677]) who opposed mind–body dualism, preferring instead a monism that more directly links mental goings-on with the body. Affective accounts, then, have less to do with abstractions, and more to do with drives, motivations, will, emotion, feelings and sensations. For Spinoza, these were not incidental to being human, but a central feature. Deleuze's (1988 [1970]) monograph on Spinoza, along with later writing with Guattari, has also done much to bring affect back to critical attention. This places the capacity for affect in relation to an expanded idea of what constitutes a body and opens up corporeal capacities of affect to visual and other image-making systems. In Deleuzo-Guattarian terms, affect is an aesthetic activity in the way that artists (and here argued advertisers) are interested in generating intense and affective experiences that take the body (including the brain) from one condition to another.

While affect-based theory suffers from being a repository of everything that is non-representational and non-semantic (Grossberg, 2010), indirectly affect provides a mode or gateway with which to engage with media, advertising and contemporary communications programmes in a less imagistic way. It allows us to think of advertising as a field of attention, attraction and affect. The idea is thus to consider creative advertising less in terms of abstraction, but more in terms of stimulation and sensation – or that which is experienced in a lived and embodied place, time, field of movement and action, and is engaged with. In spite of this, my argument has less to do with rejecting representational approaches than to broaden understanding about the means and affects that advertising generates. Rather, the semiotic aspect becomes merely one dimension of experience in what are accounted for here as *events*. This means that we might think about creativity and advertising as including ideas and corporeal experiences, rather than just the more usual symbolic dimension. More plainly phrased, although in analysing advertising through a representational lens we typically tend to decontextualise it from the context that was intended by media planners and buyers, the world of advertising is very much about affect, calls to action and moving us to behave a certain way or engage in a given act. This zone in-between idea and thing is argued here as being aesthetic, sensational and intensive.

Rather than thinking about advertising as a system that appropriates, steals (although many in advertising will readily own up to this) and re-presents meanings from elsewhere to sell and make its points, this book also accounts for what is unique, immediate and affective about individual advertising events. The idea of the 'event' is a term that will be employed throughout and goes to the heart of the methodological and philosophical orientation of this book. Emerging first from the Stoics around 300 BCE and subsequently traceable through Leibniz in the seventeenth to eighteenth centuries, and onto Whitehead and Deleuze in the twentieth century, it prefers processes to substances, happenings rather than things, multiplicity over solidity, and being as becoming (Bowden, 2011; Deleuze, 2011 [1969]; Shapiro, 2012). The event in this case is that which is irreducible to composite or fixed things and while an event or singularity is clearly linked to parts that are involved, there is also an extra dimension comprised of a novel and indivisible character. My general orientation, then, differs from representational approaches and rather than thinking about objects, things or symbols, this book privileges process as it is this which gives rise to that which we understand as objects. This perspective sees the object as the abstraction and reality as made up of ongoing processes. Indeed, the event as a point of engagement sees the coming together of a wider range of processes and happenings so to comprise a nexus, or multiplicity of becomings – each unique and novel. For Whitehead (1964 [1920]) an event is that which occurs during a period of time and is comprised of a specific character. This character comes to be by dint of being related to other events. These might be as commonplace as the noticing of the shadow of trees on the books that line my office wall, the ringing of my mobile phone, the chilli plant growing on the windowsill, my external hard-drive whirring to automatically back-up, the sharp pencil marking the paper as these notes were originally made, or indeed, as this book explores, creative advertising. The idea of the event is predicated on a sense of temporal immediacy disclosed in sense-awareness. As Massumi (2011) in discussion of Whitehead points out, there are two factors requiring attention in accounting for events: first there is the relational coming together of parts and factors so to comprise something more than the sum of these interrelations; second is the qualitative dimension of the event where a character is generated that is discerned by feeling. This latter point does not lend to post-event analysis, but rather is immediate and to be accounted for as it unfolds and happens.

Should the passage above be too woolly and vague then consider that an experience of any sort is not just about theoretical abstractions, being locked up in private intellectual processing, but that experiences emerge out of embodied engagement with things in the world that themselves exist as an outcome of other processes. After all, advertising is never solely experienced as an abstraction or assemblage of theoretical propositions so why should we conceive it so? Advertising is deeply experiential and staff of all departments in advertising agencies are interested in what goes on at the meeting place between people, their advertising and the impressions or affects that are generated at that engagement point.

The point then is to restore some balance between textual and structurally-inspired criticism, and what here is accounted for in terms of sensation, affect, quality, media, co-creativity, interactivity and machinic arrangements (to borrow the latter from Deleuze and Guattari, 2003 [1980]). The two approaches differ as textual accounts generally have little interest in the embodied practice of advertising itself. Rather, such criticism uses advertising as a way of exploring wider social structures and cultural phenomena. These are generally depicted within a critical framework of representation, commodity fetishism, and manipulative and exploitative accounts of capitalism (Marcuse, 1964; Williamson, 1978; Arriaga, 1984). Textual accounts derive from linguistics and while this lends methodological rigour and insight to accounts of representation, it also means that advertising is compartmentalised within existing frameworks, categories and out of connection with everyday experience. This emphasis is important, as much recent award-winning creative work is contingent upon real-time engagement and temporally-bound advertising events. Contemporary examples might take the form of unfolding interaction on social networking sites, activities in metaverses, the use of new media search tools to find things in real life, in-situ happenings that are simultaneously web-cast, and with wider use of more recent media forms that blurs online and offline goings-on.

Textual analysis is that where advertising is dissected, decoded, seen as mediating something else, interpreted and contextualised within larger structures. I do not disagree per se with this, but see it as a rather one-dimensional approach to understanding advertising. My emphasis here is less about critical frameworks, but more about considering advertising in terms of affective experience, interaction, embodiment, co-creation, emotional faculties and felt experiences of contemporary creative advertising. The focus here then is mostly on the aesthetic dimension understood in the older sense of lived sensational experience, rather than having to do with beauty and taste. Further, we cannot properly understand objects of our attention without knowing something of the causal conditions that give rise to them. In textual accounts of advertising, this tends to be framed in relation to critical accounts of capitalism and ideology. My chosen tack is to assess another causal factor – creativity. Undoubtedly there will be differing views on the existence of traces of creativity in the products of advertising, but what is clear is that creativity in advertising is a key dynamic and primary mover, and if not these, it is certainly a belief and ideology that impels those who produce advertising.

This brings me to my second proposition and opening definition of creativity that describes the process as an act of will in situations without clear determinates. This suggestion is underpinned by broad discussion throughout this book on how this proposed definition has been arrived at and what the constitutive words in the sentence represent. The context to this is largely Kantian, particularly in regard to his Copernican revolution where Kant (1990 [1781]) posits that we relate to objects through representations and organising principles that we project into them. This might be read as a liberational notion in that destabilisation of the given allows for all manner of shaping, forming and creative acts.

In regards to what this book is not, there are four points to be made: firstly, as will already be clear, it is not a 'how to' book on advertising and creativity. Practitioners of advertising have far more useful things to say on this than academics.[1] It is not an easy book either as a wide range of material has been drawn upon to generate unique and far-reaching understanding of both creativity and advertising. While on occasion we might enjoy being able to scan a book safe in the domain of known ideas, albeit with novel application of acknowledged concepts, this book will require more time and a closer read.

Second, it is not a generalist account of creativity. Originally the book was broader and more comprehensive in relation to the various areas of study that have something to say on creativity but as the writing of the book progressed it became apparent that was there little utility or benefit in painting a broad picture of how creativity has been treated across various literatures. While arguably some context has been lost, this has allowed space to advance what I feel are more focused and related issues. For those who want it, useful overviews of creativity include Vernon (1970), Weisberg (1993), Lau et al. (2004), Boden (2004), Negus and Pickering (2004), Pope (2005), Runco (2006) and Kaufman and Sternberg (2010), who all offer accessible overviews of discussion and debate historically associated with creativity.

Third, this book is very much Western in orientation and takes seriously remarks that Western discussion of creativity and the imposition of its conceptions have hindered scholars in the East (Lau et al., 2004). As such I am keen not to engage in the same and restrict my commentary to pointing out that differences exist, particularly in relation to the premise that Western creativity tends to be predicated on an outcome or product, and the production of ideas through divergence and originality. In some contrast to the West's insistence on the new, Eastern conceptions of creativity frequently involve re-interpreting traditional ideas or finding new points of view on the past (Lubart and Georgsdottir, 2004). Typically, rather than break with tradition, there is a tendency to express or see it in new (or novel) ways. This manifests in terms of technique and mastery, where much effort is expended on acquiring these. Creativity then adapts, reworks and extends these (see also Gardner, 1997). Many of the synonyms we use for creativity (for example, invention, novelty, individualism, newness, novelty) may also seem foreign and possibly absurd and illusionary to Easterners such as the Chinese (Rudowicz, 2004). Other factors include greater involvement of social and moral values, where notions of collectivism play a much greater role than in the West. Of course, such an account does not even begin to take into account the forces of globalisation and hybridisation that make accounting from afar so problematic.

Fourth, although I am sensitive to critical approaches to advertising from the fields of cultural and media studies, and have myself written critical books and papers on advertising (McStay, 2009; 2011; 2011a; 2012), it will already be clear that this book is different in tone. While remarkably little critical material on creativity in advertising exists, there are general approaches that might be pre-empted. These include the role of advertising as stimulating unhealthy behaviour in society and the seeking of happiness through buying things. For instance, in accounts of consumer societies, advertising does not stimulate rational choice but rather an unhealthy attachment between producer and audience formed at a supra-linguistic level generated through simulation and the rearrangement of signifiers for commercial and strategic ends (Baudrillard, 1998 [1970]; Poster, 1995). Typically frame-based representation in Marxian-inspired thinking involves the pre-eminence of the commodity-form in society and the ways in which stimulation of consumption brings about overly self-focused behaviour. Beyond the individual, advertising as the outward face of capitalism tends (unsurprisingly) to assist already dominant groups of people in society and promote social structures favourable to the advancement of capitalism. Advertising – and creativity therein – also stands accused of generating undesirable social trends, behaviours or pathologies (for example smoking, unhealthy eating or body image issues).

The association of creativity with all of this will be distasteful for some. Indeed, we might retreat to the arts that are sometimes thought of as an antidote to commodity aesthetics (Pope, 2005). However, while we tend to see a division between art as the product of free lone visionaries, and creativity in advertising as subject to the whims of patrons and clients, this has not always been the case as artists have long been supported and dictated to by religious, political and financially well-endowed figures (Schapiro, 1994). Should creativity in advertising be admitted, it might be described as being wasted on an industry in the business of promoting materialism, excess, the ideological supremacy of commodity relations, alienation, and mental and physical pollution. Although the excesses of critical opinion have been toned down and few now refer to popular culture as a "sadistic phantasy" as Fromm (2002 [1956]) did, beyond its textual and economic significance, creativity in advertising remains largely out of the media and cultural studies loop.

In such accounts, real creativity lies in a much more rarefied place away from advertisements and inducements. Raymond Williams – who remains deeply influential in media and cultural studies – exemplifies this, bemoaning the contemporary use of the word 'creativity' and its lack of emphasis, application and precise meaning to depict general kinds of activity, remarking: 'Thus any imitative or stereotyped literary work can be called, by convention, creative writing, and advertising copywriters officially describe themselves as creative' (1976: 84). Deleuze and Guattari similarly express:

> Finally, the most shameful moment came when computer science, marketing, design and advertising, all the disciplines of communication, seized hold of the word *concept* itself and said: 'This is our concern, we are the creative ones, we are the *ideas men!* ... '
> (Deleuze and Guattari, 2011 [1994]: 10, emphasis in original)

Clearly, given antipathy towards advertising, the link between advertising, capital and creativity is going to be uncomfortable.

The problem is that if we grant advertising creative status, we open the door for the hijacking of creativity by the 'cultural industries'. Here both art for itself and the applied arts become subsumed by commercial rationality, and the creative act and its output are betrayed and usurped by something foreign (for examples of critique see Lovink and Rossiter, 2007). Clearly Adorno and Horkheimer (2005 [1944]) and the wider writings of the Frankfurt School also have much to say on this, but we might summarise by pointing to their concerns about culture as being prone to quantification, innovation in segmentation and industrial logic. Ewen (2001 [1977]) similarly points to advertising as the aspect of cultural production that, by means of a science of inducements, fashions docile subjects that eschew exploration or self-determination in favour of perpetual discontent (so persuadable to buy more things).

More preferable for some is a view of creativity where value is intrinsic, without reason, utility or even purpose. Driving home changes in the status of philosophy and ideas, Deleuze and Guattari also remark that Plato could never have imagined what was to come in his most comic (or catastrophic) musings on the nature of ideas. As advertising has conceived itself as that which deals in 'big ideas', it is understandable that for critical commentators this type of discourse represents cultural poverty and is to be guarded against. Extrapolating somewhat, philosophy and creativity have been deterritorialised from intellectual and artistic preserves, and reterritorialised with a foreign set of relations involving commerce. It is not only principles, traces and outcomes of creative endeavour that are deterritorialised, but past visions are reframed so for canon to be reduced to cliché to fit the meta-discourse of the creative industries.

Moreover, from a critical perspective, the contemporary commodification of creativity has resonance with the harnessing of labour-power in industrial capitalism (Suarez-Villa, 2009). The Italian Autonomous Marxist, Berardi, likewise argues that we may think of alienation in our present post-industrial times as being 'marked by the submission of the soul, in which animated, creative, linguistic, emotional corporeality is subsumed and incorporated by the production of value' (2009: 109). Wider contemporary critical discussion is also taking place in regard to affective and immaterial labour in relation to new media and advertising (Fuchs, 2011; McStay, 2011), and the broader ways in which labour is not just corporeal, but generates intellectual and emotional output and affects (Hardt and Negri, 2000).

In *The Grundrisse*, Marx (1973 [1939]) directly comments on creativity, noting that a key aspect of being human is our capacity to engage in creative activity. For Marx this is eroded under capitalism, labour processes, alienation and the denial of individual creative fulfilment. Similarly, Raymond Williams (1977) sees creativity and self-creation as being metaphysically at the centre of Marxism by means of self-composition, developing new modes of consciousness and confronting hegemonic processes going on within the self. We can then draw attention to the commodification of creativity as occurring on three fronts: concern over the utilisation of creative and co-productive affective/immaterial labour alongside the excavation of value through data mining in advertising and/or user-generated content; that creativity becomes a form of labour and this takes creative workers away from more fulfilling endeavours; and the ways in which creativity has been reterritorialised with a more instrumental character.

Battle-lines are drawn, and there is little chance of rapprochement between advertising and its critics any time soon. This book, however, opts not to exalt or rehash criticisms made elsewhere, but to explore, and this foray into creativity and advertising begins with the specific, offering an overview of the manner and status with which creativity is held in advertising. While advertisements have creators, these people, their motives, the environments in which they work, along with the aspirations of creative directors and agency heads, tend to be left out of analyses. Omission of this background insight is a mistake, particularly as modes and discourses of creativity act as a form of affective expression that deeply influences the corporeal creation of advertising. Indeed, like the clients they serve, many agencies possess a house style that provides a discernable look and feel to the best of their advertising.

It is useful then to obtain both a sense of the make-up of the industry and that, which – after money – impels advertising: creativity.

John Hegarty, Chairman and Creative Director of Bartle Bogle Hegarty (BBH), a major creative advertising agency, remarks that creativity is that which seeks to 'adjust the viewer's perspectives in some way, either attitudinal or visual' (1998: 227). Elsewhere he comments that it is 'about breaking something down and putting something new in its place' (Cracknell, 2011: 7). Within the industry there is much chatter about creativity but, as indicated above, little about the specifics of how it works, where it comes from and what it is comprised of. While this is to be expected, as after all advertising agencies are not universities and are more interested in application than theory itself, it is worthy of remark that as a word and locus of such divergent opinion, it is used in very many conversations without a clear common referent. As intimated, critics are not alone in their disparagement and creativity in advertising may appear contradictory, with some of its practitioners questioning the capacity for advertising to produce 'authentic' creative output (Nixon, 2003).

Likewise, in my own conversations with agency practitioners, some have questioned the existence of this cornerstone of advertising practice. It is, however, a key expression by which the industry defines itself and this, I contend, is interesting. To talk of creativity in advertising is to form a blurry picture of how creativity is characterised in advertising. Within agencies themselves, creativity is appreciated differently within respective departments. Account executives who have to go and sell the work to clients will have their perspective, managers responsible for budgets will have another, and creatives seeking to make their mark and win awards will have theirs. There exist then realism and idealism, understood in the common meaning of the word. The realistic perspective is encapsulated well in agency-legend David Ogilvy's remark on creativity as 'the work I have to do between now and Tuesday' (1985: 24). More idealistic is what might be called the Bernbach School, named after William Bernbach, who is generally heralded as initiating a revolution in advertising where creativity is prized above all. The latter's insistence on intuition, provocation, humour and eschewing orthodoxy is noteworthy, particularly when contrasted with other agencies that believed in – and perhaps were led by – market research, segmentation and strategy (that has to do with brand development, positioning and campaign objectives). From the outside then, creativity might be seen in a transformational sense, akin to pixie dust. As will be returned to, it is that which is sold to clients as a form of magic that cannot be attained through logical means. After all, if it were a followable method, everyone would be doing it.

While charting and representing creativity in advertising and its concurrent influences on media culture is important, this provides only the most surface understanding of how we should conceive of creativity. To provide a more satisfying and robust account we must proceed over the horizon line, de-couple creativity from advertising, and think about creativity in a more significant and far-reaching manner. Consequently this will provide more novel means to assess the relationship between creativity and advertising. The de-coupling is necessary as the options are either to tread water and regurgitate what has gone before so for both author and reader to be on familiar, comfortable, safe and less challenging terrain, or to admit that creativity is highly protean, not readily delineated and prepare ourselves to approach the subject differently, utilising philosophical tools.

In asserting that creativity is not an object or thing whose contours and impacts we might easily describe, and that 'it' possesses no obvious structure of its own, we might question its existence at all. However, although it is virtual, consisting in potential and forming rather than form, it is that which shapes the inchoate and sits at the interface of culture and nature. More practically, and back in the terrain of practice, by engaging in such meta-discussion we might anticipate coming dimensions, actualities and instantiations of creative advertising and experimentation with media and the human sensorium.

Structure of the book

Creativity is central to advertising that itself plays a significant role in the economy and, for better or worse, wider mediatised culture. The focus however is not on the advertising that generates the most revenue, but rather on the award-winning end of the spectrum and work that is novel in approach. As will be returned to, advertising that wins awards is by no means the most effective. In beginning to address the nebulous notion of creativity, Chapter 2 orients the reader to the significance of creativity to the advertising industry and details its importance for luminaries in advertising, and the sometimes contradictory ways in which they conceive of it. Being central to advertising, creativity is something sought by all in advertising. Agencies and clients alike pursue it, although as past Executive Creative Director of Saatchi & Saatchi (1987–92) Paul Arden (2003) remarks, only a very small percentage of clients really want to see something they have never seen before. Having introduced the historical context of creativity in advertising and its centrality to agency-based conceptions of creativity, the chapter progresses to add depth and context to this understanding via a phenomenological account of creativity in advertising. Although this book in general prefers a process-based account of creativity, the language that many key figures within the industry use to account for the nuances of their creative practice is highly phenomenological in orientation. Far from being an intellectual tag-on, I argue that creative advertising indirectly draws deep sustenance from both the axioms of phenomenology and its general world outlook, particularly in relation to philosophers such as Husserl, Heidegger and Merleau-Ponty. This is to turn away from the abstractions of strategy to understanding self-conceptions of creativity in advertising as contingent on the lived dimension of culture. Often critiqued as an industry that deceives, I argue that creatives' ways of working paradoxically tend towards the belief in revealing and creating phenomenological truths of products and services.

Continuing the focus on practitioner perspectives, Chapter 3 begins by assessing the nature of what constitutes a creative advertisement. Arguing that advertising has historically possessed its own aesthetic properties generated by the functions of an advertisement, media limitations, modes of audience engagement and two-way interaction with other aesthetic fields, this chapter details what I designate the poetics of advertising. Arguing that these flow from the need to distil complexity and the deceivingly effortless interplay between the visual and textual, this chapter also highlights the irreverent dimension of creative advertising. Emblematic of these poetics is the poster that serves to destabilise easy distinctions between advertising and art. However, the chapter proceeds to highlight that while representation and advertising were once synonymous, this is no longer necessarily the case in a period where intimacy through engagement replaces interruption in much award-winning creative work. Similarly, where advertising was once discrete, bounded, a deliverable, reproducible and that which can be stored, re-run and re-analysed, the temporal possibilities have now expanded to cast doubt on advertising as that which is simply representational. As already highlighted, advertising is increasingly better thought of as an event rather than a text. The interest is less in an object capable of being reproduced, than an occasion or experience. The event is thus original, perhaps not entirely unlike Benjamin's (1999 [1968]) famous notion of 'aura' and the establishing of a unique presence of an original creative work in time and space. It is a novel encounter that comes about not because we experience something, but rather that a set of interactions occur among a given set of parts that give rise to an event.

Where Chapters 2 and 3 focus on creativity in advertising, subsequent chapters begin to address the broader topic of creativity. Chapter 4 recognises that creativity is that which is new, wilful, intentional, draws from disparate sources, and involves the generation of structures, arrangements, occasions or events considered valuable in some way in a period of time to a given group of people. On cultural contingency, Csikszentmihalyi (1997) for example points to Raphael who from the sixteenth century onwards has oscillated between being lauded as creative and a wonderful draftsman. What passes for creativity itself has also been wrangled over and subjected to discursive reconstruction. Culturally and politically it is articulated and re-articulated so to fit regimes and ends. Be this genius-based conceptions, hyper-individualism, the psychologisation of creativity, or capital-based instrumental and functional approaches, the characterisation of creativity is prone to prevailing economic and wider cultural forces.

While creativity might appear timeless, its contemporary meaning as an act of human creation did not come about until after the Enlightenment, although there is evidence of discussion of two creators (God and the poet) in the Renaissance (Williams, 1976: 82). The word we now know as 'creative' stems from human-centred art, although 'creativity' as a general name for this faculty only followed in the twentieth century. Its origins are frequently associated with the philosopher Alfred Whitehead (1985 [1929]) who presented the term 'creativity' to refer to activities that results in actualities (thought of as individual instances of self-creation) coming into being. 'Creativity' then is Whitehead's expression for that generic activity intrinsic to every instance of becoming and is that which emerges from the multitude yet contains something novel within it. This leaves the multitude from which it emerges increased by one. Such understanding has distinct implications for later (and currently quite fashionable) ecological conceptions of creativity and media (Ong, 2002; Strate, 2004; Fuller, 2005). It also allows for new and unique entities to come into being that are not entirely contingent upon their formative structure for their definition.

Although a significant amount of words might be dedicated to the cultural constructions and histories of creativity, Chapter 4 only offers a working overview so to allow for discussion of symbolic, textual and playful conceptions of creativity. David Hesmondhalgh (2006) for example writes in his influential book, *The Cultural Industries*, that creativity within the areas of commerce and practice involves handling, negotiating and manipulating symbols and texts, even going as far to reject the word 'artist' in favour of the expression 'symbolic creators'. This symbolic field is semiotic in nature but is discussed here under the wider rubric of combinatory conceptions of creativity. This approach is used so to also give voice to the creative advertising industry's interest in bisociative approaches (inspired by Koestler, 1970 [1964]) that have less to do with tracing chains of meaning but still involve combinations. Chapter 4 progresses to argue that, while there is an agreeable logic to combinatory approaches, it is a problematic and limited account of creative production that disavows other perspectives of creativity with regard to the making of advertising, our engagement with advertising and more centrally for creativity, the magnitude of what constitutes creativity. These points are explored in relation to Boden's (2004; 2010) notions of exploration and transformation.

Chapter 5 develops a separate and more original account of creativity in relation to affect and sensation. It is less about overturning than widening possibilities and is an attempt to envelop the symbolic into the affective and sensational. However, a certain amount of ground clearance is required. This involves taking to task textual processes that ignore sensation and the decisive role of affect. As Hardt writes in his introduction to Clough's (2007) canonical book, *The Affective Turn*, any foray into notions of affect quickly runs into mind/body questions and how to account for correspondence between the two. Such debates have clearly rumbled on for some time and are not going to be concluded here, although this book explores questions of consciousness, the capacity for reflection, questioning and will in terms of Spinozan parallelism. This is further articulated in terms of cognitive neuroscience, or that which involves neurophysiology, psychology and the understanding of neural phenomena in relation to the exercise of psychological capacities, along with questions about the possibility of incorporating human nature into science (Bennett et al., 2007).

This chapter specifically focuses on the role of sensation as that which sits between mind and body, and begins to think about the ways in which advertising is less in the business of symbols and more in the business of affect, sensation, intensity and the generation of artefacts and experiences that stimulate before we intellectually process. This also sees a breakaway from the hegemony of the visual so to broaden what we designate as advertising and marketing communications beyond visual media. While it is unfair to take to task too vigorously analytical tools that respond to that which they see, we should not let our propensity for visually-oriented means blind us to other sensory and image-making systems employed by advertising and marketing communication programmes. Advertising thought of this way is the attempt to stimulate, harness and modulate affect, intensity and sensation. These affective approaches are in the business of generating qualia, or the unique qualitative character of particular experiences. The emphasis in this chapter is less about abstraction and code, but rather embodied experience where we do not spectate or judge from afar but where we might see advertising as a machine, albeit one where we are not exterior spectators but bound intimately into the field of the event. This machine then is a named collection of forces, processes and affects that are immediately lived, although not necessarily consciously experienced.

Chapter 6 develops a transgressive approach to creativity and gives itself over to an understanding of creativity predicated on immanence, physicality, overflow, sensation, sensuousness and excess in its rejection of borders and boundaries. There is a dual function of this short chapter in that it highlights the importance of excess in transformation that will in later chapters be discussed in relation to bifurcation. Yet the transgressive approach also allows us to peer beyond accounts where creativity is characterised as 'good' and assess more fully the contribution that subversion and amoral being makes to creativity. This is to up-end the Hegelian dialectic and through Bataille (2008 [1932]) find that which is disavowed by mind and culture in the energy of the obscene.

Chapter 7 explores further these transgressive and rebellious tendencies by accounting for what Berlin (1997 [1979]; 2000) labels the Counter-Enlightenment as a catchall for those dissatisfied with rationalist accounts of being, knowing and creating. This sees a renewed interest and expression of what is sensational, lived and local, in some contrast to Enlightenment discourses predicated on understanding through universal, replicable and verifiable methods. I argue that it is in the Counter-Enlightenment where we find recognisable writing and practices that are both insightful in themselves yet provide depth for later accounts predicated on intensity, affect and aesthetics, understood in its original, less divisive and more sensational sense. Sometimes labelled romantic, this book demonstrates there is more to this body of philosophising and making than critics suggest. Too often derisively referred to, a proper examination of its not-always-consistent philosophical principles reveals less about self-indulgent ramblings on nature, returns to the past, divine links, wilderness and love, and more about social and intellectually engaged thinkers who have much to offer us in our contemporary assessment of creativity and development of a more affectively oriented account.

The emphasis on the subject is quite unfashionable both in terms of the symbolic account being critiqued here and in process-based approaches being aligned with. In accounting for creativity this book has no interest in resurrecting the idea of the mythic lone genius with *his* special faculties that works, acts and produces in isolation. The idea of wholly original work emerging from nowhere is not possible, but an attentive and interested force is needed to initiate, instigate, steer, organise, participate, will and move projects forward. Where symbolically-led accounts of creativity focus on the creative self as a function or cultural intermediary so to fulfil a nodal role within a meta-structure (Bourdieu, 1984; Mort, 1996; McFall, 2004), I am keen to reintegrate a willing, reflective, questioning and shaping subject back into the mix.

This is not to detract and misrecognise the co-creative or properly corporate nature of creative events (*corpus* is Latin for body of people), of which there are three parts: first, in reference to work carried out prior by others, a creation never belongs entirely to an individual (or collective) as it involves ideas, innovations or conceptualisations to have taken form elsewhere (although for creative advance to occur there has to be an element of something new, or what is definable only in terms of itself). Second, the work is constructed for people and therefore they are already participants in the creative work (audience data may also exist about audience preferences and the best ways to communicate with them). Third, as is the case in advertising and musical ensembles, people will often work in parallel on the same project, although there is no particular reason not to point to co-willed acts and events. However, just because we recognise that creativity always tends to be co-creative in both reference to past ideas and other people, this should not diminish the role of the active subject that contributes, shapes, sculpts, forms, makes links, imbues, reveals, refines, redrafts, authors and labours. While there is often a degree of luck and serendipity involved, if these are not consciously brought to form they remain just passing moments of fancy and connection.

This belief in shaping, forming and the active subject stems at least in part from a reaction to Kant's (1990 [1781]) *Critique of Pure Reason* and the role of the subject in formulating the world. Kant's efforts wrought a deep fracturing of certainty in that which is around us. Schelling (2001 [1800]), who formed part of a chronological and philosophical arc from Kant to Fichte to Hegel, adopts a highly similar position where much of what we take for reality exists as a projection. These discourses also relate to the ways in which we may take the outside world and fashion it, as opposed to being shaped or moulded by it. Creativity thus begins to emerge as an active force that shapes within indeterminate environments. Conceptualising our conceptions of the world via self-consciousness and projection also makes us more aware of the artificial but lived concepts that we unthinkingly apply about us. Such recognition and awakening allows us to free up the world from convention and begin to see the world of the familiar more strangely. That is to say, by means of scrutinising ourselves, and the ease with which we act in the world, we are able to challenge every assumption and conviction with potential to wilfully reframe reality.

Chapter 8 continues this theme. Here I develop a post-Kantian conception of creativity so to move beyond problems of subjectivism associated with idealism. It also begins to tackle some of the problems associated with notions of affect that run the risk of a dualistic swing from culture to nature. On accepting that our organs of perception constitute the qualities we perceive outside the subject, we recognise that these sensations and nerve excitations come together to form external objects and things, and act as perception marks. Whether these are the blue of the sky, the green of a leaf or the more complex construction of a poster advertisement, the qualities apparent in these external objects are created subjectively. As Whitehead (1997 [1925]) points out, we should give ourselves more credit for what we find beautiful in the world as these are not properties out there but qualities that belong to us.

Semiosis and sign-making are not only linguistic in origin, but also deeply biological. As sign-making animals we weave the fabric of our own relations (between others and the external world) into reality or what Uexküll calls a 'solid web' (2010 [1934]: 53). The truth of our existence is inescapably and immanently located within signification, but we need not flee to metaphysics to explore this as what passes for the transcendental emerges from the immanent. Signification is not simply that of the Saussaurean sort, being predicated on linguistics, but rather where meaning making and biology merge as in biosemiotic accounts, Batesonesque (2000 [1972]) accounts of difference, and the ways in which organisms create contexts and make connections. Biosemiosis provides a means of reframing affect so to straddle mind/body relationships and see the two aspects as working in parallel. We do not have to jettison symbolic accounts, but they do have to be reframed or enfolded into a sensational and biosemiotic account that begins to question what is going on between mind, body and that 'stuff' which constitutes both processes. Semiosis then is not simply abstract 'code', but a very complex series of differences that contestably goes to the heart of what constitutes life for us. Reality and the world thus exist in a relational and co-creative fashion and it is signification that allows us to escape the potential Kantian impasse of subjectivism. Semiosis then is that which transcends both naïve realism and maddening loops of self-representation.

Signification in this context is a deeply creative act involving the generation of new worlds and the ability to construct, deconstruct and ultimately employ the faculty of imagination. At root of being in the world are interpretation, creation and the ways in which we sensationally represent the world to ourselves, and others. Advertising in a biosemiotic context is a wilful attempt to transform reality for the gain of another in a world where reality as conventionally understood is absent. Instead, together, we make up the multifarious constructions of our world as we go along, albeit not in an abstract fashion but a highly immanent one. While advertising is not the only practice professionally engaged in signification, it is one with enormous reach and this alone gives it a special role and need for scrutiny. As is becoming clear, transformation and creativity are deeply linked. This relationship goes to the heart of being in the world. As sign-making and interpreting animals, creativity is that which forms and remakes our sensational experience of being.

This sense of malleability is expanded upon in Chapter 9 so to account for the possibility of the new. I begin with Whitehead's notion of concrescence that involves the means by which what is novel might emerge. Creativity here has to do with realising potential and making actuality out of virtuality (note, virtuality has nothing to do with digitality in this context). It is in this virtual space that this chapter positions itself arguing that deterministic accounts of the world are problematic, and instead we live in a stochastic and irreversible one (Prigogine and Stengers, 1984). Chance exists, newness may occur, and we should be cautious of accounts that treat creative artefacts as part of a mapped continuum with beginning and predictable end. As the pragmatist William James (1897) tells us, without the chance that possibility can spill over from actuality, the difference between future and past is wiped out. Not only is the new possible – it is necessary. Such a view recognises that all systems and their subsystems are fluctuating and on occasion a subsystem may undergo a process of positive feedback so to become more powerful and disrupt and destroy the pre-existing organization. This is the bifurcation point whereby it is impossible to tell which way change will go. At this moment, deterministic description breaks down and we reach the stochastic moment, as with the tossing of a coin. By definition it is a point of unpredictability. Emergence then is not guided and chance may exist and play a role. Here order is pushed into a state of disequilibrium until a critical or bifurcation point where chance prods what remains of the system into a new mode of being where a new mode of order or creative logic arises – at least until the next bifurcation point threatens the stability of that system. These reactions compete with the system's previous mode of functioning. If a system is stable it will see off these challenges to change and the norm will be re-established. Conversely if the invading forces are quick enough to scale the system then a new mode of being or functioning will occur. The reactions that seek to change the system are characterized by evolution, subversion, innovation, creativity, anti-conservatism, transgression, emergence and that which seeks a new order. These stand in some contrast to conservative self-correcting systems that seek to maintain the status quo. This then is a process-based approach where the world is not seen as a large collection of objects and things, but rather as the interplay of forces, consonances, differentials, relationships and events. This Whiteheadian (1985 [1929]) view sees objects as abstractions from a much more real condition of process and becoming.

The logic of stochasticism, emergence, events and the new is carried into Chapter 10. This investigates the relationship between creativity, and newer, more technical forms of mediated experience. While the reader with only a casual interest in advertising may indexically link advertising with images, much investment and time goes into media planning and creative exploration of the means by which media choice may maximise campaign effectiveness. In decoupling the process of advertising from ideas of media as a blank vehicle, we might ask what possible materials can be imagined as media, how can they be hacked and repurposed, and how might they engage people? This chapter examines work on media affordances, transduction and ecological conceptions of media, and positions these within a sensational, affective and aesthetically-led account of media, creativity and advertising. Exploring the ways in which media are taken up by artists, activists and advertisers, media in this context may be subverted and transformed to realise opportunities in the potential grammar and structures of misplaced concreteness (borrowing from Whitehead, 1997 [1925]) of standard [media] objects found in culture. That is to say if, as established in earlier chapters, fixity is an illusion, what opportunities arise and how might we best understand the philosophical implications of hacking and the capacity to repurpose media objects? Heidegger's discussion of care and being is useful as a means of establishing how we might interact with technology and media. This is sensational rather than observational knowing, and different from intellectual and symbolic accounts.

So, how does this play out in an advertising context? The beginning of an answer to this is that through interaction, audience engagement, repurposing media, intra-media stimulation and feedback, media become more than the sum of affordances immediately possessed. They are transversal and transductive. Going beyond their prescribed remit and being in excess of themselves, they become ecological, allowing for novel and more technical experiences in which the sum of parts is exceeded.

Chapter 11 concludes by reflecting on the two propositions stated at the beginning of this chapter and assesses their analytical usefulness.

Note

1 For practical material on creative advertising have a look at trade associations operating in the UK and US, such as the Institute of Practitioners in Advertising or the Internet Advertising Bureau, who offer a range of publications on best practices in digital advertising. Likewise, D&AD and The One Club (among many other associations) have many examples of best practices in creative advertising.

2 Strangely revealing

This chapter provides insights into how people in advertising conceive of creativity so to provide non-specialists with a sense of agency perspectives, intra-agency discourses and the degree to which creativity is valued. It also provides a working overview of the numerous actors that play a role in the co-creative development of advertising. While some of the practitioners mentioned here will be very familiar to those practising or studying advertising, this chapter will help those unfamiliar with the internal workings of advertising to obtain a better sense of how central creativity is to the advertising industry. Insights into creativity in advertising are derived from a number of sources and approaches. These include having myself taught advertising and worked alongside creatives and creative directors, as well as formal interviews and informal conversations I have had with advertising practitioners. However, the scheduling of interviews into a busy working day too often leads to clichés, or the repeating of agency and trade dogma, so also consulted are books written by practitioners as these provide space for practitioners to develop their arguments, metaphors, analogies and insights on creativity. While ostensibly promotion for themselves and their agencies, the reflective space allotted by book-writing arguably provides a rich source of information for the researcher.

Although discussion of creativity within advertising can tend towards hyperbole, the practice of creative advertising can be read in deeply phenomenological terms, particularly those provided by Husserl, Heidegger and Merleau-Ponty. At the outset this degree of philosophical engagement may appear surprising, but certainly at the creative end of the spectrum (where awards are won by means of peer-recognition), the practice of advertising is best seen as that which reveals, highlights and intensifies experiences of objects and advertising. The latter half of this chapter thus accounts for the ways in which creativity in advertising involves engaging people at an ontological level and attempts to shape new relationships, experiences, and the *as suchness* between people and objects they encounter.

The rise of creative advertising

While advertising exists to promote sales, brand equity and awareness among given groups of people for a named client, the role of creativity in advertising has been fundamental from the earliest of its professionalised days. Stanley Resor for example, who in 1916 purchased the J. Walter Thompson Company, one of the first full-service advertising agencies, remarks that the creative part of advertising comes first and that 'everything else is plumbing' (cited in Jones, 2004: 141). However, perspectives on creativity are not uniform and past titans of the advertising industry have a variety of views on what creativity is, its role within the advertising process and what constitutes creative advertising.

While it might appear straightforward enough to link creativity and originality, many within the industry see this as a misguided and dangerous view of advertising. As remarked upon in the introduction, David Ogilvy (1985), a founder of modern advertising, paints a down-to-earth and instrumentalist picture of creativity as a highbrow word for everyday work. Describing the C word as hideous, he goes on to point out that while agencies might win awards for work, there is no necessary connection between prizes and a rising sales curve. Leo Burnett similarly eschewed originality for its own sake quoting an unspecified ex-boss of his: 'If you insist in being different just for the sake of being different, you can always come down in the morning with a sock in your mouth' (Ogilvy, 1985: 201).

Thus, while novelty is useful, creative ideas in advertising operate within specified parameters and eschew the bizarre in favour of what is *both* original and useful. Ogilvy comments that when he writes an advertisement he does not want us to comment that it is creative but instead he wants us to buy the product. Likewise, he chastises those who eschew research in favour of self-proclaimed genius, 'who gravitate to the type of clients who, bamboozled by their rhetoric, do not hold them responsible for their sales results' (1985: 8). Instead he urges those with an interest in working in advertising to study in depth the products they are selling, to exorcise pseudo-literary pretensions and concentrate on what he calls the obligations of advertising: that is, to sell. He credits this to Claude Hopkins' book, *Scientific Advertising* where Hopkins (1998 [1923]) sees the practice of advertising as a process of trial, error, review, the learning of principles, application, more feedback, refinement and the use of data through tools such as coupons and other methods of enabling feedback so to understand what works and what does not.[1]

Influentially, in the US during the 1950s and 1960s, Rosser Reeves embodied hard-sell formulaic advertising. Champion of slogans and the Unique Sales Proposition (USP), messages were relentlessly beaten into consumers. Reeves' approach is encapsulated in advertising for Anacin, a painkiller that for seven years featured hammers banging away in a cartoon head. In addition to being intrusive and irritating, it was also effective. Cracknell characterises Reeves' approach to advertising:

Hit them hard, straight between the ears, painfully, mercilessly – and keep hitting them until they give in. Boring, repetitive commercials, usually featuring quasi-scientists in white coats or basic graphic devices with a voice-over slamming home a product virtue – over and over again: 'Four out of five doctors …'

(Cracknell, 2011: 26)

For Reeves, communicating a message at the lowest possible cost was paramount and creativity was considered a dangerous word. Advertising was driven by rules and research. This led to a conservative cycle of production in that only what had been done before could be produced and the creative component of an agency existed to give form to these unadventurous strategies. This is contra to contemporary thinking and empirical research that highlights the more that people like advertising, the more they tend to remember it (Du Plessis, 2011). If Reeves represents the reason-to-buy-hard-sell method, then Ogilvy represents the inception of softer, more branded advertising, of which Reeves was deeply sceptical due to the potential for misinterpretation and polysemy. Arguably a halfway house between Reeves and more daring or radical approaches, Ogilvy (1985) emphasises consumer research and the need for creative work to be driven by clearly defined audience insights.

If Hopkins and Ogilvy symbolise research in advertising, then William 'Bill' Bernbach represents originality in advertising, although earlier architects of modern advertising had insisted on novelty. For example, on retiring from Young & Rubicam in 1944, Raymond Rubicam left his agency no rules of practice, but instead the aphorism 'resist the usual' that continues as the agency's mantra to this day (Y&R, 2012). Bernbach's position is clear and deeply influential to this day: research kills creative ideas and renders, at best, mediocrity. Creative advertising is intrinsically associated with the US agency Doyle Dane Bernbach (DDB) and their work from the 1960s and 1970s. This is due to the ways in which they altered what is considered creative in advertising in regard to working practices (copywriter and art director teaming), format, simplicity, tone, mode of address, humour and layout, with their influence continuing to hold sway over the most lauded of contemporary boutiques and creative agencies, and also the most conservative ones. The full story of DDB[2] in the US and Collett Dickenson Pearce (CDP) in the UK has been recounted too many times (see Tungate, 2007; Cracknell, 2011) so I will not go over old ground here. However, their insistence on higher levels of honesty, authenticity, inclusivity, intelligence, humour, intuition and provocation is noteworthy, particularly when contrasted with other agencies that believed in, and were led by, market research and segmentation. Also, part of Bernbach's novel approach to advertising involved the requirement of good taste. Recognising the power of mass media and the various ways in which it might influence society, he remarked that creators of advertising could either brutalise society or raise it to another plane. Building an ethical case for creativity in advertising, he noted the intrusive nature of advertising and that it is better to entertain and provide light relief. Alongside critics, he argued that not only is the majority of advertising crass and soulless, but that it is corrosive and debilitating. But, as advertising exists regardless, and we are all exposed to it, Bernbach's point is that both parties might as well enjoy the process. This collection of points might as well function as a manifesto for creativity in advertising.

Creative advertising in this setting is pleasurable, represents a conspiratorial wink between two parties, and makes an ally rather than a target out of the buyer. Creativity is not merely a part of advertising, but for many of its practitioners it is the atmosphere that attracts and sustains them. Paul Arden (2003), best known for his work while a creative director for Saatchi & Saatchi, notes that creativity is the lingua franca with which advertising agencies operate. Being a discourse that both forms and permeates agencies the notion of creativity flows through all its tendrils, its output and internal goings-on. As highlighted in the introductory chapter, Arden describes that clients say they want creativity, but that, 'Only one in ten thousand really mean, "Give me something I haven't seen before". So, before you make your pitch, find out exactly what your client means by the word "creative". It's probably different from your definition' (2003: 105). Arguing that people in advertising should rely less on safe decisions that go only to familiar places, but that they should opt for unsafe options that generate reaction and achievement, Arden's call to action arouses many modern conceptions of creativity including recklessness, fearlessness, anti-conformity, childlikeness, originality, and avoidance of the reasonable, steady and middle path.

Selection of the unsafe option often means pushing the boundaries of what is appropriate as with, for example, the infamous 'Mission Iraq' campaign 2011 created by the agency Droga5 where the New Zealand distributor for gaming-headset company Turtle Beach sent a gamer on a mission to an Iraqi war zone. Having generated controversy and spectacular footage of 24-year-old Phil Cummings (or StatiC) escaping dangers, it was finally revealed that the entire thing was staged in Turkey. The campaign line? 'As real as you want it to get.' Other campaigns or stunts that flirt and possibly cross the border of what is appropriate include BBH's 2012 stunt for the technology conference South by Southwest (SxSW) in the US that involved homeless people wearing t-shirts saying 'I'M [person's name here], A 4G HOTSPOT' and carrying around mobile 4G Wi-Fi in exchange for donations.[3]

A reoccurring trope in the industry literature on creativity and advertising is the capacity for an agency to do more than the next with the same amount of money or less. John Hegarty of BBH likewise comments that creativity in advertising is all about reduction: 'Write less, say more' (2011: 7). Ideally, for clients, agencies represent contracted creativity on tap, able to deliver attractive and effective advertising campaigns. Jeremy Bullmore, originally a copywriter, but also ex-chairman of both the advertising agency JWT and the

Advertising Association, remarks that a good creative is someone who can make things happen in a manner that might be quicker, more economical, more rewarding or lasting. He comments:

> They can help people understand complex arguments; they can bring freshness to old promises; they can engage people's minds and self-interest; they can develop a narrative; they can forge connections through visual and verbal metaphor. And they do all these things and many more not just for the sake of it but as a calculated means to a clearly understood end.
>
> (Bullmore, 2003: 204)

Within agencies themselves, creativity is seen differently depending on the department: account executives in a client's firing line have their views, those in charge of budgets have theirs, and creatives looking to get ahead have theirs. Miller (2003) observes that there is a structural fault between creatives and account executives (or managers). While one believes in the power of novel and unique ideas, the other centres on the brand and product. Each side will grossly stereotype each other, along the lines of failed artist vs. business-headed boor (Mazzarella, 2006; also see Malefyt and Moeran, 2003). There are a number of additional but related factors influencing creative endeavour. These include: marketing and strategic objectives; clients; budgets; the advertising brief[4] that keeps creatives on track and aids in the production of originality; hierarchical approval of creatives' work (copywriters, art directors, creative directors and others from the creative department within an advertising agency); and collaborative influences from outside services where production expertise is bought in.

Firmly of the creative camp, Trott (2009) somewhat brutally describes that researchers and those who plan advertising strategy are out of touch with popular culture and everyday life, and that creative briefs harm the creative process. The brief for Trott, as an outcome of consumer research, is that which puts limits on creativity. These limitations might involve the correct strategy, but also lead to uninspiring work. Similarly, this leads Arden to proclaim that 'it is wrong to be right, because people who are right are rooted in the past, rigid-minded, dull and smug' (2003: 55). Of Crispin, Porter and Bogusky (CP+B) fame, Bogusky and Winsor (2009) make a similar point arguing for the importance of intuition. They comment that they frequently meet successful people who credit intuition as the key to their results, also positing that: 'Not everybody has great instincts, and in all probability, the rise of quantifiable analytics was powered by those poor souls who need a way to navigate a business without it [intuition]' (2009: 94). The idea of the creative antagonist is a frequently reoccurring one in advertising and we might quickly summarise with a couple of quotes from John Hegarty to make the point:

... creativity isn't an occupation, it's a preoccupation ... you are leading people who are driven by the need to do something great. That desire comes from deep within their psyche ...

(Hegarty, 2011: 72)

You cannot create great work unless a little bit of you goes into it, be it your heart, your soul or your beliefs ... it has to have an integrity and humanity that touch people, and those qualities come from within ... That's why creative people can be so insufferable – they're not just doing a job, they're expressing their beliefs.

(Hegarty, 2011: 21–22)

Ogilvy (1985) in an open letter to prospective clients warned that they should not ask to meet the staff that might be working on their accounts on the basis they might find them repulsive, also regaling that, 'Few of the great creators have bland personalities. They are cantankerous egoists, the kind of men who are unwelcome in the modern corporation' (2004 [1963]: 50). Similarly, a past chairman of Wolff Olins remarks: 'The most irritating aspects of working with creative people are their arrogance, their egotism and their total self-centredness, their feeling that the world has to revolve around them, that time doesn't exist' (cited in Mort, 1996: 101). However, this equating of the advertising creative with hackneyed romantic stereotypes does not account for the problem of authenticity that gnaws at these types of accounts of creativity in advertising. Nixon's (2003) ethnography on advertising agencies points to mixed perceptions within the industry on the existence of 'true' creativity in advertising where some consider themselves authentically creative, but others feel themselves to be commercial hacks. This is perhaps best crystallised in the title of Jacques Seguela's 1979 book, *Please Don't Tell My Mother I Work in Advertising, Tell Her I Play the Piano in a Brothel*.

While ideological divisions between departments exist, these borders are increasingly less absolute as creatives are more frequently involved in client meetings and asked to articulate decisions for their work. Particularly within smaller boutique-like agencies too (Adam & Eve, Dare, Fallon, Mother, Naked or St Luke's in London for example), there is an emphasis on creativity throughout the agency. Moreover, when pushed, most account managers and creatives will agree that the best advertising is that which manages to stay on strategy (understood in terms of matching advertising messages to target markets and their motivations to try a new product or remain with an existing brand), although the campaign itself should feel fresh and original. Indeed, Droga5, an agency currently globally revered as a creative hothouse and described by *The Guardian* (a UK newspaper) as the world's most exciting agency, has a mission statement comprised of 'Creatively Led. Strategically Driven. Technology Friendly. Humanity Obsessed.' The need for relevance to both product and audience will of course be foremost in the mind of account executives given that they are directly answerable to clients. Needless to say, this may lead to conflict. Tensions also exist between clients and agencies. Arden notes that:

> ... there is a continuous battle between the client and the ad agency's creative department. The client wants to advertise his name, his product and its benefit. The creative person wants to advertise him or herself. The creative idea is what the agency wants to explode on the page. The client would be happy with his logo. Yet, oddly enough, they need one another. The creative person has to have someone sponsor his skill. And the client knows that the creative mind increases sales.
>
> (Arden, 2003: 79)

It is a familiar practice within agencies to criticise unadventurous patrons and this schism is not a recent one. Exasperated commercial poster designers in the nineteenth century complained along similar lines. W.S. Rogers writing for *The Poster* in 1899 remarked on clients who 'would rather I made a base imitation of a hackneyed design, than produce an original design of my own' (cited in Bigham, 1998: 182). Little has changed today and online discussion on Facebook groups such as Ads of the World attracts complaining comments from creative staff about work being mauled in client presentations, and for lesser work to be subsequently agreed and approved. There are many gripes about clients to be found, but they tend to centre on the accusation that clients rarely have a clear initial idea but later want to make wholesale changes that ruin the idea to be communicated and its execution. This leads to an agency truism that clients get the advertising they deserve and while some clients will seek challenging work and give their agencies relative autonomy, others will be more active in regard to the direction, strategy and appearance of the advertising.

The client/agency distinction is akin to longer-standing patronage-led art and the ways in which the benefactor might potentially interfere in the realization of a vision (Gibbons, 2005). The client and paymaster is thus an important input into co-creative endeavour and ultimately decides the degree of novelty that takes place in advertising. There are a myriad other actors that prove the point that the production of advertising does not belong to an individual, but to a collective. Although there is much lonesome machination in the wider process of production, the creation of advertising is social and collaborative. It is a co-creative endeavour both requiring and benefitting from the efforts of many actors. Creative attributes in this setting emerge from the group, although this is not to say that advertising is without a personal signature – it is just that the signature belongs to the agency and not one individual. While one creative may have a strong hand in how an advertisement appears (and will probably be seeking awards), it is subject to the verification and production skills of a wider range of actors, along with internal and external pressures, constraints of marketing objectives, budgets, the advertising brief, hierarchical approval of creatives' work and collaborative constraints. The sequence of production of advertising is less than smooth and tensions and contradictory wishes plague the process. Problems occur, including aforementioned difficult clients, deadlines, legal restrictions, unavailability of music, actors, directors and media space. These all lead to the potential for strategies and ideas to be jettisoned in favour of new ones halfway through campaign development, and on occasion later down the line. In some contrast to those who see advertising as calculating in its execution of persuasive communication, more often than not it exists 'in a state of precarious uncertainty' (Malefyt, 2003: 140).

A key gatekeeper for the aspiring agency creative is the Creative Director, or some equivalent. This figure raises questions about what literally passes for a good idea, what the criteria are, potential relationships between creativity and experience, and what makes one innovative idea better than another. This person will also understand that as agencies do not formally advertise (in the sense of having to pay for space in the media), their creative capacity is judged by the advertising ideas and campaigns they produce. In discussion of ideas dismissed, Ogilvy comments: 'I shudder to think how many I have rejected. Research can't help you much, because it cannot predict the cumulative value of an idea' (1985: 16). Similarly, John Hegarty when asked 'What exactly is good creative judgement?' replied, 'You are talking about taste … And you can't teach taste' (in McCracken, 2009: 39). Trott remarks that an advertising creative has to be able to 'stand back and judge it as if we'd never even heard the idea before' (2009: 71). This involves bracketing out personal tastes and measuring the work by objective criteria, although it is unclear what these might be. He continues:

> We're no longer experiencing a piece of advertising any more. No we're doing a job. Now we're professionals. We have to think about what we're doing. So we no longer say, 'I like it', or 'I don't like it'. Now we must always begin with a criticism with, 'it works because … '. Or, 'It doesn't work because … '
>
> (Trott, 2009: 94)

This involves a difficult shift in perspective and stipulates that one is not only able to 'think outside the box', but is able to stand outside the box and critically evaluate dimensions, context, applicability and value of the original work against what are highly indeterminate criteria.

The role of judgement has lineage in the field of aesthetics, particularly in regards to detachment, impersonality and disinterestedness (note, not the same as uninterested). This mode of discernment is rooted in Kant's (1952 [1790]) *Critique of Judgement* where one must remain indifferent so to engage in disinterested pleasure and aesthetic experience. While not a perfect fit, as Kant was more concerned with the sublime and beauty, the point remains in relation to the origins of indifference to the object, the cultivation of distance, critical detachment, and the focusing on appearance and representation. This is to leave aside emotional engagement as, after all, we do not care for the object we are dealing with, but are only concerned with how it affects us. Expertise largely comes through practice, familiarity with the wider field of advertising, and the application of loose and unwritten formulae ('have I seen anything like it before?'). The question remains however, what are the criteria by which the work is judged, particularly if not benchmarked against the brief or research? Much of this stems from non-verbalised insight or intuition that quickly perceives differences, similarities, makes connections and disconnections, and benchmarks against past and existing work.

Awards play a central, if somewhat mixed role, in advertising. Bullmore (2003) is scathing of awards arguing that the intensity of interest in these, and the impulse to produce work that is an artistic end in itself, promotes self-indulgent advertising that is irresponsible to clients. He goes on to point out that the conflation of art and advertising is dangerous, as advertising exists to fulfil a commercial purpose. Hegarty (2011) in some contrast characterises the agency itself as an addict, with winning being the cocaine of the industry. Key recognised awards include the Art Directors Club, Cannes Lions, Clio, Cresta, D&AD, The One Club and the Webby Awards (among many others, see IPA, 2011). They are the means by which practitioners gain recognition among their peers with many creatives placing sizeable stock on visible markers of success, peer recognition and approval. Acting as a currency of trade within the industry, they can be indexed against salary and seniority. Seniority does not only take financial form, but also serves as fuel for a social status and fantasy, not dissimilar in advertising circles to the transformations that pop stars and celebrities undergo (Nixon, 2003). Yet, some practitioners argue that awards should be recognised as representative of opinion, and not be held as creative authorities themselves. This is a difficult idea, particularly if one holds that creativity is socially agreed and nothing is intrinsically creative, but rather it is an accolade awarded by the machinations of a social system (Csikszentmihalyi, 1997). For Arden (2003), however, among others, awards involve the mediocrity of the known and are too influenced by what is fashionable. Trott (2009), on a different tack, makes the observation that where in art an elite group dictates the rules, in advertising millions of people decide whether creative work is any good.

'Wow, I wish I'd thought of that': the Big Idea

The review from *The Sunday Times* on the back cover of Dave Trott's book, *Creative Mischief*, describes him as a genius – in capital letters no less. Inside he accounts for advertising as being applied creativity and that which makes one think 'Wow, I wish I'd thought of that' (2009: 1). Advertising is obsessed with ideas, or what Ogilvy (1985) dubbed 'Big Ideas', and the vast majority of creative awards are based on the originality of concepts or ideas, and the quality of their execution (the ways that advertising ideas are carried out or presented). Ideas are the turning of advertising strategy (what message is to be communicated and to whom) into a memorable, convincing, palatable and potentially enjoyable advertising experience. The most successful will stand out, become iconic and translate across all media, however different their properties may be. Ogilvy offers the following requirements for a big idea: 'Did it make me gasp when I first saw it? Do I wish I had thought of it myself? It is unique? Does it fit the strategy to perfection? *Could it be used for 30 years?*' (1985: 16, emphasis in original).

Within the industry, the expression is a collective noun for solutions to problems that can be judged in terms of how attractive and useful they are, how long they last and the degree to which they surprise and entertain. In common sense, an 'idea' is shorthand to express a concept or theory, a new technique or mode of production, or a new style of representation (Boden, 2010). An advertising idea might be akin to a melody that may be played on any media instrument. It is a theory or premise that explains in simple terms the directionality and *raison d'être* for the advertising. It is a crystallisation of research, product functionality, brand personality, and cogitation and simplification on and of these, translated into a deceptively simple affective experience.

In regard to how ideas are arrived at, James Webb Young's (2003 [1965]) *A Technique for Producing Ideas* offers a clear exposition of how this is achieved. Lauded by creative advertising luminaries such as Bill Bernbach, Young borrows from Pareto (1935) and explains the need for systems, process and principles, offering five stages in his approach to creative advertising: *collection* and the acquisition of intimate knowledge of the product and its intended audience; *organisation*, so for this information to be organised and accessible; *incubation and mastication*, the examination of information to understanding its significance, the combining of informational items with other items of information and the jotting down of unworkable yet interesting ideas from which a jumbled mess will be the result; *birth of the idea*, where if the first three stages have been properly done, the idea will appear perhaps at the unlikeliest of times; and finally *shaping*, and making the idea workable for the practical conditions that it should meet. This type of creative process follows a well-known path also described by Wallas (1926) and Young is somewhat disingenuous by not citing Wallas more directly.

This approach is also found in Ogilvy (2004 [1963]; 1985) who advises that one should fill the conscious mind with information, cast aside rational thought, go for a walk or drink half a pint of claret, then allow messages from the unconscious to come through with the result being a big idea. Although not in discussion of advertising, Csikszentmihalyi (1997) cautions that this framework is frequently distorted, over-simplified and taken too literally, particularly the latter stages when ideas more often than not are tweaked, nuanced and potentially turned upside-down before finishing.

Making the familiar strange ...

A customary refrain among advertising tutors and students seeking to be professional advertising creatives is that they should 'make the strange familiar, and the familiar strange'. Deriving from Russian formalism and defamiliarisation, Shklovsky (1917) pointed out a desire within literature to take the familiar and to make it strange so to challenge the formulaic, wake readers from stupor, increase attention, and disturb conventional and lazy, uncritical patterns of perception. Citing Tolstoy and his use of a horse as narrator in *Kholstomer: The Story of a Horse*, Shklovsky went as far as claiming that this is the essence of all art. Brecht offers a similar notion in his account of the estrangement effect[5] whereby an object is turned from something ordinary, familiar and accessible into something peculiar, striking and unexpected (Willett, 1964). Like many modern artistic endeavours, defamiliarisation has to do with an imperative to render perception anew.

While Brecht sought a view of theatre and estrangement (or alienation) within the context of Marxian practice, in advertising this has to do with joining up ideas, links, situations and events and building connections between hitherto unthought-of associations. Arguing for a structural, relational or combinatory view of advertising, Young similarly asserts that ideas for advertising are 'nothing more nor less than a new combination of old elements' (2003 [1965]: 15), although Pareto (1935), from whom Young draws, makes the same point about creativity itself.

As we will return to in Chapter 4, fashioning connections and making strange or familiar involves intertextuality, appropriating, borrowing, and outright stealing. On this latter point Arden is unrepentant and quotes the independent filmmaker Jim Jarmusch by telling his readers to 'steal from anywhere that resonates with inspiration or fuels your imagination' (2006: 94). Trevor Beattie makes a similar point, arguing 'advertising is a world of magpies and we steal sparkling things ... We go to a club and steal a trend and go on to appropriate whole chunks of youth culture. ... Advertising never sets trends, it only follows them' (cited in Nixon, 2003: 80). Arden and Jarmusch alike quote Jean-Luc Godard: 'It's not where you take things from – it's where you take them to' (Arden, 2006: 94; Jarmusch, 2004). To continue the theme, Bogusky and Winsor (2009: 98) cite T.S. Eliot stating 'Immature poets imitate; mature poets steal'. Eliot (1999 [1920]) also goes on to observe that a good poet creates something new out of that which has been stolen. This occurs through the alteration of language, juxtaposition of words, novel combinations and newfound density of meaning.

Revealing and disclosing

Jeremy Bullmore remarks that creative components of advertisements involve the creation of emotional ingredients. This occurs via 'an excursion into irrationality; into inspiration and creativity; into a field of fantasy where numbers have no place' (2006: 61). Creativity tends not to be discussed in intellectual terms, but in relation to empathy, gut-feelings, intuition, attitude, mood, tone and an attempt to see the world from another person's point of view. This experiential dimension is affective and immersive. Bernbach, in the 1960s, puts it in a similar fashion urging fellow ad-writers:

> You've got to live with your product. You've got to get steeped in it. You've got to get saturated with it. You must get to the heart of it. Indeed, if you have not crystallized into a single purpose, a single theme, what you want to tell the reader, you CANNOT be creative.
>
> (cited in DDB, 2012)

The way that practitioners discuss creativity in advertising is frequently reminiscent of phenomenology as espoused by Husserl, Heidegger and Merleau-Ponty. This is certainly not a grafting-on of philosophy for the purposes of academic pontificating, but rather a means of teasing out the nature of experiential engagement required in the creative process, particularly in the way it is held that a key principle of making good advertisements is that they should 'reveal' (Bullmore, 2003). This involves exploring the object or service to be sold in all its possible dimensions to get to the core of what it is; to recognise dimensions of affordances and corporeality; to understand incorporeal significance; to ingratiate these into customers' cognitive and bodily worlds, and to paradoxically do all of this by engaging in a significant degree of intimacy with a large body of people. Among actually designing the advertising, there are two processes taking place: first, to understand the object in the richest levels of experiential and affordance-based detail; and second, consideration of how it fits into a person's life, what it will be like to use that object, how the object will fit into a customer's own scheme of meaning, and the search for an idea or truth located in the product or service itself that is meaningful for potential customers. The mode of knowledge is not always initially easy to verbalise, but involves an experiential mode of knowledge in which differences, resemblances, connections and disconnections, ratios, balance, significance, sensational value and relevance are assessed without recourse to overtly identifiable criteria. The act or practice of branding, and positioning objects and services in people's minds, involves dealing in what exists for people. It has less to do with *what* things are, but *how* things are so to be the *beings* they are.

As Heidegger (2011 [1962]) explains, phenomenology is a method and approach interested in how things come to be rather than in what they are. Stemming from phenomenon and logos, phenomenology is the 'science of phenomena'. This has value for advertising and its endeavour for detail, and to relay and communicate the perceived essence of an object or service. While hucksterism most certainly exists, it is, however, remarkable that on receiving a new brief, creatives in agencies will seek to discern and interpret the character or experiential essence or, if need be, create it. While such level of care does not always occur, it is notable that much of the best advertising (both adventurous and cautious) finds its advertising ideas in the product, service or brand itself.

Heidegger calls on the Greeks to highlight that the word phenomenon means to 'show itself' or make manifest. As such we must, according to Heidegger, '*keep in mind* that the expression "*phenomenon*" signifies *that which shows itself*' (2011 [1962]: §29, 51, emphasis in original). Reading creativity in advertising this way, it has less to do with making, sign play, fashioning clever combinations, or even novelty, but rather revealing and disclosing. This differs considerably from established critical and semiotic opinion on what creativity in the advertising process is. The phenomenological interpretation of creativity given here sees creativity as a means of disclosing experiential properties while the semiotic view of creativity in advertising sees creativity in terms of transference and sign-value. This occurs by means of leveraging one or more signs to give credibility to an otherwise dull object or service. While there is validity and critical value in reading advertising this way, it is useful to take a few steps back if we seek to understand creativity in advertising. In the process of idea generation, creatives will interrogate the product or service, and the people who are being sold to. Much creative advertising work flows from an interesting aspect of the product or even how it was produced. While advertising might be seen as that which covers up, or adds irrelevant excitement and noise, this is not the case – at least in advertising deemed creative.

The point is to show what might be considered mundane in new ways. This is not entirely unlike still-life painting of apples, teapots, flowers, plates and other items from domestic life. Creativity in this setting is about highlighting, renewing vision, bringing into focus, perceptual shifts, making exotic, enlarging and intensifying experiences of objects. It is to bring to the fore a sense of 'thisness' and what will later be accounted for in the jargon of haecceity and qualia, and that which is unique, individual and accounts for a thing's particularity. Thus rather than parachuting in other signs with which to cover up the fact that a product or service has nothing to say for itself, in creative approaches ideas frequently emerge from the being of the product or service. While signs from outside of the immediate sphere of that which is being advertised may be used as an interesting way of telling the story of the product or service, creative solutions are not driven by texts outside the domain of the brand but are simply employed as vehicle to tell a phenomenological story. Thus the semiotic component of the advertising process broached in the next two chapters is a useful and interesting way of accounting for the being of a given product or service, but it is not the totality of the process. Rather, much creative advertising begins with experiential dimensions of the product or service itself.

Experience in this setting has to do with high levels of sensitivity to affective cues imbued into products, and their marketing and advertising. Where strategists put the map before the territory, creative advertising takes on phenomenological qualities in relation to its accounting of micro-elements of culture. To quote Kevin Roberts, Saatchi & Saatchi's Chief Executive Officer:

> Strategy is dead. Who really knows that [sic] is going to happen anymore in this super VUCA [volatile, uncertain, complex, ambiguous] world? The more time and money you spend devising strategies the more time you are giving you [sic] rivals to start eating your lunch.
> Management is dead. To win today you need a culture and an environment where the unreasonable power of creativity thrives. Ideas are today's currency not strategy. Martin Luther King did not say 'I have a vision statement' did he? He had a dream. You have to make sure you have dreams and your brand also needs a dream.
>
> (Draycott, 2012)

While some hyperbole is to be expected from the CEO of an advertising agency known for its high levels of creativity, addressing fellow business leaders, the quote reflects well the phenomenological nature of creativity in advertising that places emphasis on multiplicity and being present in the moment over abstract strategy. It is to focus on what Merleau-Ponty (2002 [1945]) refers to as the unity of experience, subjectivity over objectivity, and an emphasis on the lived dimension of culture. The idea of the lived in this context is temporal, or that sense of being in, connecting and engaging with an immediate present that we did not bring about ourselves. It is to deal with the world by means of first-person subjectivity, rather than with the objectivity of the dead. This objectivity is predicated on a rejection of quality and the reduction of the complex to the simple (by only including that which can be measured, repeated and/or predicted). In reality, to call it objectivism is not quite right given that disavowal of the territory in favour of the map is a decision to ignore the living.

Detachment from the subjective gives rise to advertising that is impersonal, objective, strategic, yet mostly conventional and unoriginal. This may involve repetition of advertising formulae, celebrities, or crass appeals. It is not that causal or reductionist types of knowledge are denied, but rather that for Merleau-Ponty they are somewhat dishonest in that they conceal the subject, eschew the world of which they speak, and are naïve by refusing to acknowledge the primacy of consciousness, and the lived aspects of experience and life. In turning away from what is clear, distinct, reasonable and understandable, indeterminacy becomes a positive attribute in relation to experience, as it is when this is admitted that we are able to allow notions such as quality to arise as a mode of expression, rather than simply logical signification.

Phenomenology then is the study of being and there are clear reasons why those preferring positive knowledge will reject a mode of understanding that attempts to account for that which has no shape, delineation or definition that we can talk about in terms of traditional or repeatable logic. As Heidegger borrows from Hegel, phenomenology involves the study of the 'indeterminate immediate' (2011 [1962]: §2, 22). As we do not live our lives in absolute clarity where all lines, objects and meanings appear without blur or indeterminacy, Merleau-Ponty's point is that out of this opacity arises quality and subjectivity. This is due to localism, contingency, ambiguity, shifting, the eschewing of objectivism and a celebration of rootedness in the world.

Positive indeterminacy

Context is all-important and attempts to abstract and strategise inevitably shift the focus from lived and experiential aspects. For advertising creatives, over-emphasis on strategy and the map reduces the quality and impact of the advertising, and it is out of multiplicity and indeterminacy that expressive, rather than logical, ideas and creative artefacts emerge. In contrast to the experiential blindness of the formulaic, adherence to locality and the refusal to take a bird's-eye view (if such a thing were possible) outside of spatial and temporal cultural happenings provides what we might designate *positive indeterminacy*.

This is tantamount to *insight, quality, sensational understanding* and *engagement*. In contrast, over-emphasis on strategy diminishes presence and provides only deadened formulae and stale advertising. The interest in presence is to understand intention, although not in the common sense manner of promising to do something. Rather intentionality is that which structures experience as we are bound to the world by dint of experiencing every object we come across. In a Husserlian fashion, it is our outward propensity to experience things in the world. It has to do with the premise that as we engage we are conscious *of* something. The 'something' need not be what the thing actually is, but rather what and how it appears to us as, in our given state of temporal awareness. This is not to suggest that phenomenological approaches involve passivity but rather that whether active or not, the emphasis is on the living experiencing subject. At least with Husserl (1970 [1936]) phenomenology stands opposed to any form of reductionism or abstraction. We might also see the creative process in advertising in Heideggerean (2011 [1962]) terms as a mode of engagement, a way of life, sensitivity to environment, an orientation to the world, or a less formal or objective way of engaging with Being.

Creative advertising in this setting is the act of revealing, fashioning and communicating the being of an object, service or initiative, and the attempt to steer behaviour so as to benefit the people responsible for these enterprises. To put it in phenomenological terms, it is to 'make the Being of entities stand out in full relief' (Heidegger, 2011 [1962]: §27, 49). Where critics of advertising might denounce the advertising process as that which fosters lies and mis-truths about products, people in advertising often see it the other way around. Their task is to try to recognise the lived thing in itself and to impose this consciousness on others. Methodologically, that which is to be the advertised product will be used, consumed, gazed-upon, touched, manipulated, tested and taken apart so to establish physical and immaterial affordances, and the core form of the product or service in question. It is an attempt to put aside purely intellectual understanding so to understand the primordial and sensational dimension of that which is being dealt with. This 'beingness' will then be used as the source for creating engaging expression. Dewey (2005 [1934]: 108) comments that art 'throws off the covers that hide the expressiveness of experienced things' and 'intercepts every shade of expressiveness found in objects and orders them in a new experience of life', but perhaps this observation better describes creative advertising?

The endeavour of advertising then is to intuit and express the phenomenological and experiential truth of the thing in itself. This means being aware of, and exploring, all properties, attributes and connections about the object that typically go unremarked upon, passed over and unsaid. So while advertising is said to deal in representation this is not quite the case as there is first the process of ascertaining and identifying what is to be expressed. This property, quality and experiential truth is important for advertisers and it is this dimension of the lived that is the true creative playground. This mode of engagement involves recognition of that which affectively structures our world, drives our propensity to it and fashions our memory of things in the world. This is where advertising is confused with mistruths: its purpose is not to tell the physical truth of a product but to fashion the experiential truth of objects. Truth-in-itself is unknown to advertising.

Conclusion

Practitioner perspectives in advertising tend towards a pastiche of creativity through allusions to excess, overload of being, dramatic living and authenticity, despite or perhaps even because of its tools of trade being highly imagistic. However, if we push past the hyperbole, the emphasis on vivacity, experience, emotion and engaging with the present permeates accounts of creativity in advertising. Creative advertisers believe that over-emphasis on strategy in advertising leads to decontextualisation and sterilisation that fails to recognise the complexities and idiosyncrasies of lived life. Further, they argue it is from this experiential rather than scientifically fostered understanding that creative advertising draws strength. There emerges an emphasis on creating immediate experiences and the process of advertising is less about construction, but rather as revealing, so for the creative work to emerge from the brand, product or service itself. In practical terms this means visiting factories, knowing as much about the product as possible, using it, and meeting the people that use it so as to develop and be able to reveal new insights and ways of thinking about a particular product or service. This goes to the heart of creative practice in advertising and is expressed by the requirement that creatives interrogate, describe, disclose and eventually unfurl the true nature of a product understood experientially.

While metaphor and rhetoric play a key role in expressing ideas, these are only vehicles to tell a particular story about a unique entity.

The language and discourses that creatives in advertising employ are at times highly phenomenological and particularly redolent of Husserl, Heidegger and Merleau-Ponty. In exploring the relationship between creativity in advertising and phenomenology, we can see that the best of its practitioners are not just able to fashion a snappy headline or an attention-grabbing image but, by means of renunciation of strategic dominance, to play with experiential being. Although later chapters shift from the idea of being as that which is found or indeed created, and towards a process-based view where being emerges through interaction, events and engagement, the deep level of engagement that the best practitioners go to is worthy of remark and exploration. This engagement is seen in creative advertising circles in terms of revealing, highlighting and intensifying experiences of objects and advertising among specified groups of people. It is to deal in the immediacy of the present and how things come to be objective, true, unique in experience, and the variety of processes required to make such 'events' happen. The emphasis on uniqueness is important, particularly as we progress to discuss the lived, circumstantial, affective, sensational and process-based dimension of advertising experiences (or events) in later chapters.

The strength of an idea in advertising, then, is the extent to which the truth appears to be self-evident and natural after engaging with the advertising and/or the product/service advertised. Another way of putting this is that a strong advertising idea is the invoking of a perceived phenomenological essence without which the object would not be properly recognised (as defined by the purpose and objective of the campaign). A strong advertising idea is distinct and stripped-back with all non-essential elements bracketed-out. It is to create an experience that is immediate, clear and that purposefully alters or maintains attitude towards a given object. So while we may already be accustomed with an object or service, a strong advertising idea may potentially renew that which has faded with familiarity.

While many accounts of creativity tend to deal in creativity as novelty (as this book does to some extent), in offering a phenomenological account we might say that creativity in advertising has more to do with revealing than invention or innovation. There is then a sense of primitivism about this approach to advertising that reflects the original archaic language of poetry, as well as the powerful illusion of the imagination and communication that does not tell, but expresses and is in excess. The best of advertising is that mode of creativity that evokes and reveals rather than describes.

Notes

1 The need to control all aspects of the advertising process continues today, most notably in online behavioural advertising that sees application of segmentation techniques taken to an exponentially different magnitude. My earlier book,

The Mood of Information (McStay, 2011), addresses both the genealogy of segmentation, data-mining and the consequences of such practice in granular detail.

2 Founded by Maxwell Dane, Ned Doyle and William Bernbach.

3 The UK's Advertising Standards Authority has a litany of campaigns that have caused controversy and come under threat of a ban.

4 The creative brief is the crystallisation of much work done prior to reaching agency creatives. Based on market research, analysis and reflection, the brief details: the advertiser, why they are seeking to advertise and what the role of the communication is; the target audience; insight into the consumer and why X product/brand is different; the proposition and the core message to be delivered; how consumers should respond to the advertising; why they should believe the claims of the advertising; the identity of the brand; the tone of voice of the advertising; and also mandatory elements that should appear in the advertising (such as a logo). Briefs differ between agencies but it will usually be a single page long (for more detail see Yeshin, 2005).

5 The translation of *Verfremdungseffekt* is the subject of some controversy and has also been understood to mean alienation from the familiar (see Willett, 1964).

3 The poetics of advertising

Chapter 2 provided detail and background on how creativity is perceived within the advertising industry, and then proceeded to theorise the creative process within advertising as deeply phenomenological and predicated on what is phrased here as positive indeterminacy that, in regard to advertising, is the action of privileging engagement with phenomenological and experiential dimensions of culture. However, this focus on formative processes and rootedness-in-the-world does not tell of the fruits of this engagement, nor does it provide much insight into the craft of making. This is what is meant here by poetics, that is, the ways in which advertising is assembled to produce a desired effect of some sort.

The aim of this chapter is to first isolate what a creative advertisement is and how this is constituted. In developing this I argue that, until recently, creativity in advertising may be defined as a distillation of complexity. The first part of this chapter considers some of the influences to have given rise to this premise. While the 'distillation of complexity' idea still holds for the majority of advertising, recent years have seen a weakening in what is a proposition supported by a pictorial conception of advertising where stimuli are fashioned upfront to make a point or achieve a goal of some sort. The second part of this chapter examines creative advertising practices in a digital context, particularly in regard to participatory influences on production, social over semiotic substitution, and the ways in which advertising might be better thought of as an event rather than a text.

Arts and crafts

Taken as a whole, the predominant belief within the advertising industry is that creativity is characterised by simplicity, economy and the somewhat modern idea of less being more when it comes to representation. Advertising then is an exercise in techniques of compression and composition. This has occurred because advertising is employed to fulfil a specific function. Being required to convey a large amount of information in a short period of time has shaped advertisements over the years and given rise to aesthetics that quite clearly belong to advertising. However, in arriving at this, advertising has plundered and cannibalised wider aesthetic practices, often paying little lip service to the intent of styles, techniques and visions it has outright stolen from. This said, influence has not all been one way and many artistic movements have pilfered or appropriated from advertising.

Before we proceed, we should clear up the question of whether advertising, as an aesthetic practice, should be considered art. One way of dealing with this is to ask to what extent is advertising a craft? Crafts involve closeness to materials, and the application of design and aesthetics to objects of utility. Collingwood (1997 [1938]), for example, remarks on a number of differences between arts and crafts: the first is that the result is preconceived and the craftsperson will know what he or she would like to make before making it. There will then be a right or correct way of doing things, where haphazard and chaotic approaches are to be avoided. Indeed, if a craftsperson begins with an outline for a table and chairs and ends up with something only vaguely resembling this, then the craftsperson is unlikely to be a successful one. For Collingwood, art in contrast has to do with *indirectly* arousing emotions. Although art can, of course, arouse emotion, there is possibly less intentionality involved compared to a crafted object where each component or factor is carefully considered so to engender a desired response. While it is commonly held that artists might seek to express, this does not necessarily translate to an intention to evoke. This avoidance of overt arousal leaves us with questions, perhaps most obviously that although art representatives might claim expression over vulgar sensation-mongering, how might we ever know the difference and what was really intended? Indeed, as detailed in Chapter 5, artists such as Cezanne and Francis Bacon predicated their work on the bringing-about of sensation. An intention to stimulate involves knowledge of: the audience; the medium and its potential for affect; the reaction sought; the language or means with which to communicate; suitable content; and tone of voice.

Moreover, while craft can be conceived in general replicable terms where one might seek to fashion the best and most functional table ever produced, in advertising, one would soon feel the wrath of a Creative Director for advertising that is 'correct'. Indeed, in addition to being strategically appropriate, award-winning advertising tends to be that which is novel in terms of content, evocation, the strange/familiar dyad, feelings generated, insight or use of media; damnation arrives in 'This has been done before'. Advertising then is not solely a craft.

In regard to art, it is instructive to go back to Kant's discussion of how art might be distinguished from handicraft. Art here has to do with intellectual enrichment and being free to choose what to create while the industrial arts are a form of labour. Labour, in an eighteenth-century context, is a strong term to apply to the process of creative advertising, so we might consider positioning it within what Kant calls the agreeable arts and those that 'have mere enjoyment for their objects' (1952 [1790]: §43, 165–66) – namely that which fosters a genial spirit where few would pay attention to its composition. The position of creative advertising among art, craft and the agreeable arts is unclear, but it does sit between these bases, as creative advertising possesses a functional dimension and overtly interacts with a range of aesthetic practices. However, while functional, it rarely follows rules or Platonic blueprints to do what has been done before, as craft traditionally does; conversely, while participating in aesthetic production its purpose is ostensibly to serve the needs of a named client. The designation 'applied art' seems to perform well.

Questions over the distinction between artists and advertising creatives find wider expression in the dyads of authentic/derivative, fine/applied and originality/craft, and the dyad of commercial imperatives vs. autonomy in cultural production is well recognised within the industry. More recently, industry bodies such as D&AD (2011) have responded to such distinctions by highlighting the value of commercial creativity and craft skills, but also invoking tropes of restlessness, agitation, brilliance, pushing boundaries and experimentation more usually associated with art. Instead of bemoaning that advertising creatives should serve two purposes (creative excellence and the specifics of clients' needs), in commercial creativity this is celebrated.

The idea that art and advertising exist in different domains is further problematised by the history of creative advertising, and poster art in particular. During the late nineteenth century, for example, Jules Chéret ensured that colour lithography was not just a reproductive technique, but also an artistic one. Chromolithography facilitated the mass production of posters that emulated the sensual effects of oil painting, yet along with new chemical inks, afforded colossal print runs and massive posters more easily handled by printers. As Salsi observes, 'for the first time art and graphics – including lettering – printing technology and free innovation, business advertising and artistic work all coincided and fed one another' (2007: 14). Moreover, quite arguably, Art Nouveau and its combining of the fine arts and applied arts was inspired by advertising (particularly Alphonse Mucha's lithographed poster for the play *Gismonda* that appeared in Paris in 1895). Indeed, posters received 'high art' status and were recognised by the French art establishment as a credible medium when in 1889 Chéret was made Chevalier of the Légion d'Honneur (a form of knighthood) for creating a new medium for art by applying art to commercial and industrial printing.

Importantly for the subsequent status and reputation of posters, many leading artists such as Boccioni were co-opted into designing them. Poster art is perhaps best encapsulated by the work of Leonetto Cappiello and the pieces he created for Campari and Cinzano. While not a formally trained artist, Cappiello was insistent that attention be paid to maintaining the aesthetic of the street, and the artistic and visual education of the masses. In regards to purity of form, inspired by Edward McKnight Kauffer's graphical work for Shell, British Rail and London Transport among other clients, Abram Games from the late 1930s onwards was insistent on poster messages being delivered quickly and vividly through the arrangement of familiar objects in new ways.

It is notable too that Games described himself as an 'Advertising Artist' in the letterhead he used for correspondence with clients. Games possessed little in the way of an overt signature style, although his creative process gave rise to a unique vision for each client. While creative advertising is often said not to be art as it serves more than one purpose (client objectives as well as aesthetic value) for Games there was no confusion of purpose: his dedication to his clients lent a purity and singularity of vision ironically also found in art. With Games' aphorism famously being 'maximum meaning, minimum means', his point is that posters should not tell a story but make a point. Whereas other artists contemporary to him designed posters without a client in mind and appropriate lettering was added once a client was found, Games' approach was that all aspects of the poster interrelate, and that elements and the sum of these should identify with the client. This involves 'logic, feeling, atmosphere and more tangible characteristics such as colour, trademark, lettering etc. All parts of the design should work together, inseparable from the whole' (Games, 2008: 7). While simplicity and power are important, they are over-ridden by content: nothing should appear that does not add to meaning-making. What was thus required from the creator was clear, powerful and precise communication.

The poster form remains quintessential advertising, superseding television or any newer mediums by far in terms of purity. Posters are, by definition, a mode of persuasion to take place in the public domain. Their strength comes from directionality, capacity for impact and the means by which successful posters wrench their viewers from the world and demand attention. This impact born of simplicity, synthesis, bisociation (involving the combination of unrelated elements to form a novel and valuable outcome) and intensity is reflected well in John Hegarty's observation:

> The more an idea is distilled, the more forceful it becomes; it is part of the fascination and strange allure of the poster that it can say so much by using so little ... It is an essential factor in the art of communication.
>
> (Hegarty, 1998: 223)

The employment of lone illustration-based realisations had waned by midway through the twentieth century. Part of this had to do with changes in the poster form itself that was deeply affected by photography and more realistic modes of representation, with other factors having to do with the rise of other mass media. Working practices changed as a result of this and creative output began to receive input from a variety of people both inside and outside the advertising agency. While television advertising rose in terms of popularity of media choice and expenditure during the 1950s and 1960s, and enjoyed its extravagant heyday in the 1980s (Tungate, 2007), the aesthetics of distillation and interplay of modal elements continued as a defining characteristic of what is deemed creative in advertising.

While advertising has always involved co-creative processes, perhaps most pointedly since copywriters and art directors began working as teams in the 1950s, the house or signature style of an agency or luminary creative is still quite evident today. Generally speaking, however, as mass media such as television moved into the ascendant, this shifted the emphasis from the advertisement as a creative object to that which is a part or outcome of a larger co-creative practice. This sees creativity as being more about process, unfolding, emergence and interaction – all themes that will be returned to in more depth in later chapters.

Undermining hierarchies

While the essence of creative advertising tends towards maximising impact through minimal means, irreverence is another characteristic that frequently recurs in accounts of what constitutes creativity in advertising. It is also a common component of much award-winning and lauded work. One cannot help but be reminded of Dada (that stole from advertising) and Tristan Tzara's observation that 'Dada began not as an art form, but as a disgust' with a world racked by war, boring dogmas, conventional sentiments and pedantry (Alexandrian, 1995: 29). Like many proponents of creative advertising, Dada also sought to destabilize distinctions between fine art and popular culture.

The two-way influence between Dada and poster advertising is perversely notable (given Dada's anti-capital stance), particularly in regards to photo-montage and its capacity for association, metaphor, juxtaposition and flexible picture language. Indeed, while Dada and Pop (accounted for below) have been most overt in their plundering, Picasso, Duchamp and Bruce Nauman among many others have all appropriated mass media and advertising content (Gibbons, 2005). Similarly Barbara Kruger, Lawrence Weiner, Edward Ruscha and Tracey Emin have all fused the verbal and the visual in a way that, at least indirectly, points to an advertising influence. This interaction between advertising and art is perhaps best seen in the work of Dada's Hannah Höch (an originator of photomontage) who, through juxtaposition of pictorial and linguistic elements, exploits the way in which advertisements were held to play with the unconscious. Here there is an irreverent intellectualism present that preceded and pre-empted postmodernism and late twentieth-century advertising with its enticing headlines and imagery that interact with each another. Dada's full legacy, at least in relation to advertising, was to come later with the recognition of postmodernism, its destabilising cultural practices, and also in stunts, swagger, irreverence, twists and bizarre headlines that made strange familiar items from popular culture.

In regard to advertising Jeremy Bullmore (2003), for example, goes as far as to say that showing the familiar and potentially mundane in a new light is one of the most important functions of advertising. In the annals of creative advertising, there are many examples of 'reality with a twist'. David Ogilvy's *Man in the Hathaway Shirt* from the early 1950s is one of the more famous examples that employed an eye-patch to evoke intrigue, mystique and societal interest in Hathaway's distinguished gentleman (and via a supposed process of transference, their shirts). There are surrealist overtones here, although the objectives of advertising and surrealism are of course quite different with one of these seeking to liberate the unconscious. As with copywriters and art directors in advertising, surrealism saw poets and painters team up, with Apollinaire stating that the poet must always be the accomplice of the painter – a firm ally in the triumph over the unknown (Alexandrian, 1995). Similar too is the emphasis on not only possessing technical ability, but also the intellectual ability to engage in processes of destabilisation, creating audience uncertainty, and the charging of images with a new power so to reveal an insight. In both too there is an element of play-along with a healthy dose of subversion, irreverence and an awareness of the instability of lived life. Magritte provided many templates for the processes of exaggeration and reversal that are common in creative advertisers' toolboxes. This is not to suggest that Magritte was sympathetic to advertising as clearly he was not. He even went as far as to state that what he hated most in the world is advertising, and that he found it imbecilic (Cook, 1992). However, despite his misgivings, he provided numerous tools for 'reality with a twist' that characterises much advertising considered creative.

The aesthetics of creative advertising are embodied in *Lürzer's Archive* that collects and publishes in magazine and web form advertising deemed outstanding. As with Magritte and surrealism, advertising therein often involves transformation, visual puns, changes in matter, content, location, oversized objects, messing with size constancy, changes in colour, taking something away, adding things, and distortion. Sometimes they are of absolute graphical simplicity, as with the bird's-eye close-up of Kikkoman's red soy sauce bottle-top against a plain white background so to be indexical to the Japanese flag – produced by Leo Burnett in 2005. Another for Coke by Ogilvy & Mather, Shanghai, that won the Outdoor Grand Prix in Cannes 2012, simply depicts the Coke's vertical white stripe present on all their red cans as two elongated hands passing a bottle from one to another in the manner of a relay baton. Another by Welcome to Orange County in 2005 for Koi Living depicts a knife placed into a wooden holding block that has descended and cut right through the block itself. Less simple, but also taking without consent from the surrealist's store, is a 2005 advertisement by The Dukes of Urbino.Com depicting what appears to be a giant floating duck peering into a Matchbox toy boat. Also from 2005, produced by Sil, Kuala Lumpur, is Burger King's smile in which a bap acts as upper and lower mouth, onion as teeth, a burger as cavern of a mouth, and a slice of tomato as salivating tongue licking teeth and lips. In addition to distillation and irreverence then, we can add reformulation to our account of what typically makes up the poetics of creativity in advertising.

So far we have been looking at mutual influence and crossovers between art and advertising, but where the boundaries between advertising and art become utterly blurred is with Pop. While Warhol is the most famous proponent, we might also remember Stuart Davis and Charles Sheeler who in the 1920s and 1930s developed Standard Still Life that drew from and celebrated everyday items such as the rubber glove and the electric fan. Deriving from Dada, Warhol's commodity-based art turned a mirror against mass society, delivering useful testimony on the pre-eminence of mass production, consumer goods, advertising and cultural norms in the mid- to late twentieth century. The art's value, intrigue and power are generated by the isolation, detachment and enlargement of items from mass culture. Popular culture to one side, Warhol also called into question the nature of originality in art and profited by repetition with works that were nearly identical.

While the textual interaction between popular culture and the art establishment is widely understood, the mode in which the work was produced is also noteworthy. Warhol's Pop factory was not entirely different from an advertising agency where work is co-created by a number of people. Indeed, Warhol was not only interested in advertising and mass production but had worked in agencies and received awards for his work. Despite dominant conceptions of authorship and art as that which is produced by individual artists, the factory method had antecedents too in Renaissance master artists, their assistants and the studios of Verrocchio, Leonardo, Cranach, Titian, Rubens or Rembrandt (Honnef, 2000). However, in advertising authorship is reduced even further through the wider range of input that feeds into the production of the visual aspect of advertising. While art directors have the final say on what is included in visual imagery, there is now a vast range of input from those outside the factory/agency environment including television producers and directors, post-production houses, colour graders, illustrators, musicians, technicians, web and multimedia designers, art buyers and photographers.

Television

While advertising has plundered from art, it has also appropriated from a much wider field of cultural production and society itself. While the form and poetics of posters led to the privileging of simplicity and the distillation of complexity, television advertising on first reflection seems more excessive, or perhaps even bloated. The truism remains the same, however, in that every second of a television commercial should involve distillation and compression. By the 1990s we saw what is quite possibly the zenith of commercials, intricate sign-use and leveraging of meaning systems in culture to create branded differences among products that were often quite similar. Perhaps the densest and strangest is Reebok's UBU (Reebok lets you be you) campaign produced by what was then the agency Chiat\Day, directed by David Bailey and edited by Lawrence Bridges in 1987. Containing a voice-over of Ralph Waldo Emerson's *Self Reliance* and a highly kitsch musical score reminiscent of Romani music, it depicts a number of scenes predicated on being non-conformist. In *Reading Ads Socially*, Goldman (1992: 205–10) offers a wonderfully rich description of this advertisement that includes square-dancing, a grown man with a bolo bat, two punks collecting milk from a cow, a pair of dancing elderly women in red trainers exiting an American diner, a man with three legs, three boys on rope swings moving in mechanical unison, ballerinas vacuuming a lawn, all of which (and much more) employed to destabilise traditional conventions of representation and interpretation in advertising. This took the lessons from Dada and Pop to the extreme through high levels of pastiche, parody, bizarre juxtapositions of signs and, as with photomontage, remixed, remade and cut-and-pasted. The theme of irreverence underpins this and many of these postmodern shenanigans were highly tongue-in-cheek. On occasion this turned advertising inside-out as spots highlighted the artifice of semiotic transference between unrelated signs, and turned this into a selling point. Others possessed at least a hint of deconstructionist posturing leaving viewers to fill in the gaps as to what an advertisement might be saying. Imbued throughout is irreverence and a mode of representation that was, and still is, self-reflexive. This involves taking on board criticisms of consumerism, advertising thought of as the detritus of capitalism, and turning this angst and appeal to realism into Baudrillardian hyperreal signs with which to generate more consumption (Goldman and Papson, 1996).

As both the amount and semiotic sophistication of advertising increased (definable in terms of intra-genre knowledge and reflexivity) we might ask from the perspective of 15 or so years later, what happened? As all areas of public and private life, along with the past and the future, became hyperreal and ensnared within a sea of commodity-signs, where could advertising go next? As advertising intensified its referents, sped-up, fed-back on itself, did we reach and breach an impasse and someone forgot to tell us? No, the answer is that the game changed and there is now more to advertising than representation as outlined above. This point has three dimensions to it: one, media targeting has come to play a greater role (as discussed in Chapter 10); two, advertising is realising opportunities outside of visual and aural communication (as discussed in Chapter 5); and three, possibilities are emerging of getting closer to potential customers without sacrificing the positive economies of scale that mass media delivered.

The poetics of improvisation

The coming into being of online media in the 1990s could not have come at a better time for advertisers as clearly the traditional line-up of media were being saturated. Lindstrom (2009) provides figures stating that by the time we reach 66 most of us will have seen two million television commercials, also highlighting that recall of advertising has dropped enormously from 34 per cent in 1965, to 8 per cent in 1990, onto a hard-to-believe 2.21 per cent in 2007. While we might question the numbers and methodology, we can take away a correct impression of both a saturated advertising environment and tired communicational strategies. Both of these for Lindstrom add up to developed consumer filtering systems and shorter attention spans.

Practices of co-creation extend beyond production into consumption and prosumption (Ritzer and Jurgenson, 2010). Although advertising is still typically a frame-based practice (whether this be mobile, web, poster, television, cinema or press) that seeks to draw its spectator into its representational and, as argued more forcefully later, sensational environment, there exists a degree of confusion about what advertising is today. It is revealing to search the front-end webpages of the top ten advertising agencies in the UK. One will find that advertising is rarely mentioned and none refer to themselves as advertising agencies. While containing shots and footage of advertising work, agencies are unsure of how to define themselves in a period when their self-identity is less assured than in previous decades. Where it was once quite clear that creativity in advertising is about a deep understanding of the product and the capacity to speak and embellish upon a basic truth using minimal means and paid-for and recognisable media; digital media and novel modes of audience engagement have generated unique challenges, opportunities and self-questioning within the industry about the nature of creativity and advertising. Whereas the advertising business once sought to interrupt as a means of obtaining attention, new methods of persuasive communication or promotion seek to engender participation, interaction and intimacy with potential customers and brand ambassadors. Moreover, the advertising object has changed somewhat. Where it was once a bounded object, a product or deliverable, an artefact, and that which can be stored and replayed on a reel of some sort, the temporal and spatial possibilities of advertising have expanded. The spatial dimension refers to the capacity to cross borders and geographic boundaries with minimal media spend, but more notable are temporal developments in advertising. This is driven by an interest in soliciting engagement and means that advertising is less about circulating an object then engaging in a mediated event and dialogue over a period of time. While the poetics of advertising have historically tended towards product-based representation, more recent forms for advertising may involve extemporisation. The capacity to react quickly, engage, respond and interact in a free-form manner sees the mediated creative process as a significant part of the deliverables. As Sawyer (2010: 107) highlights in discussion of creativity and jazz, 'musicians and improvising actors alike compare their ensemble interaction to conversation'.

Much of this change in discourse involves breaking down the perception of one-way information flow and encouraging consumers to connect with a brand's endeavours. Indeed, at times it appears that the less advertising involves advertisements the better. There is an almost theatrical dimension to this as agencies working on behalf of brands seek to stimulate attention and fellow-feeling between the brand and its potential consumers. Where commercials, radio spots and frozen print and poster advertising effectively denied participation and encouraged distance, the character of advertising developed in the first decade of the twenty-first century so to take advantage of wider participatory discourses occurring in the wider inter-connective media milieu.

Although advertising has always been predicated on interpretive play, deciphering complex texts and covert feedback mechanisms (for extended discussion of feedback and advertising see McStay, 2011), more overt feedback is now quite clearly desirable. The language of conversation and experience is now preferred (although data-mining has concurrently and exponentially intensified). While poster, television, radio, cinema and press advertising all continue, their pre-eminence has been irrevocably fractured by the arrival of digital modes of seduction (for wider discussion of digital advertising see McStay, 2009). Creativity and representation no longer equate to the same thing. Moreover, as media are not conduits through which information is relayed but are conduits for people and organisations, this requires that advertising adopts strategies usually found in public relations, having to do with influencing conversation in non-representational ways.

There is then a balance to be struck between the generation of brands, spectacular ontologies, meta-messages and shared experiences, and more subtle attempts to engage with interested people and steer chatter and conversation taking place both on- and offline. These types of endeavours are quite different from those based on aesthetic production and minimal means where advertisers only have a short period of time in which to solicit attention. In an advanced media culture there exists common discourse and language that advertisers and audiences alike will both engage and perform in. If handled well, advertisers no longer need to worry about seconds of engagement and exposure. Where the poetics of advertising in the past have been shaped by media affordances that limit interaction and time frames for engagement, this is now not necessarily the case. This provides opportunity for advertisers to play with the form of advertising and on occasion parody its very conventions. Take for example Wieden + Kennedy in 2010 and the Old Spice viral commercial featuring the actor, and former NFL player, Isaiah Mustafa asking women whether they would want their men to smell like him. Winning the Grand Prix at the Cannes International Advertising Festival, this campaign successfully utilised social networking sites including Facebook, Twitter and YouTube. On Twitter, the Old Spice Guy tweeted, 'Today could be just like the other 364 days you log into Twitter, Or maybe the Old Spice man shows up.' He subsequently answered fans' queries on YouTube videos ranging from 'how many teeth do sharks have?' to 'If there was an epic battle between you and a rabid lion, who would end up looking better after?' For example, wspencer tweeted, '@oldspice Am typing while running from stampede of scantily-clad female admirers who appeared after trying #oldspice. Is there an antidote?' Old Spice Guy even engaged in matrimonial duties when a fan named Johannes S. Beals tweeted, 'Can U Ask my girlfriend to marry me? Her name is Angela A. Hutt-Chamberlin' to Old Spice. A video appeared up on YouTube within an hour, and Old Spice tweeted it at Beals.[1]

While self-parody in advertising is nothing new with much television adver-tising in the 1980s and 1990s drawing attention to its mode of construction, wider media formulae, literacy of past advertising, recycling of other cultural signs, the adoption of ironic poses or even seeming attacks on capitalism itself, the Old Spice man is emblematic of all this plus engagement and the wish to more deeply interact with communities.

Community

Concurrent with the desire to influence conversation is the wish either to be part of a community or to found a community. There are a number of advertising examples that reflect this, particularly in integrated approaches. UNIQLO's *Lucky Line* highlights this trend well, making a virtue of queuing for sales, but in an online environment. Created by Dentsu Tokyo in 2010 this involved a mini-metaverse hosted on UNIQLO's website through which the company sought to boost sales and create brand awareness by means of a virtual queue populated by avatars managed by people through Twitter and Facebook. While a virtual shopping queue might not have obvious appeal, #UNIQLO Lucky Line became a top worldwide trendword on Twitter and generated a virtual queue consisting of: 180,000 people in Japan; 630,000 in Taiwan and 1,300,000 in China. This campaign also linked into their real-world stores where discounts could be redeemed, and where in Japan UNIQLO set a single-day sales record of 10 billion yen. This is not the only example with many companies now building social components and game structures into their websites (involving challenges, prizes and races against the clock).

Volkswagen and their agency AlmapBBDO in 2010 engaged in similar endeavours mixing up the virtual and the real by giving away tickets to a music festival in São Paulo. Hiding the tickets in ten different places around the city, interested people had to use the hashtag #FoxatPlanetaTerra and the more they collectively tweeted about the VW Fox at the festival, the closer Google Maps would zoom in on the location of the tickets. Twitter users called on other Twitter users to forward the hashtag and push the Google Maps zoom on with some users simply adding the hashtag to their daily tweets. While the idea of a treasure hunt is not especially novel, although it is unusual in an advertising context, #FoxatPlanetaTerra became a trending topic on Twitter within two hours, remaining there for the duration of the four-day campaign. A campaign for Dulux paints by Euro RSCG London in 2010 titled *The Let's Colour Project* employed a more literal interpretation of creativity and community. In four cities in four different countries, this involved painting grey urban spaces with bright colours. The advertising agency worked with local communities painting streets, squares and schools lacking colour. Film and written content was uploaded to blogs, YouTube, Twitter, Facebook and Orkut pages in real-time. A documentary director also made films depicting the partnerships between locals and visitors.

Subsequently an architect in Italy, the governor of Bangkok, a girl in Kosovo and a community leader in Chile asked the campaign's project leaders to bring the project to their area of the world. In terms of exposure, this achieved 2,000 posts on independent blogs; one million views across online channels; 500,000 film views online in less than four weeks; twelfth most tweeted video in Twitter film category; one of TED's ads worth spreading; and film of the week on YouTube UK.

Creative advertising in this context requires engagement and sustained dialogue, or at least close monitoring of users' activities, and represents an aspect of advertising quite different from representational creativity whose lineage is frame-based art. Where traditional frame-based advertising is fixed, in the sense that it is enduring, communitarian creativity is performative, temporally-located, transitory and event-based.

Ironically however, it is a broadcast advertisement that perhaps best represents contemporary discourses of community, sociality and a version of creativity in advertising that appears less remote and representational. Whereas earlier representational forms of advertising involved semiotic substitution, much advertising now utilizes what we might call social substitution. Take for example a 2009 campaign by Saatchi & Saatchi for T-Mobile, a brand owned by Deutsche Telekom AG. The first advertisement titled 'Dance' depicts an apparently spontaneous flashmob in London's Liverpool Street station, and later in the campaign at Heathrow airport. The idea for this campaign derives directly from the site-specific dance and performance company *sevensistersgroup* and the group's Susanne Thomas-choreographed, *Trainstation* (1998). It is in the performative overlapping with the everyday and the shift from the stage to more familiar environments where *Trainstation* gains its power. Deriving from situationist and surreal endeavours that push us to reveal a little more of ourselves, this type of work involves interventionist dance, social disturbance, the blurring of performance and everyday life, and the conventions and idiosyncrasies of the social world around us. T-Mobile's 'Dance' also reveals a subtle change in approach to sociality. Rather than attempting to be the most popular, it is the facilitator.

Indeed, sociality is appropriated and folded-in to the commodity-sign so for T-Mobile to brand connectivity, joy, spontaneity, frivolity and community by means of a planned accident. Thus not only do we enjoy the advertisements themselves, but we are hailed by the meta-discourse of sociality. While this may appear that advertising is leveraging an authentic sign, we might scratch a little further and realise that the discursive construction of sociality is itself too a highly mediated sign. Transparency, openness, uncritical tendencies and performativity are all words readily associated with the branding strategies of well-known social network services. While the emphasis on sociality is not surprising for a brand and company whose business is 'communications', it is an important point to mark. Where traditionally brands have fought via straightforward representational means to make an impression and be number one, T-Mobile has sought to leverage sociality and community as a standing-reserve and the creative strategy is thus to commodify that which rebels against anomie and advertising as depicted within Capital Realist discourse. In doing so, T-Mobile offers a sugar-sweetened simulation of a counter-articulation against advertising-filled liminal and soulless non-places.

Conclusion

This chapter has disturbed easy distinctions between art and advertising, particularly in relation to Abram Games' insistence on a purity of vision that emerges out of the commercial task at hand. The interplay between art and advertising also points to porous and less-than-clear borders. What we designate as advertising is changing too and where advertising was once clearly understood as being content that utilises paid-for media space, this definition is increasingly less encompassing. Nor is even the association with representation certain as participatory and interlinked media events become more popular.

Note

1 Available from www.youtube.com/watch?v=-fLV28SkZ8&feature=player_
embedded.

4   Playful combinations

The aim of this chapter is to account for combinatory conceptions of creativity. There are two parts to this: the first relates to what Koestler (1970 [1964]) labels bisociation; and the second has to do with more familiar semiotic, structural and critically-led accounts of advertising. While these share similarities, there are also significant differences worthy of exploration particularly in regard to surprise and the requirement of audience involvement. In exploring the role of combinations, the chapter also accounts for the centrality of play, reflexivity and meta-communication to creativity. The chapter progresses to expand the premise of creativity beyond combinatory logic, to explore what Boden (2004; 2010) designates as exploration and transformation, and positions these in relation to advertising.

Generation

Creativity tends to be linked with divergence, or that mode of thinking that involves multiplicity over convergent and singular solutions (Wilson et al., 1954; Getzels and Jackson, 1962; de Bono 1990 [1970]; 2007). Convergence in these accounts is framed as being akin to elementary mathematics involving answers that are demanded by the given information. Divergent thinking is different in that it requires another order of thinking. For example, we might ask: 'can you give words that mean the same as cold?' to which one could answer, 'chilly, impersonal or infection'. Where one person seeks practical solutions that preclude anything but the correct answer (or the shortest route to it), the other tends to be more imaginative displaying less commitment to practical solutions. To quote one example from Hudson, he asks a mathematical near-prodigy and an arts specialist to give uses for the common brick. While the scientist answers 'building things, throwing', the diverger responds with:

> As a weight. As a weapon (missile). As a grindstone and sandpaper. To build with. To make a flower-bed edge. To keep something from blowing away. To make a bookshelf out of. As a hot water bottle. As a paper weight. As a book end. As a bolster to level a table or something similar.

Instead of an asbestos mat on a stove. As a tile to pave a courtyard. To block a drain. To break a window. As a hammer. As an ornament. As a draught excluder. As a scourer. As a ruler, or set square. As a stepping stone. As a practical joke in cake or as a present. As a nutcracker.

(Hudson, 1966: 90–92)

Thus, in contrast to thinking where thought-processes converge on a solution, divergence involves a degree of inventiveness. We should be very careful of privileging the diverger over the converger, or even directly linking it to creativity. This is because although the generation of multiple solutions may be fruitful, this does not necessarily equate to originality or anything of value. However, this mode of thinking is clearly evident in advertising where numerous solutions to problems are both desirable and possible. It is notable too, as highlighted in earlier discussion, that both divergent and convergent approaches are required in advertising as strategic acumen combines with churn and idea generation.

Akin to divergent ideas that involve connecting ideas and objects between multiple planes is bisociation through which two seemingly unrelated dimensions of thought are combined to form a novel outcome. Koestler states:

I have coined the term 'bisociation' in order to make a distinction between the routine skills of thinking on a single 'plane', as it were, and the creative act, which as I shall try to show, always operates on more than one plane.

(Koestler, 1970 [1964]: 35)

It involves combining for novel effect different types of items and ideas from different domains, dimensions or discourses. While sharing characteristics with semiotic approaches in that it involves bringing together two or more domains to create another province for stimulation and meaning-making, it is done for a different effect. For example, a 2012 poster advertisement[1] by RKCR/Y&R London selling Land Rover's 'Defender' off-road vehicle simply depicts a line-up of syringes, each labelled with what one would be inoculated for if going on an intrepid mission, possibly to Africa or Asia (diseases include hepatitis A, yellow fever, tetanus, diphtheria, meningococcal meningitis, rabies, tick infection, typhoid and tuberculosis). It is an arresting image and possibly one that falls under the slightly dumb category of 'shock advertising', particularly as rabies, the more obviously visceral disease, is privileged. While there are chains of semiotic association to be argued but not conclusively stated, the actual event of the advertisement is in the co-creative joining up of the domains being referred to that makes the wider branded meta-point (that the Defender is for hardcore off-roaders). The 'aha' moment of a creative act (whether it be making or enjoying a creative event) comes through disturbance of the familiar, and when we realise there are two (or potentially more) planes being referred to and the means by which they have been linked together. While applicable to endeavours ranging between comedy and the sciences, this conception also underpins creativity in representational advertising as broached in Chapter 3. For example in 2000 the advertising agency Leo Burnett on behalf of the canned tuna manufacturer John West[2] used a visual pun titled *Fishing* involving a close-up of the top of a tin can to depict concentric circles in a pool of water with a fishing line cast into the middle of it. The bisociation is not just tenuous but used so to market John West's fish as simple, pure and not caught with nets.[3] Another example from 1998 by Saatchi & Saatchi for Burger King titled *Fiery Fries* depicts a chip (or fry) dipped in red sauce so to resemble a matchstick[4] (see also Pricken, 2002: 15).

Hegarty comments, 'Creativity is a manic construction of absurd, unlikely irreverent thoughts and feelings that somehow, when put together, change the way we see things' (2011: 28). The capacity to express brand ideas through bisociative approaches provides a sense of freshness and originality. Not all combinations or bisociation is obvious or 'aha'-like and it is worth considering how absurd some of the juxtapositions are. Hegarty's and BBH's pitch for Flat Eric, the yellow puppet character made by Jim Henson's Creature Shop, to Levi Strauss for Sta-Prest One Crease Denim Clothing cannot have been an easy task. Released in 1999, Flat Eric rode with his friend Angel around California evading the police as a wanted criminal in a Chevrolet. With *Flat Beat*, a tech-house tune by Mr. Oizo playing in the background, Flat Eric driven by Angel taps his fingers on the sill of the open window also head bobbing enthusiastically but coolly along to the music. Similarly, Budweiser's croaking frogs from the mid-1990s created by DMB&B/St. Louis ('bud', 'weis', 'er') must have made for an interesting client presentation. Featuring three frogs in a swamp at night one frog croaks 'bud', another, 'weis' and the last 'er'. Initially in random order, the frogs eventually begin to croak in sequence and the camera eventually pulls back to reveal the bar on shore with Budweiser in red neon lights. Time and again in the realm of entertainment, audiences of arts and advertising have unexpectedly warmed to incongruous and seemingly unrelated juxtaposition and bisociation. As discussed below, audience readings of meta-communication co-creatively add to the stock of a brand as aspects of advertisements are shared in a mnemonic fashion in workplaces, schoolyards and other public spaces.

For Koestler the creative act does not result from fashioning a creative product from nothing. Instead, 'it uncovers, selects, re-shuffles, combines, synthesizes already existing facts, ideas, faculties, skills' (1970 [1964]: 119), and the more unrelated the objects or ideas, the more scope there is for creativity. While elements of the combination should complement, there should also be a jolt of sorts so to create surprise and awareness of novelty. In creative advertising there is a balance to be found in that bisociation should make sense for the target audience, as well as for organisations giving out industry awards. If advertising is obvious, this reflects poorly on the brand; but too tenuous, then the advertising fails to communicate. The role of the audience member then is an important one as they are co-creatively required to spot the analogies and make the links themselves. Creativity then requires more than originality, but it should also be relevant and appropriate to the task or endeavour. Moreover, while novelty is useful and important, we should not misrecognise creativity as a free-for-all celebration of the weird and random. Rather, creativity to a greater or lesser extent operates within parameters of some sort, if only to transcend them.

Play

While we might associate playfulness with fields of open creativity, abandon and being free from rules, actually the opposite is true. Although we mostly use the word without restraint it has quite a precise and bounded meaning. Huizinga (1955 [1938]) depicts that play pre-dates culture and that the distinction between human and animal play is little, if any, as both are predicated on ceremony, attitude and gesture. It is also something that is voluntary, cannot be forced, is not a task, is done at leisure, involves separation from everyday life, has a defined duration and is predicated on freedom.

Caillois (2001 [1958]) picks up the baton from Huizinga, delineating a clearer-cut and more rules-based account of play. Among other descriptors, he posits that play involves: uncertainty, where meaning outcomes are not known in advance; rules, when ordinary conventions are suspended in favour of another set; awareness of another reality; absence of creation of capital or goods; being unproductive; an occasion of pure waste; that it is free and voluntary; a source of diversion, joy and amusement; and that the player is free to leave or stop. In regard to zones of play, Caillois draws attention to: competitive games such as boxing (*agôn*); games of chance such as gambling (*alea*); simulation-based games such as tag played by children (*mimicry*); and vertigo, as found in fairgrounds, snowboarding or downhill mountain biking (*ilinx*). These four categories also exist on a continuum of ways of playing where on the one hand we have high levels of spontaneity, liveliness, exuberance and free improvisation (*paidia*); and the other that involves rules, thought, patience, skill, discipline and calculation (*ludus*). Ludus is a disciplining of paidia – the reservoir from which the impulse to play emerges. Both paidia (play) and ludus (game) find their origins in ancient Homeric, Platonic and wider Greek accounts of education, and that which helps achieve perfection and excellence (Jaeger, 1986 [1944]).

Caillois argues that play involves local rules, uncertainty of outcome, pleasure and that it is separate from wider goings-on in life. Although correct on the first points, there is no clear reason why the opposition between 'real' and 'play' should be so absolute and dualistically determined. If Caillois is insistent on divorcing play from the multiplicity of everyday life, is play rendered unreal by the cutting of all ties and relationships with life that give rise to the playful situation? At this point then we might give up trying to make associations between play, creativity and advertising. After all, as people are paid to do advertising, this is surely work? However, in both Huizinga (1955 [1938]) and Caillois (2001 [1958]), definitions of work tend towards utility, necessity, repetition and work from which little pleasure is derived. This does not characterise all work as some of us are fortunate enough to do work we enjoy and find enriching. Advertising is one of these pursuits and agency environments are usually designed in such a way as to foster a sense of leisure (sometimes containing pool tables, for example). Many agency environments are architected, designed and brightly decorated to be more open, fluidic and unlike traditional office environments. Demarcated from the world so to foster inspiration, they encourage interaction, and sharing of space, time and ideas. However, deadlines do have to be met and few would observe that the advertising business is stress-free, but this also applies to other areas more frequently associated with play, such as sport or even computer gaming. For example sportspeople train hard and get nervous before races, and adult gamers' cortisol levels increase during the playing of exciting mainstream games containing techno music (Ritterfeld et al., 2009). In regard to motivation and why people work in creative advertising, this is intrinsic as well as extrinsic. Although rewards and accolades motivate (as with games), and while financial rewards are high for those at the very top, starter salaries in the UK are not especially high and possibly as low as £15,000 (Creativepool, 2012). It is also a notoriously difficult industry to enter both in terms of a high candidate-to-recruitment ratio, and that placement schemes to gain experience may involve little or no payment along with the financial hardships of getting-by in the most expensive cities in the world.

We can look at the relationship between advertising, play and creativity in two ways: one, that the connection exists; or two, that managers of agencies seek to foster a sense of play within agencies to engender a more stimulating environment in which to create and work. It is worth noting too that agencies tend not only to group in specific cities, but also zones of a city (for example Soho and Charlotte Street in London) where very few employees will actually live. In relation to play and ritual, creative work tends to be practised in teams of two. Absorption occurs as teams pontificate, posit, test, probe and exchange ideas, and along this path there will be highs and lows as ideas emerge only to crash through irrelevance or lack of originality. Among other reasons, lows occur through poorly constructed and possibly prescriptive briefs that leave little room for bisociative and playful manoeuvre.

Remarking on the playful work of poetry, Huizinga (1955 [1938]) accounts for this in terms of rhythmical and symmetrical arrangement of language; use of rhyme and assonance; the creation of motifs; expressions of mood and tension; play with symbols and ideas; image-laden writing; relaying of human empathy; and artificial and artful construction of phrases. All of this and more apply to copywriting, as the best writers are able to draw in, enchant, seduce and modulate affect. Indeed, aspiring copywriters have it drilled into them that they should be writing *to* the person who is their archetypal consumer.

Moreover, although advertising is a very real business in the sense of people getting up and going to work, undergoing meetings, dealing with clients and so on, its output is quite virtual in terms of cultural, symbolic and modes of affective production. There is also playful but fierce competition among teams and between agencies as they seek to win prizes and creative validation from peers (as well as career progression and money). Later in his book, *Homo Ludens*, Huizinga admits of commercial competition and play 'when trade begins to create fields of activity within which each must try to surpass and outwit his neighbour' (1955 [1938]: 200). While Huizinga was no fan of advertising (referring quite aptly to it as 'sensation-mongering'), he recognises that there is a sporting dimension to economic life in which business becomes play and that businesses will 'instil the play-spirit into their workers so as to step up production' (1955 [1938]: 200). We might add a dose of *alea* too, particularly in regard to ludic capitalism or that which involves entrepreneurialism, gambling and what is inherently a game of chance.

Beyond playfulness and competitiveness within the economic realm, there is a more nuanced and focused application of Caillois' notion of mimicry. Mimicry is based on closed imaginary universes and communication that sit outside the normal order of things. So, as cats and dogs nip rather than bite, and children play with Lego rather than build houses, we display implicit knowledge of codes and meta-behaviour. Bateson (2000 [1972]) builds a convincing argument out of mimicry (unrelated to Huizinga or Caillois' usage of the word) and the ways in which play can refer to higher orders of messages. Predicated on Russell and Whitehead's *Theory of Logical Types*, Bateson argues for play as a form of meta-communication and tacit understanding. Speculating on the development of communication, Bateson notes that we do not automatically respond to signals in the environment, but assess them so as to discern the type of signal they are. Bateson develops the idea of play as meta-communication where signals are exchanged carrying the message that play is occurring. This happens through actions and behaviour that do not denote what they denote. So, as a child or animal play-fights, and while blows, nips and trips may occur, this is not fighting in the sense of combat, but in a playful sense.

There are then multiple levels of communication and in playful acts, one level comments on and modifies the message of the other. The latter playful message subverts the former and cancels out the former. The idea of meta-messages is an important one for defenders of advertising as it is akin to Bernbach's point in Chapter 2 where he tells us that creative advertisers and audiences collude in an agreement that states: 'we're all in this together; you know we're going to try and sell you something – let's both enjoy the process' (cited in Cracknell, 2011: 13). This brings us back to reflexive modes of address and the familiarity between two parties that facilitates this capacity for nuance and meta-communication. This competence for messages about messages provides a platform for creative advertising, particularly in regard to textually complex advertising. Advertising then is inherently paralinguistic.

As Bateson puts it: 'The logician's dream that men should communicate only by unambiguous digital signs has not come true and is not likely to' (2000 [1972]: 418). In everyday life, paralanguage is often more influential than the text itself and although we might utter the correct words in a job interview, a momentary break in eye contact may indicate untrustworthiness. Similarly, whether it is a glance, smile or raising of the eyebrow, the capacity to fully describe the workings of this is beyond language as it belongs to a different mode of communication from language (Cook, 1992). Bill Bernbach similarly asks 'How do you storyboard a smile? Yet the quality of that smile may be the difference between a commercial that works and one that doesn't' (cited in Jones, 2004: 53).

Combinatorial approaches

Within many psychological, industry-based and critical accounts of advertising, creativity tends to be thought of in terms of combining the right elements or ideas for novel effect. This is predicated on expertise in redundancy, or the ability to transmit information with bits missing and for the receiver to have a better than random chance of recompiling the entire message. This follows the familiar logic of creativity involving a symbolic environment and workers or bricoleurs being paid to create novel combinations of symbols for given purposes.

The understanding of textual and combinatory logic employed here derives from the Latin *textus*, meaning cloth, and the ways in which parts might be bound or basted (only loosely held together). In more classical structural readings, a text is an assemblage of other texts bound together, and it is through these constituent texts that the text we seek to understand is made intelligible. In the Derridean (2001 [1967]) post-structural sense, texts are much more loosely held together (basted) and the texture of a text is only ever temporary and rearrangeable. In this latter version, meaning does exist before or after the event but comes into being through active dialogue with the text. The former tends to see meaning as anterior and ordained.

Practice and discussion of advertising reflects both structural and post-structural tendencies in that mainstream critiques of advertising tend to focus on reading advertisements (for example, Williamson, 1978; Vestergaard and Schroder, 1985; Jhally, 1990; Goldman, 1992; Dyer, 1993 [1982]; Goldman and Papson, 1996; MacRury, 2012), while production of creative advertising is often somewhat more playful and open in textual creation. This involves a tendency towards slippages of meaning (Derrida, 2001 [1967]) and writerly texts (Barthes, 1971) where meaning is co-produced. The structural dimension points to advertising as being comprised of a wider language that gives meaning to an advertisement. Indeed, in this context, the surface of an advertisement means little – what is more important is the governing reality that lies beneath the surface of the text and how meaning is structured. That is to say, they are comprised and part of a much larger structure that possesses grammar or rules governing interrelations. Being part of such a system or set of conventions thus means, by and large, predictable responses can be obtained from people. The heart of this is Saussurean, with such functional combinatory logic reflected in Saussure's assertion that 'language is a system of pure values which are determined by nothing except the momentary arrangement of its terms' (1959 [1916]: 80). Further, signs do not have intrinsic value, but rather come to be through their relative position. Value (in the functional sense) comes to be as a result of internal relations of a given cultural system. This field of symbols is characterised by complex and interacting domains consisting of ideas of ideas and thoughts about thoughts, and the various ongoing results of these interactions that are shared and, ideally for advertisers, understood by audiences.

As detailed in Chapter 3 and here in relation to bisociation, this sees the appropriation of signs from one domain so to be leveraged within an advertisement. These image and frame-based combinations are said to be valuable in the sense that a sign has currency. This occurs because combinatory arrangements of signs within an advertisement boost the stock value and/or sales of the company that owns the brand. Industry accounts of combinatory play in this arena tend towards bisociation of cultural elements or signs, while cultural and critical analysts of advertisements employ the language of transference in which a positively received sign is used to propagate another sign. The appropriation of signs from a system of signification reflects an ongoing assessment (of sorts) of appropriate language with which to engage consumers. Put simply: in an arguably Pavlovian fashion, advertising links socially desirable ideas with products to be sold. The combinatory approach to advertising put more technically involves an ongoing process of appropriation of domains for the purpose of translating sign value into brand equity and then into capital.

Critical elements

Advertising as that which embodies and exemplifies commodity relations, social power dynamics and ideological structures has been taken to heart by areas of the cultural studies project that employs Marxian-inspired organising principles, as originally associated with the Centre for Contemporary Cultural Studies at the University of Birmingham. This canon, almost exclusively, equates advertising with being visual. This sees a frame-based mode of re-presenting meanings originally belonging elsewhere to make a point about a commodity. In doing this, meanings are borrowed from elsewhere, reframed and subject to the logic of commodification (Goldman, 1992). They are a bricolage in that ideas and images, or whatever else happens to be at hand and available, are appropriated and put to work for a novel purpose (Lévi-Strauss, 1974 [1962]; also see Derrida, 2001 [1967]).

The idea of the commodity sign is deeply Marxian and, as Lukács (1971 [1923]) expresses, has to do with ideological autonomy from the process of production. The concern in this critique is that social relations themselves become objectified and that which has hitherto been outside the sphere of production becomes embroiled within it. In branding and advertising this is more overtly apparent than elsewhere as the process of commodification pulls from far and wide to be more appealing and convincing. The root of fears about advertising is that it is perceived as taking what we hold dear so to appropriate, deterritorialise and transform a given set of relations, ways of being or areas of representation hitherto outside of commodity logic. Not only do the wider gamut of life and domains of experience become commodified, but perhaps the galling part of this is that redefined or rearticulated social relations are then sold back to us by means of images and products. The appropriation of signs from different domains, subcultures and even oppositional voices to capitalism consequently results in the commodification of wider cultural phenomena as they become linked to commodity signs themselves. Critics from Marcuse (1964) onwards have consequently argued that the commodify form and the ways in which cultural signs and artefacts are operationalised flatten all other interests in society.

Logic of representation

In the wider fields of art, design and commercial modes of representation, creativity tends to be thought of in terms of combinatorial play and the ability to conceive of ideas through unconventional, playful, and sporadic approaches. A key commentator on the cultural and creative industries, David Hesmondhalgh, remarks that creativity involves 'the manipulation of symbols for the purposes of entertainment, information and perhaps even enlightenment', even going as far as to eschew the term 'artist' in favour of the term 'symbolic creators' for those who 'make up, interpret or rework stories, songs, images and so on' (2006: 4–5). Rejecting the word 'art' in favour of 'symbolic creativity', Hesmondhalgh promotes a text-based account of creative production. This is done to reject the idea of creativity as self-expression, to avoid divisive connotations of genius (often linked with creativity) and to highlight the social nature of meaning-making. He describes that texts are cultural artefacts produced by the cultural industries. These are ensembles of symbols manipulated for a purpose. The possibilities of what a text might be are broad, but Hesmondhalgh is restrained in identifying texts as the collective name for products such as television programmes, films, books, newspapers, advertisements and other mediated artefacts. It is noteworthy that this definition of creative production involves the idea of a text as a distinct, contained and bounded item capable of being circulated throughout a system, and separate from the means and media by which it is circulated (this will be addressed in full in Chapter 10). Another contemporary influence within media and cultural studies to have recently discussed creativity, David Gauntlett (2011), similarly rejects genius-based accounts in favour of a symbolic approach, seeing the cultural sphere as a symbolic environment.

Disavowing creative gatekeepers who might validate what is and what is not creative, he promotes the idea of creative communities in which all participants to varying extents express symbolic creativity. He also argues that creativity does not require accreditation, but rather should be seen in light of everyday life and micro-decisions we make in writing emails, making speeches, updating social media pages, cooking and other aspects that involve symbolic decisions.

Although a seemingly infinite array of choices exists, combinations cannot be randomly made, as certain combinations will not work for given strategic purposes. As semioticians tell us, combinations should make sense and possess an agreed cultural logic or reason for being together so that the network of association is recognisable and meaning can be made. This 'cultural logic' is symbolic logic, deriving from similar conceptual schemes as arithmetic and language where signs are defined through their position within an overall system and if we substitute one sign within a set of signs, the overall meaning of a sentence, formula or advertisement is affected. The premise of meaning through combination permeates language and the wider communicational sphere. This means that any proposed sign or element must be determined within a wider set of publically understood networked relations.

Combinatorial conceptions are characterised by causal conceptions of mind ('If I do A, then B, C or D might occur particularly if a little of E is added'). This is due to the language-based root of combinatorial conceptions of creativity that is comprised of semantics (meaningful content) and syntax (how these meanings are structured). This requires a capacity for comprehension and contextualisation. There is logic in this and combinatory conceptions of creativity are not greatly different, as they have to do with known outcomes from the mixing of given elements. In two senses this is a functional and structural account of creativity. We have on the one hand the potential for instrumentalism and on the other a geometric and algorithmic account where a text does not so much contain ideas or concepts but functions, as with a system of coordinates.

Following this view, there are rules to creativity in regards to what is possible. Having more to do with regularity and changing conventions of use, these rules are looser than mathematical rules, but this does not excuse symbolic creativity from being predicated on logic, albeit one whose rules develop. This derives from tacit societal convention and provides what is possible. As with the later Wittgenstein in *Philosophical Investigations*, it gives 'the given' (1953: II, 226). While people might deviate and challenge the rules of the given, communal conventions limit what is communicatively possible for the individual. To know something then is to know all possible occurrences (and possible combinations) that might happen with that object, and it is in combination and configuration that states of affairs are produced. For Wittgenstein a thought is a sign that expresses a situation only understandable in relation to the wider world of signs. The thought or proposition does not contain its sense, but rather this is established through determined relations best considered spatially. This shifting geometric arrangement of signs within individual and multiple planes is the terrain of the algorithm. That is to say, the text itself is an algorithm, or a point, that is a representation of given variables and ingredients of particular proportions drawn from respective dimensions and domains.

This is where practitioners in advertising demonstrate what they do as they exhibit deftness in understanding complex signs and arrangements, and repurpose these within combinations for a novel effect. Creativity seen this way has much less to do with torrents of originality, but instead expertise in genre, conventions and expectations (Negus and Pickering, 2004). This is the 'novelty in combination' approach in which tweaks and twists in conventional meaning give rise to newness. Thus, in advertising, we might say that a good creative agency or boutique will churn out much combinatorial creativity. They will win awards, delight clients, allow its creators some satisfaction, and grace publications such as the well-received *Lürzer's Archive*. However, as Boden (2004; 2010) points out, creativity involves three sorts of surprise. The first involving *combinations* have now been well covered; but there are two more, predicated on *exploration* of conceptual spaces and *transforming* spaces.

Beyond combinatory conceptions

A conceptual space is 'any disciplined way of thinking that's familiar to (and valued by) a certain social group' (Boden, 2010: 32). Some spaces are more complex than others; for example, games with simple rules that only allow for a few possible moves. Boden uses the example of noughts and crosses versus chess. Where one has limited options, the other grants a larger amount of options and strategies. Exploratory creativity involves the possibility of recognising hitherto unseen possibilities. It involves a mode of behaviour that involves doing things differently within a given space. Whereas combinatorial conceptions involve a novel juxtaposition of elements, exploratory conceptions involve unusual ways of working or seeing things differently within a given space. It is that which is possible within a given space, but only seems obvious after the event to those who understand the rules of that given space. This may have to do with technique, materials or noticing something about what is possible that no one else has spotted or discovered. Be this gymnastics, cookery, mathematics or advertising, it has to do with exploring the nature and boundaries of a discipline. As discussed in Chapters 3 and 10, advertising is undergoing a prolonged period of media exploration and experimentation that is altering the ways that we think about advertising. Exploration then is not simply textual and combinatorial, but in the case of advertising currently involves an expansion of what can be achieved with interactive media and participatory practices.

Transformation is slightly different and has to do with redefining problems. This approach recognises that we cannot change the way games are played, or alter a universe of discourse, by playing within its rules of practice. Instead of working within constraints the aim here is to re-draw principals of practice, or, in the case of seeing creativity as play – potentially cheating, although Caillois' (2001 [1958]) somewhat conservative view of creativity (in the cybernetic sense of maintaining a stable system) sees transformation as corruption and invokes precautions against cheats and rule-breakers. Boden's (2010) notion of transformation involves thinking of something that is not possible out of a given set of elements. For this to occur, the pre-existing order of things must be changed so to allow new possibilities, combinations and horizons. Bohm (2004 [1996]) makes a similar point, arguing that while insights of a combinatory nature may involve valuable discoveries and inventions, they are not creation. Instead creation for Bohm is the coming into being of a fundamentally different order. He is quite clear that creation is not play within a structure, or the connecting together of two different structures, but rather the bringing about of a new kind of structure and paradigm.

Transformational creativity in advertising has perhaps only been seen twice, although a third possibility is discussed in the following chapter. As briefly mentioned in Chapter 2, the first occurred in the 1960s as DDB changed how advertising was done. They altered the rules of the game so to change the nature of advertising and the boundary of potential therein by re-creating the format of advertising, working practices, and perhaps more importantly, the meta-communicative relationships agencies are able to create with consumers. Particularly in the US, where much advertising was cluttered, DDB's layouts gave their clients a much simpler format. The tone, humour and mode of address was also different to what had gone before containing higher levels of sophistication, or what we can now define in terms of playful and reflective meta-communication. Explained in Barthes' (1971) terms, this involved a shift, or at least the appearance of which, from readerly to writerly advertising. That is to say, where advertising once followed a very presentational or readerly approach that ignored the interpretive and playful acumen of audiences, DDB revealed and revelled in the artifice of advertising and made a co-conspirator out of viewers and listeners. Examples are many, but perhaps most famous is their 1960s work for Volkswagen, and in particular the print advertisement comprised of a black and white photo of a Beetle along with the word 'Lemon' in bold sans serif font underneath. In trying to sell to the American public, in an age of over-sized Cadillacs, a small car made by a company founded by Nazis, the advertisement first appeared to be calling its own car a lemon, but after intrigue and longer exposure to the advertisement the reader works out that it is about the quality control process that Volkswagens go through. In addition to facilitating greater closeness with target audiences, this allowed for greater latitude in destabilising audiences' expectations, and possibly more interpretative and writerly freedom than traditional hard sell approaches. This involves less overtly passive advertising, but advertising contingent upon the playful creative constitution of meaning and interpretation (for example, bisociative links). Of course we might rightly question, but not conclusively answer, whether this is true dialogue or just another layer of manipulation?

Less overt or obvious in the line-up of transformational advertising, but possibly more profound, is the influence of behavioural targeting strategies and the ways in which areas of advertising are shifting toward being predicated on data, feedback and what elsewhere I have accounted for in terms of autopoiesis, co-emergent advertising materials and the pre-empting of intent (McStay, 2011). While audience feedback research in advertising goes back to the early 1900s with national practices such as the Audit Bureau of Circulations (ABC) being established in the US in 1914, data-mining today presents a radically different proposition due to the real-time nature in which information is gathered and put to use. Admittedly this is an unusual understanding of creativity given that we tend to think of it in aesthetic and representational terms, but this innovative trend represents not only bisociation of computer science, profiling and personalising experiences of advertising (heterogeneity), but more centrally involves the creation of a new order, structure and paradigm in which advertising is done.

One might wonder how long it will be before sophistication in content and targeting are merged so to comprise bisociative and algorithmic creative behavioural advertising? While speculative, in principle the idea of combinatory approaches, bisociation, profiling, statistical matching, sentiment analysis and big data is conceivable. There are some obvious questions, particularly for computer scientists: for example, how do they test reliability when the difference between what is perceived as creative and non-creative can be minute but seismic; how are rules of association established; and more generally, can the nature of advertising be changed *and* also be privacy friendly? Privacy has to be maintained for this idea to work as it is contingent on people opting in and providing more data about preferences, as complex algorithms only work reliably on large amounts of data. The upside for audiences is that they receive more interesting and novel advertising.

As will be explored in the next chapter, we might also posit a third option that sidesteps advertising conceived of as the offspring of visual culture altogether, and progresses to explore the role of non-visual imagery and modes of advertising that exploit and affect other senses.

Conclusion

This chapter began by highlighting the role of divergence in accounts of creativity that privilege multiplicity, expansionism, and the generation of options by means of the exploration of multiple domains. Combinatory play between domains characterises both bisociation and semiotic conceptions well, although where the former seeks surprise, a reveal, or an 'aha' moment on comprehending the link, the latter in its critical guise is interested in highlighting the ways in which what was once outside the sphere of production becomes incorporated within commodity logic by means of transference.

In regard to the exploration of domains and meta-communication, this chapter highlighted play as a key factor within any discussion of creativity. What was discussed was not as obvious as we might have thought at the outset, particularly given the rules-based nature of play. However, on closer inspection the divisions between 'real' and 'play' are less rigid than supposed.

This chapter also provided a more formal conception of combinatory logic as predicated on a structural understanding that, in the strictest of senses, is best understood in shifting geometric and algorithmic terms. However, while combinatory dynamics play a key role, Boden's three-part taxonomy proves useful in getting beyond combinatory perspectives, particularly in regard to rule breaking, exploration and that rare situation where entire discourses and modes of practice are overturned within a short period of time. In advertising there are three possible transformative points: the development of meta-communicative advertising in the 1960s; more recently in regard to feedback, data-mining and heterogeneous content (since the 1990s); and as the next chapter explores, affective modes of imaging and advertising not contingent on visual or aural content.

Notes

1 Available from http://theinspirationroom.com/daily/print/2012/5/land_rover_jabs. jpg.
2 Available from www.aef.com/images/museum/clio_2000/IMG0009.jpg.
3 The Wikipedia article on John West Foods records that in August 2008, John West was 'assessed by conservation group Greenpeace as selling the least sustainable tinned tuna in the UK in its Tuna League' although it was committed to source all of its tuna through sustainable catch methods by the end of 2016. 'The first step towards this was the launch of pole and line tuna in September 2011' (en.wikipedia. org/wiki/John_West_Foods).
4 Available from www.coloribus.com/adsarchive/prints/burger-king-fiery-fries-495455/.

5 Sensational dimensions

In creating a meal we select ingredients from different regions, planes and domains, and do this for a purpose – to intensify flavours, and to stimulate an experience for a given end. The end result is the generation of properties and affects that do not belong to its constituent parts. While combinatory approaches might be the dominant mode to understanding creativity in advertising we should not lose sight of the purpose of using multiple ingredients, which is to deepen and enrich sensory experience. The initial question then is less 'what do we think?', but instead, 'how do we feel?'

The aim here is to further the task of de-coupling discussion of advertising away from representation, signification and ideology to one that is more affective, sensational, embodied and machinic in orientation, where the idea of the machine is far in excess of its usual association with hardware. One simple reason for doing this is that affect is that which both determines and exceeds cognition (Whitehead, 1948 [1933]; Shapiro, 2012). Another related point is that while 'the science of signs' may provide some means of tracing association, and drawing schemes and diagrams of operation, it ignores swathes of human experience in the process. This chapter begins to account for the role of affect in advertising by highlighting its connection to postmodern critique, as broached in the previous chapter. It then examines current practice in relation to advertising and marketing interest in neuroscience. This account provides us with an understanding of the centrality of affect, sensation and a less representational account of advertising. This awareness is employed in the second stage of this chapter that more fully addresses thinking on affect. The practice and implications of commercial interest in neuroscience supply form, depth and illustrations for affect-based critique that, although right, correct and valuable, suffers from being vague and imprecise in comparison to more finely honed and longer-established tools for assessing representation in advertising. A key outcome of this is a questioning of the hegemony of the visual in practice and critique by means of reconsidering the nature of images, and the assessment of production that harnesses the full gamut of sensory and image-making faculties. In considering the affective consequences of advertising, the chapter proceeds with a Spinozan understanding on affect and mind/body parallelism, and via a foray into Deleuzian thinking on bodies and machines, shifts advertising away from a metaphysical ontology to a more immanent understanding of advertising and creative potential therein.

Viscerality

Goldman and Papson's (1996) book, *Sign Wars*, is highly symptomatic of the heady days of representation, textualism and combinatory sign-play in advertising. Mostly drawing upon Baudrillard's (1988) discussion of the hyperreal, and indirectly Barthes' (1972 [1957]) *Mythologies* and Judith Williamson's (1978) *Decoding Advertisements*, it also contains a small passage remarking that advertising is tangible and substantial as well as that which is to be read and interpreted. This observation sits within the milieu of MTV-styled imagery and discussion taking place in the 1980s and 1990s about postmodernism, hyperactivity, interruption, fast-editing, loud music, bombardment of visual stimuli, frenzy, acceleration, channel zapping, fragmentation and so on (see for example Fiske, 1986; 1987). This palpability and breakdown of signs begins a more tactile approach to advertising better thought of in terms of intensity, sensation and affect. In regard to the media environment of the 1990s that still saw the pre-eminence of television, this affective dimension is also the gist of Kalle Lasn's (1999), and Adbusters', psycho-environmentalist and 'brandalist' critique of advertising. Reflecting the 'hyper' part of the 1990s, it has less to do with representation as abstraction, but advertising thought of more affectively and autonomically as noise, reflexive behaviour, content and orchestration of 'jolts' for the mind, and the engaging of our brains at neuronal levels and physiological levels. This has less to do with advertising passively, structurally and imagistically understood, and more to do with campaigns or barrages of commercial noise and pressure modulated in high (and sometimes low[1]) frequency waveforms. In *Camera Lucida*, Barthes (1981) puts this only slightly differently in relation to photography. Drawing a distinction between *studium* and *punctum*, he asserts that the former involves linguistic, political and cultural constructions; the latter involves sensational, physical, emotional dimensions that puncture or wound the individual. While his discussion is not on advertising, it serves here to highlight that combinatorial conceptions are inadequate as a means of entirely understanding people's engagement with mediated artefacts.

Affect

Combinatory choice then is also a sensuous decision-making process, and not only a symbolic or abstract one. This brings back to mind early Wittgenstein and his point on the relationship between language and mysticism where language limits the expression of thought, and that anything outside of language is nonsense. While something might exist without language, it cannot be demonstrated or communicated. He remarks: 'There are, indeed, things that cannot be put into words. They make themselves manifest. They are what is mystical' (2010 [1921]: §6.522: 97). Famously too, he ends the *Tractatus* with 'What we cannot speak about we must pass over in silence' (2010 [1921]: §6.522: 98). Indeed, the lived dimension of affect is difficult to put into words, but it does make itself manifest and it does make a difference.

That which we have difficulty putting into words is precisely what must be addressed. While linguistic, textual and combinatory accounts of advertising provide analytical clarity (at least to those within media and cultural studies), there is much missed in these accounts of advertising and by focusing so exclusively on associative and derivative meaning we miss the capacity for affect. The primary faults are that ideas about representation do not account for the ways in which advertising affects and operates. This is three-pronged in that there is habitually little interest in agency practice and how the industry works; the second is that focus on visual texts, meaning and structure eschews other senses and image-making systems; third is an ontological critique, developed below, where over-focus on text and meaning fails to properly recognise affect. Representational approaches say a great deal about images and what they could possibly signify but pass over in silence the situated and experiential dimensions of advertising. They are also quiet on interaction that does not involve visual images and, as also explored later, there are many ways for brand owners to make positive impressions. These may be aural, olfactory, tactile or involving a combination of sensations in addition to the visual.

Affect is not equivalent to representation and meaning, although it involves these. An image or mediated experience for example can be affective and captivating without us, or a helpful textual analyst, knowing why. Whitehead (1948 [1933]) phrases this 'affective tone' as that which we both in part create and are drawn to. It is the emotional experience or connection that both fashions and goes beyond cognition. Importantly too, these relations are that which gives rise to objects for us. Wissinger (2007) highlights the beyond-reasoning part of this well in her discussion of modelling and how models, their agents, art directors and other interested parties are often unable to explain why one model is successful and another is not, but know that one provokes a visceral reaction. This means two things: (1) that an image or mediated experience might have an effect that does not equate to a meaning; (2) that such an experience may have no meaning at all. There are significant parallels in advertising and perhaps the classic example of this is Ogilvy's *Man with a Hathaway Shirt* (1951), also broached in Chapter 3, that gained a surplus of attention by providing the man in the shirt with a black eye-patch. This invigorated the campaign with affect and also effects, in the form of a large rise in sales of Hathaway shirts. Although we might subsequently work to place this within a narrative and a textual story (what happened to this aristocratic gentleman that resulted in the wearing of an eye-patch?), this tells little of the arresting nature of the advertisement and the sensational ways in which we might be affected without knowing why – even after reflection. It also misses the possibility that power may lie in a lack of precise meaning and that the most potent images are polysemous, open and not easily accounted for even by the closest of readings (Wissinger, 2007). Indeed, as accounted for in discussion of bisociation in the previous chapter, ambiguity provides a mode of affect that captivates and enraptures.

Connecting neuroscience and affect

In digressing from the pre-eminence of representation and privileging affect we focus on more immediate local events and experiential happenings. The advertising industry has never lost sight of this, and since the inception of professional consumer research at the beginning of the 1900s[2] has sought to know more about the role of emotions, feelings, memory and recall in relation to advertising messages so to aid in engineering attention and engagement. Currently, much interest revolves around neuroscience, the brain, and how the effectiveness of advertising might be improved by means of scanning areas of brains and obtaining feedback on how certain regions are stimulated. This has important implications for conceptions of affect.

On mentioning neuroscience (particularly in relation to advertising) we might recoil and shudder believing that neuromarketing seeks to strip away self-determination and the role of consciousness, leaving us prey to internal colonisation by advertisers and marketers. However, it cannot replace explanations for us having reasons, intentions, purposes, goals, values, rules and conventions (Bennett and Hacker, 2007), and caution is required so not to overextend the reach of neuroscience and its implications for affect and advertising. For Damasio (2011), we might think of consciousness as a result of a mind that possesses a sense of subjectivity that can consequently be defined in terms of a mind that is able to ask questions about itself, what it is made of, and what its environment is. This provides our known self with a somewhat semiotic character that cannot be understood without recourse to mapping and image-making systems. This brain or mind does not possess a consciousness button, but rather exists as an event by dint of a range of sites interacting therein. By means of additional sensory faculties, the mind understands both itself and the world by means of images, and records the consequences for the organism of what it finds.

This brings us to an important point. The mind does not represent the world around it in solely visual terms and if we are to better understand creative possibilities we need to step outside the hegemony of the visual and break the seemingly indexical link between image and optical faculties. Images may be aural, visual, tactile and so on, and conceivable in reference to maps and circuits of association that are also not dependent on the visual. In neuroscientific terms, maps are crucial as they are the means by which we manage ourselves, and our relationship with the world. In addition to providing records of past encounters and experiences, they also act to get around having to consciously evaluate every situation in full anew. Mapping systems are a key target for advertisers and marketers that seek to influence behaviour and orientation. Importantly too they do not transparently record, but are biased and prejudiced. Created in the cerebral cortex, maps fashion both our sense of self and environment, and permit image-making, expanded memory capacity, imagination, reasoning, and as an outcome of these, language. They emerge when we *interact* with things (people, objects, places and so on), giving rise to mind and the means by which we know sights, sounds, touches, smells, tastes, pleasures and that which all come under the heading of images (Damasio, 2011). An image then is not necessarily visual. Further, it is not contingent on awareness and images may form and influence without our noticing them.

In engaging with advertising and marketing events there is arousal, an embrace and narcotic-like temporal moments. This is not suggested so to elicit renewed attention from the reader, but to observe that narcotics and brands are both in the business of modifying the transmission or mapping of body signals. This is achieved through stimulating structures in the limbic system, and the generation of anticipatory desire, pleasure, the release of dopamine and what is accounted for as the reward pathway. Expressed one way, advertising is interested in contributing to marketing efforts to release as much dopamine as possible when a possible customer thinks about a particular brand (Du Plessis, 2011). This is not in the sense of stupefaction or enlightenment, but what are experienced as positive sensations. This is only to suggest the most basic but frequently neglected of questions. Asking how we feel might be less intellectual than asking what we think, but it is a more appropriate means of judging advertising and aesthetic content. At the very least, it should be the starting point of analysis.

Advertising thought of this way around begins to be connected (again) with autonomic and involuntary responses, that which is not conscious, and what in the past has involved cognitive psychologists and stimulus/response research in advertising (see for example Simon and Arndt, 1980). This tends towards thinking about the quantitative relationship between a prescribed input and an output. Factors here include elements within a message, frequency, placement, recall, attitude, behaviour, intention to buy, and reaction of individuals versus groups. Deceptively simple and attractive for those seeking to advertise, this raises all sorts of methodological questions about the longer history of a brand and/or product, and possibly overstates the importance of advertising in the wider line-up of marketing efforts.

Advertising has for a long time been interested in feelings and emotions, and thereby affects. In psychological and neurobiological terms there is a significant difference between emotion and feeling in that the former are bodily autonomic programs of actions comprised of chemical and neural responses, and the latter are perceptions of what is happening to us when we undergo an emotive process. The difference here is that while animals and simpler organisms may have emotions, they do not have reflectively constituted feelings. Emotions then may be triggered by current events, or those recalled from the past, and are those bodily reactions we have to particular stimuli. Importantly for advertising emotion is much more than what we experience consciously and affect may be created even when there is no consciousness of exposure to a stimulus (Thorson, 1999). Emotions do not sit collectively in one area of the brain, but rather are associated with different parts. For example, the amygdala is linked with fear and the ventromedial prefrontal cortex to compassion (Damasio, 2011). More than one centre may be stimulated at one time so giving rise to mixed emotions. Centres are stimulated *both* by combinations of signals and degrees of intensity, or that level of amplitude required to transform and stimulate. Feelings of emotions are the becoming aware (or perceptions) of emotions going on in the brain and an idea (or representation) about the state of the body, and Damasio (2003) posits that feelings arose as a by-product of the brain's involvement in managing and mapping our body functions. With a wink towards Descartes, Damasio simply posits that 'Emotions play out in the theatre of the body. Feelings play out in theatre of the mind', and that although we tend to think of them as one thing they are instead connected processes (2003: 28). Moreover, feelings are not only expressions of emotions, but in descending scale of complexity are also connected to: deeper-seated drives and motivations; pain and pleasure behaviours; immune responses, basic reflexes and metabolic regulation (2003: 37).

All of this is linked to advertising by dint of the premise that when we feel a certain way about an image or item before us, what we are referring to is that which accompanies our imaging of the item. This means there is emotional engagement, however mild, and then feeling that is the mental expression of emotion. Taken together, this equates to affect. Interest in affect then is clearly evident in both creative departments and advertising research. Redolent of stimulus/response, presentations on research and campaign strategy will involve accounts of affect, intensity and impact in terms of 'neuroscience proves … ' (Du Plessis, 2011: 134), but we might also consider the other dimension of affect that sees this process in lived, phenomenological, aesthetic and sensational terms where a quality, nuance and feeling is sought with which to express a brand. To modify the discussion of Abram Games in Chapter 3, not only is a purity of vision for a brand or client sought, but also a particular tone, resonance or mode of intensity to help position brands and provide unique experiences and gratification of some sort.

Research and creative dimensions are not mutually exclusive and research can impact on the creative stage. Du Plessis (2011), of the market research firm Millward Brown, for example tells that eye-tracking technology indicates levels of engagement with: campaign protagonists; elements of an advertisement that might be edited-out or retained; and focus and attention. This leads to advertisements being re-edited so to make sure attention is not dispersed across the advertisement but focused on key areas such as the logo (Du Plessis uses the examples of RoC skincare and Skoda). Similarly research into

Dove's 'Evolution' commercial from 2006 was conducted in relation to affect, heart rate and the crescendo of emotions experienced as the online advertisement continues. Interestingly too, measurements pointed to a rise of positive emotions as models were being made-up, although this was not verbally reported. Such techniques then are useful to advertisers in probing sensitive situations. Page (2011), also of Millward Brown, suggests key areas where neuroscience should be used in advertising that includes dealing with material sensitive to distortion (for example, understanding why heterosexual men like looking at chiselled males), dealing with abstract and higher-order ideas, and probing for the nuances of experiences of an advertisement and the peaks and troughs they may undergo during an advertising event. Similarly, as already accounted for, neuroscience may be used as a means of understanding particular elements of an advertisement, responses to these, along with the depth and intensity of these reactions.

Given its intellectual bias towards chains of meaning and transferences, feeling is something that critical/semiotic/cultural analysis has never really engaged with. However, as a means of bringing the rational and the emotional together, such as assessment of mood, tone and that which orients intellectual reaction, feeling is important. Damasio (2011) posits 'somatic markers' and emotion as playing a significant role in reasoning and decision-making, particularly when all other things are equal and there is no obvious decision to be made. These provide a shortcut of sorts and connect emotions to objects. He defines these in terms of perceptions of items past, present and future that generate emotions and feelings. Importantly for advertising too, the background emotions and maps we bring to any event influence our dealing with that event.

Memory plays a key role as neurons (cells in the brain) conduct signals to other neurons or cells by means of synapses. These are a joining point where two neurons connect together and one neuron releases neurotransmitter molecules into a small space adjacent to another neuron that bind to the neuroreceptors on the receiving cell's side. Neurons not only influence other neurons but also modify and influence other cells (endocrine and muscular), and comprise and regulate behaviour. What is important for advertising and conceptions of affect is what causes a neuron to 'fire', or send a signal to the other neuron. This is determined by chemicals inside the synapse that possess a threshold and if an incoming signal from a neuron is above this threshold it will carry the electrical nerve impulses across the synapse from one neuron to the next. Each time these neurons fire or engage in signal transmission the chemical changes in such a way that the threshold decreases. This means that the likelihood of future transmission goes up. In lived phenomenological terms, the chemical composition of synapses changes when something is experienced. Synapses are important in affective terms as it is in these where memories are 'stored' or 'registered'. Although ensuring we do not ascribe agency to neurons, we might say that neurons store memories by way of the state of the synapses, and construe things based on the condition of the synapses. Marketing, advertising and branding by means of affect might then be said to be changing the brain.

However, although neuroscience and advertising may invoke past dystopian visions of Packard's *Hidden Persuaders*, there is no way of measuring how memories are formed in the brain and, as Du Plessis (2011) points out: there is no specific spot where Coca-Cola memories reside; and there is no way to assess whether there is a memory of a brand in the brain, nor how strong memories are, nor what these memories are associated with. This associational point is an interesting one in regard to the previous chapter that examined combinatorial creativity, as it is mostly in the limbic system that pleasure is associated with an object or stimulus that is the subject of our focus (otherwise known as a gestalt). This leads to a feedback loop and as more pleasure is generated, the more we focus on the stimulus. Although there are many stimuli or gestalts that will not grow large for us, others will and this depends on the strength and significance of the stimuli for us. The question then is what is the scope of the neurons that can be recruited for a given cause? Are these neurons chained together and already associated so to help create a large gestalt? To clarify, this is why for many of us Coca-Cola's Christmas advertisement 'Holidays are Coming' featuring a train of glowing Coca-Cola trucks is significant and potent – it is able to recruit many neurons that are already linked together, enlarge the gestalt and comprise a potent and affective event.

Outside visual culture

Even a passing interest in neuromarketing quickly leads one to question the pre-eminence of visual communication in commercial persuasion. As we recognise that images in the brain are not visual but associated with all of the senses, the hegemony of the visual possibly comes into question. The UK's Royal Mail for example creates for advertisers direct mail that is sensational and sensory in nature. Options for advertisers include the use of taste, smell, touch and sound, as well as visual imagery. Benefits listed on the Royal Mail Sensational Mail website include: greater impact for enhanced interruption and customer acquisition; the capacity to hold attention for longer; higher recall; an increase of value in relation to the product being advertised; and the possibility of bringing the product experience into the communication. While the pre-eminence of sight-based media is unlikely to be challenged, there are reasons to question why it is so absolutely dominant. For example, Martin Lindstrom (2005), a brand consultant on consumer behaviour, conducted an extensive study examining the relation between the senses and branding finding that only 37 per cent of his participants ranked sight as the most important sense when evaluating our environment (followed by smell at 23 per cent).

Hearing also plays a vital and under-accounted for role. While jingles, mnemonics and other points of recognition have long been part of advertising, certain sounds are more affective than visual stimuli. The sound of a baby laughing, the crack of an opening can, fizzy drink being poured over ice, the sizzling of steak and so on, are all powerful triggers and mental image-builders (Lindstrom, 2011). To again use a televisual example to make a non-television point, in 2009 DDB London, on behalf of Volkswagen, ran a commercial that makes a virtue out of the sensations experienced when closing the car door of a Volkswagen Golf. This depicts a number of people in different situations presented with vehicles described as 'like a Golf' and concludes with a woman in a car showroom visibly unimpressed by a sales-man's assertion that a closing door sounds just like a Golf. A man closing the door as he parks his Golf is accompanied by the screen message 'Why drive something like a Golf when you can drive a Golf?'. This is predicated on the premise that the depth, bass and low resonance of the closing Golf door indicate quality. Likewise, a third of Lindstrom's (2005) participants in a global study on sensory branding claim they can distinguish one car brand from another by the sound of their closing doors. This is particularly the case with Japanese and American markets. This has consequently led to the development of departments of sound engineers, product designers and psychologists to ensure that brands relay a sense of trust, safety and luxury. The Volkswagen commercial is remarkable as it highlights a different approach to affect and eschews the standard account of a car speeding across remote mountainous landscapes, but rather adopts a less abstract approach employing the senses more directly as a means of establishing emotional connections and preferences.

Lindstrom (2005) accounts for the senses as 'sensory touch points', also remarking that these have largely been ignored by advertisers and marketers. Indeed, many of these touch points are better equipped to fashion more intense and affective bias, maps, images and recognition of brands than sight. Lindstrom goes on to point out that while few brands have managed yet to colonise all the senses, religions have. These involve: architecture, iconography and symbolism; evocative smells (oils, herbs and incense); sounds (organs, choirs, bells, and so on); and tactility (wafers, forehead marking, worry beads or even the texture of sacred books). In contemporary media parlance too we might also point to co-creative occasioning and community-building so for consumers to participate, live-out their brands and possibly evangelise them (some Apple users provide useful examples). Indeed, Lindstrom's (2009) three-year neuromarketing study that employed functional Magnetic Resonance Imaging (fMRI) scanning on 2,081 people shows that when his consumers viewed images associated with strong brands (Apple, Harley-Davidson and Ferrari among others), participants' brains registered the same reactions as they did to religious icons and figures.

Quality and image-making

If we think in terms of a market of attention we can see that the visual is satura-ted, leaving much space for creative work with other image-making senses.

This however is not to point to the other senses as poorer and less affective/ effective brethren, particularly given transportational olfactory links between emotion and childhood memory, and the capacity for taste to engender loyalty to a brand. This leads Lindstrom (2005) to highlight that if products and advertising are to survive, they have to expand the range of senses that they appeal to and that the most successful communication will be multi-sensational (visual and smell for example). Indeed, and possibly alarmingly, the aim is to create strategic synergies across all senses to bring about different types of mental affect for specified objectives. The objective then, ultimately, is to build brands without dependence on logos, images, props, sounds, languages, icons, campaign lines, and build somatic markers that are of themselves and do not refer beyond themselves for qualia, haecceity or a sense of individuation and 'thisness'.

Searle (1997) draws attention to the unique qualitative character of particular experiences seeing quales, conscious phenomena or events, not as abstractions (such as numbers) but as 'concrete phenomena that go on in space-time' (2007: 99). In affective terms, they are immanent and sensational. William James phrases this only slightly differently conceiving it as 'pure experience' meaning that it is 'plain, unqualified actuality, or existence, a simple *that*' (2003 [1912]: 12, emphasis in original). In relation to affect they are sensory qualities that comprise experiences of the world (pleasant ones include the smell of fresh coffee and roses or the sound of plucking a guitar, for example), but also images (Damasio, 2011). There is an important point here as in considering the relationship between affect and advertising we might seek to pay more attention to the overall impact of 'qualia' in an advertising event. This sense of vitality, experience and embeddedness within a lived affective environment helps us begin to address a problem that has dogged textual and symbolic accounts – vivacity, sensation and *the role of quality* in creative production. By reintroducing quality defined through sensation we are able to repair the mind/body split that negatively impacts on textual accounts and build bridges with sensational (and neuroscientific) understanding.

Dewey (2005 [1934]) handles these issues well remarking upon differences between intellectual and aesthetic experiences. He points to intellectual and cognitive engagement in which signs and symbols have no intrinsic quality of their own and are that which refers to some other thing or sign. Analysis here involves a cataloguing of networks of interaction and for the analyst to convince us that this scheme is meaningful in terms of wider cultural goings-on. This diagrammatic and codified endeavour misses the unique quality or aesthetics of a particular occasion, moment, experience, meal or advertisement conceived of as an event. For Dewey aesthetic and affective experiences are about engendering affect through sensation, stimulation, and intensification, also recognising that individual experiences possess lived unique characteristics that are not simply compounds of functions and rules. As Dewey remarks, 'An experience has a unity that gives it that name, *that* meal, that storm, that rupture of friendship. The existence of this unity is constituted by a single *quality* that pervades the entire experience' (2005 [1934]: 38, emphasis in original). Fellow pragmatist, James, makes a highly similar point noting that the 'instant field of the present is always experienced in its "pure" state, a plain unqualified actuality, a simple "that" as yet undifferentiated into thing and thought' (2003 [1912]: 39).

This is not to deny intellectual and textual engagement, but rather to recognise that it is only one dimension of the event. This said, James goes further describing every item of post-event analysis (or 'therefore') as a betrayal. As Stengers (2011: 70) observes in discussion of James: 'Pure experience is "plain", that is, mute with regard to what it will signify retroactively.' The tack taken here is to both shift representation from a metaphysical conception to a more immanent and experiential account of communication and advertising; and to highlight that combinatorial conceptions run into trouble when accounting for lived affect, reception and engagement with content that is in excess of language. While we might pass over the event in silence as tends to be the case in critical accounts of advertising – this is to wilfully misrecognise the dynamics of what was intended to take place. Moreover, admittedly paradoxical: what gives rise to a phenomenon or object need not necessarily have a great deal to do with it. As Bachelard (1994 [1958]: xxiii) puts it, a poetic or creative image 'has touched the depths before it stirs the surface'. Put in a more straightforward manner, we are affected and stimulated before we intellectually process experiences and events. Physically this makes sense too as we intake the world before we consciously perceive it. By this we might recognise that in the rush to explore the textual dimensions of the image, we omit to consider the lived, affective and sensational moment of engagement in the communicative event where creative and cognitive affect actually takes place.

Similarly, Bergson (1998 [1911]) offers the example of a poem where we are much less interested in the letters of which the poem is composed than the poem itself that enriches. This is to point to what Massumi (2002), borrowing from Deleuze, refers to as 'intensive', or that dynamic aspect of experience that cannot be indexed to anything outside of itself. Above, this has been framed in terms of Searle's (1997; 2007) discussion of qualia. Bergson (1998 [1911]) compares this to the arc of a hand moving from A to B. From within it is an indivisible act, although the intellect from without may plot positions of the arc. These positions are potentially both infinite in number and spring from the indivisible act by which the hand has moved from A to B. James (2011 [1909]: 77–78) in discussion of Bergson uses the example of motion and that although mathematically we might understand it as 'the occupancy of serially successive points of space at serially successive instants of time', this is a highly static notion of what is not static. We might also say that its intensive and affective dimension has been lost. For Bergson, dissection misses the event itself and creativity thought of this way is better thought of as a continuous stream. What we are seeking to avoid then is what

Rancière (2009 [2004]), in regard to the wider issue of aesthetic occasions, phrases as the fatal capturing of art by discourse. In this we see again the pre-eminence of regimes of representation and the privileging of the symbolic. This returns us to the algorithmic mindset of codification and geometry, bound by notions of proportion, relation and quantity discussed in the previous chapter. Affect, put most simply, has to do with quality.

Bodies of ideas

For reasons not fully known we seem to have a predilection for thinking in terms of opposites, and most notable for this discussion are mind/body and physical/non-physical propositions. These are false dualisms as much goes on between these poles, perhaps most obviously states such as anger, arousal, fear, happiness, contemplativeness, revulsion, joy and other conditions. Indeed much of our waking life seems to be spent in these in-between states of affect. A sensational approach to advertising recognises the ways in which advertising acts directly on the nervous system in a manner best thought of as *affective presence* that has more to do with a play of corporeal forces than traditional conceptions of representation. We have to be careful here to steer away from direct effects ideas of advertising (although we should also avoid a reactionary dismissal of this, particularly in relation to subtle in-store marketing techniques), yet retain from discourse on the 'affective turn' (Sedgwick and Frank, 1995; Massumi, 2002; Gregg and Seigworth, 2010) its interest in intense moments of experience, everyday life and physical dimensions of culture that are frequently lost in textual analysis. It is to recapture that which emerges out of engagement and interaction with the world. This is not just intellectual (if much of it is actually that at all), but is aesthetic in its original sense of sensational experiences. This conception of aesthetics is distinctly cognition-free and pre-Baumgarten (who from his writings in the 1750s is largely responsible for the inception of modern intellectual conceptions of beauty and taste-based aesthetics), and more akin to earlier Grecian and Aristotelian modes of aesthetic understanding that conceived of it in terms of materiality, and the ways in which the sensual world interacted with the sensual body. Sensation is immediate and best seen in relation to intensity and that which is considered in terms of itself – as with a feeling or experiential state (Massumi, 2002). As Deleuze (2011 [1981]) in discussion of Cezanne and Francis Bacon puts it, whereas abstract form is addressed to the head, and acts through the intermediary of the brain, sensational rendering acts upon the nervous system. One cannot help think of the Futurists too, who help underline the point. Deleuze also urges that in relation to painting (and certainly not advertising) artists should '*paint the sensation*' (2011 [1981]: 26, emphasis in original). Elsewhere Deleuze, with Guattari, remarks:

> It should be said of all art that, in relation to the percepts or visions they give us, artists are presenters of affects, the inventors and creators of

affects. They not only create them in their work, they give them to us and make us become with them, they draw us into the compound.

(Deleuze and Guattari, 2011 [1994]: 175)

For Deleuze a body might be 'an animal, a body of sounds, a mind or idea; it can be a linguistic corpus, a social body, a collectivity' (1988 [1970]: 127). This type of conceptualisation arises out of an interest in philosophies of force and affect, as per that of Scotus, Spinoza, Nietzsche and Whitehead, among others. Spinoza (1996 [1677]) some time ago depicted that the mind and body are not autonomous but rather work in parallel (as with neuroscientific accounts). This means that mind and body are indivisible and are somehow made of the same substance. Two phenomena then are seen as an outcome of the same substance, which gives rise to the expression 'abstract dualism' which is another name for parallelism. Particularly in relation to the influence on Whitehead and subsequently Deleuze, the premise perhaps becomes clearer if we highlight the impact of James, who remarks that there is 'no aboriginal stuff or quality of being, contrasted with that of which material objects are made, out of which our thoughts of them are made' (2003 [1912]: 2) and that the [conscious] 'entity is fictitious, while thoughts in the concrete are fully real. But thoughts in the concrete are made of the same stuff as things are' (2003 [1912]: 20). Spinoza's monism and univocity is famously the single substance and infinity of attributes idea on which Deleuze premises much of his own thinking on immanence. Indeed on 'univocity' we might go back to the late thirteenth century and Scotus who also maintained a single unified notion of being that applies to all substances and outcomes (Williams, 2003). Scotus' univocity is a metaphysics of sorts, but one that encapsulates both the material and immaterial, and sees being as that which in itself is indivisible, as underpinning both what we can and cannot know, and is only recognisable derivatively.

The usefulness and foresight of Spinoza lay in the fact that in building his account he steered between mind as a metaphysical entity and dumb materialism that eschews free will and conscious action, and privileged neither position. Instead his radicalism lay in the opposition to mind/body dyads. Recent affect-based conceptions of sensation derive directly from Spinoza, and Deleuze and Guattari (2011 [1994]) note that in going about its business, art does not produce concepts but rather affects, sensations and intensities. This is delivered through the physical aspects of communication that symbolic approaches tend not to discuss. Perversely and paradoxically then, the Rosser Reeves camp of advertising accounted for in Chapter 2 may have a point when it argues that advertising has become too clever. Although his advertising was of the jackhammer drill variety, it was predicated on sensational dimensions. Of a more refined disposition, Bernbach accounts for affect thus: 'The fragile structure of logic fades and disappears against the emotional onslaught of hushed tone, a dramatic pause, and the soaring excitement of a verbal crescendo' (DDB, 2012).

It is in Spinoza then we see the origins of the somewhat curious premise that ideas themselves are bodies. This becomes clearer if we think of bodies in terms of that which are capable of affect, thus meaning that we can think of advertisements as bodies. This moves the entire gamut of communication and ideas into an affective conception of being, or what Deleuze and Guattari designate a plane of immanence. Definitions differ across Deleuze's writings but in *Cinema 1* he discusses this in terms of images and that the 'in-itself of the image is matter: not something hidden behind the image, but on the contrary the absolute identity of the image and the movement', also progressing to comment, 'The *movement-image* and *flowing-matter* are strictly the same thing' (2009 [1983]: 61, emphasis in original). Denying a split between image and matter, the idea then is to raise both the image and the aesthetic event to its proper corporeal status, and out of unreachable metaphysical domains. Elsewhere, in exposition of Spinoza, Deleuze offers one of the clearer accounts of the plane of immanence idea accounting for it as,

> composed of an infinite number of particles; it is the relations of motion and rest, of speeds and slowness between particles, that define a body, the individuality of a body. Secondly a body affects other bodies, or is affected by other bodies; it is this capacity for affecting and being affected that also defines a body in its individuality.
>
> (Deleuze, 1988 [1970]: 123)

Machinic advertising

The points being made in this chapter have less to do with denial of the importance of the visual, but an opening out to amodal sensation and image-making systems. Indeed, in regard to what tends to be a visually-dominant medium, cinema studies has also shown an interest in more tactile, sensory, embodied, post-linguistic and post-semiotic approaches to cinematic experience. Perhaps more tangibly, we also experience this every time we enter a supermarket or department store and fields of strategically arranged forces intended to generate bodily and affective events. Similar to what is presented here, Kennedy builds a Deleuzian-inspired account of sensation and cinema and develops a phrase that applies equally well to advertising – 'material capture' (2004: 5). We can shift focus away from spectacular conceptions of representation towards conceiving of advertising as a machine. Here we are not exterior spectators, but in part comprise the event or the machinic arrangement of affective production. As Whitehead remarks:

> Our 'percipient event' is that event included in our observational present which we distinguish as being in some peculiar way our standpoint for perception. It is roughly speaking that event which is our bodily life within the present duration.
>
> (Whitehead, 1964 [1920]: 187–88)

Bearing in mind that machinism in Deleuzian parlance is an expanded notion that encompasses all sorts of affective operations (for example ideas, books, lathes, bombs or computers), advertising is to be thought of in bodily terms that in itself is more accurately recognised as an event. For Kennedy, a sensational account considers 'connections, the energies, molecular connections of consciousness and nervousness within the mind/body/brains of those who experience film as a material encounter' (2004: 53). Linking well to the discussion of neuromarketing, Deleuze himself, in discussion of cinema, affirms that the moving image is that which produces '*a shock to thought, communicating vibrations to the cortex, touching the nervous and cerebral system directly*' (2012 [1985]: 151, emphasis in original).

Crucially, because of the capacity for affect, we can see what was once inert representation more actively – as bodies. The language is slippery, but this means that advertising agencies do not create texts to be read from a distance, but fashion bodies that interact and perform in machinic arrangements, or events, to generate affect. (And the bodies themselves, of course, are not static forms, but temporary sets of connections, processes and differentials.) Advertising events then are not simply representations, but are better seen as processes, occasions, interactions and bodily in that advertising is able to affect us and, increasingly, we are more overtly able to affect it. Advertising seen this way is an assemblage of forces and processes rather than form. While this may appear highly abstract, if we place this in context of communicational endeavours employing neuroscientific techniques and tweaking campaigns so to affect respective areas of the brain more potently this becomes less fanciful, and possibly a little obvious. This process and field-of-force account also factors in location, environment, circumstance and coordination of social factors (being on the Tube on the way to work for example), so for advertising experiences to be better thought of in terms of materiality of involvement, kinaesthetics, participation, interaction and engagement in the world. This coordination of forces, events and circumstance involves all departments (strategic, media and creative) within an advertising agency.

In taking advertising out of the local event for which it was designated much is lost, particularly in relation to affect. In decontextualising advertising and pinning it to a wall for analysis to be deconstructed, theorised, intellectually dealt with and placed within a meta-structure, we *dissect from a distance*. This is to remove it from the flow of everyday life where the advertising and affective event was intended to take place. There are practical problems then as by examining only the image and its operations within a network of other signs, large parts of *that* advertising experience, qualia or haecceity are missed. This point is the opposite of abstract as media planners and buyers for example go to great financial lengths to ensure that advertising is engaged with in places, times, situations and contexts (drive-time in the car, on the Tube, while walking through certain areas of a city, or being midway through the final match of the Champions League football season).

Indeed, it is worth reflecting on where most of a marketer's advertising budget is spent. By taking advertising out of its context we offer it up to passive analysis that has little interest in the sensational dynamics of the field from which an image (and it is nearly always visual) is drawn. This is not even to explore the fact that the majority of advertising is not aimed at textual analysts working within a university environment and therefore will not have the same resonance as it might with its target audience/engagers.

On participating in and co-constituting such events we step outside of ourselves and, for a few moments, merge into a scene that itself is machinic where advertising materials and selves come together so to function as one in executing the strategic objectives of advertising. Note too, that we do not need to be conscious of marketing and advertising activities to machinically participate in them, but rather we might unconsciously collude in our own contamination. This brings thought and materiality together as one, and rather than representation and ideas sitting in one area, and sensation and materiality on another, Deleuze's point is that these are born of the same stuff. While one might question the physics, pragmatically the observation works. Ideas and thoughts are capable of affect, participation, collusion, of forming larger machinic assemblages, and are connected with what we take to be materiality (that itself is better expressed as a temporary arrangement given the emphasis on process and becoming).

All of this is not to generate 'a representation', but an event or experience of a new order that possesses a quality or intensity of its own and contributes to fashioning images in the mind. This mode of experience fashioned by the entire advertising chain is beyond language and the process of advertising, conceived of in a functional sense, is that which connects bodies with other bodies so to form larger temporary machines for image and sensational impression-making to occur in the brain. In thinking of advertising we might recollect the front cover of Guy Debord's *Society of the Spectacle* and its legions of gazing cinemagoers, but this spectacular and optical conception increasingly makes less sense as we do not so much spectate but participate in affective events and their fields of interrelations. Whereas spectacular conceptions of advertising elevate and autonomise human sight from the wider sensorium, what is sought here is reintegration. As Crary (1992) points out, the Latin root of spectator is *spectare*, or 'to look at'. This carries a connotation that one passively looks at a spectacle and implies distance from the event. This is a mischaracterisation as there is no passivity or removal from an event – we are either there, or not. Moreover, although sight gives rise to the lie that we are separate from that which we see, this is not the case as vision is as inescapably corporeal as other senses. Moreover, as Crary continues in discussion of Walter Benjamin's temporal and kinetic account of city life, there is no pure access to singular objects but vision (along with other incoming sensory information) is always 'multiple, adjacent to and overlapping with other objects, desires, and vectors' (1992: 20).

Indeed, this dimension of experience and advertising is that which media planners must negotiate and deal with, and if we wish to understand advertising we must step beyond representation.

Why so much insistence on sight and optical imagery? The seeing part of this event is merely one possible image-making tool (as we have other senses), but more important is the implied distance in seeing. In affective accounts we do not participate from a distance, but are necessary components of advertising thought of as machinic, intensive and event-based processes. Mechanisms associated with representation remain (referral, deferral, transference and so on), but these take on machinic, operational, bodily and affective form as what we take to be representations are 'cut' out of the world and exist as post-perceptual events (also see Kember and Zylinska, 2012). They are also only one part of the process and in providing a sensational account of advertising we play down the emphasis on metaphysical and linguistic dimensions of advertising, and fold what was once representation into the plane of sensation, modulation and intensity. In Whiteheadian (1968 [1938]) terms this is to recognise that language is the carrying of systematised expression (or data of feeling) into the present from the past. Put otherwise, it is the reproduction in the present of sensa generated by events and mappings gone by. Language then is not thought itself, but it is central to transcending the immediately local. The symbolic is not denied, but rather the idea is to expand the symbolic (as addressed directly in Chapter 8) and that dimension of experience that elicits 'consciousness, beliefs, emotions, and usages, respecting other components of experience' (Whitehead, 1928: 9). As various parts come together, the symbolic is the character of an event that we undergo on a given occasion. Importantly too, symbols, empowered by meaning we ascribe to them, act as bodies empowered by our own reactions to them.

Manning provides a good phrase that echoes the need to respect the importance of language, yet also places it within a wider domain of affect, in that we 'must conceive of language as the eternal return of expression in the making' (2012: 8). Later she highlights that 'Words are not language's termini; they are only one of the events along the way' (2012: 224). There is then an affective feedback relationship in that affect and feeling exist, this needs expression by the original few, a suitable vehicle is found, and then positive feedback occurs as that domain of expression feeds back into the wider affected who then also participate in expression and consumption. Be this feminism, a typographic style, Detroit techno, abstract expressionism or even Whiteheadian and Spinozan inspired affect-theory itself, representation is the outcome of broader affective events.

Being intensive, we move from the metaphysics of representation to sensation. This becomes doubly apparent when we recollect that advertising does not have to be noticed to be affective. Indeed, certainly with marketing, much communication or stimulation is predicated on going under the radar and not being overtly perceived.

Conclusion

Creative advertising is that affective form of communication that develops unique ways to stimulate and simultaneously engage mind and body. This is done by aesthetic means that are sensational and poetic in their generation of qualities. Advertising is interested in intensity, in both short- and long-term impact, and is, as pointed out by Hardt and Negri (2000), emblematic of the affective economy. It seeks to captivate, enliven and modulate affect by means of unique intensities that do not necessarily connect to networks of meaning. Seen this way, creativity is fluency in play and modulation. Sign-making, graphical techniques, typography, filmic and photographic style along with other representative processes are all subsumed under discussion of modulation. The point is that these are tonal and bodily, viscerally and affectively experienced, and machinically engaged. These latter points become more readily apparent if we step away from the hegemony of the visual in advertising and marketing communication, and recognise the multisensory nature of image-making. In addition then to the more usual rendition of advertising people as manipulators of signs and signification, we might situate this proficiency as a means of facilitating biotechnical or aesthetic events that are affective in nature. This is the capacity to capture attention in a crowded environment, modulate affect so to engender unique sensations, and achieve a desired strategic outcome.

Notes

1 A low frequency campaign is the same as a drip campaign that operates as a reminder or slow-build type of advertising campaign. Rather than spending a media budget in a burst (as with a product launch), money is spent utilising low frequency over a longer period of time. Sitting between these two, advertising content and the buying of media space may also be pulsed.
2 Data-gathering techniques were employed throughout the 1800s, but the formation of the Audit Bureau of Circulations (ABC) in 1914 along with use of a range of other methods such as house-to-house calls, attitudinal and opinion surveys, retail sales, audience monitoring (AC Nielsen), statistical-sample surveys amongst other techniques represents a professionalised effort with which to generate consumer profiles (McStay, 2011).

6 Vivid living, excess and the marketplace

We tend to think of creativity in relation to what is good, fruitful and positive. Historically this makes sense given that it is only since the Enlightenment that creativity has become associated with human endeavour rather than divine action. Critical perspectives will see advertising as populated by some of the best creative talent of society, but tend not to admit that advertising itself might be considered creative as this would indicate a positive evaluation rather than a neutral observation (see for example Jhally, 2006). Instead advertising is seen – sometimes at best – as that which is distasteful but original. This brief but important chapter strips away this imposition of moral value and investigates amoral conceptions of creativity in relation to heterogeneity, excess and useless production. It begins by exploring archetypes of transgressive being and subsequently investigates the relationship of this to advertising and the marketplace interpreted through the lens of folk culture, Bakhtin's (1984 [1965]) carnival, along with Bataille's (2007 [1967]; 2008) fascination with the profane.

Transgression

As possibility for creative making passed from divine to human, the notion of creativity as that which is good and positive was also imparted. Such value systems are not as pronounced in contemporary assessments of creativity and creative output as they once were, but there is a residual dimension to this as creativity tends either to be discussed in positive terms (often in relation to aesthetics) or in neutral analytical terms as with symbolic and structurally-inspired accounts (as is the case with contemporary assessment of the creative industries). These are not mutually exclusive and what is combinatorially creative is more often than not read in positive terms.

Creativity, however, might also be associated with transgression both in the figurative and moral sense. Transgression is an interesting idea as it involves dialectics of limit and force that need each other for their continued existence. After all, once a limit has been transgressed that which seeks to transgress becomes devoid of purpose, and both dies and emerges into a new arrangement (or event). Transgression then is that which pushes boundaries, spills over and, if forceful enough, potentially gives rise to a new mode of order. This view has some lineage. Hamann, for example, depicts that God is closer to the abnormal than the normal having more to do with thieves, prostitutes, sinners and publicans than the philosophers of Paris, continuing that all the great masters who excelled were sick men with faults and wounds, possessing little in the way of good sense (Berlin, 2000).

Transgression and creativity have long been partners. As perhaps best exemplified by the Marquis de Sade's *Philosophy in the Bedroom* (1965 [1795]), a life lived creatively will come up against censorship. This archetype is the life of the libertine, the debauchee, the heretic, and those who will deliberately depart from accepted doctrine. Degas similarly celebrated the criminal seeing the artist as resourceful, cunning, roguish and devious (Gamman and Raein, 2010). Such anarchic conceptions see norms of morality, civilisation and shame as fabrications that a life lived authentically has a duty to expose and debunk. These Dionysian accounts tend towards the rebellious, creative, tribal and criminal. Phrased otherwise, Nietzsche's (1967 [1886]) archetype emerges as the rogue, the illicit, the scandalous and that which is in excess. This amoral figure comes about in distinction to Christianity (and the Good) that relegates art to the sphere of lies, damns life and that which has to do with semblances, points of view, perspectives, errors, deception and art. Indeed, Nietzsche argues that Christianity arose out of a hatred of the world, a condemnation of passion along with fear of beauty and sensuality.

Morality then, by definition, is a conservative braking force whose tendency is to maintain order and negate life. Those who seek to live otherwise are known as Dionysian. Another name is the Antichrist. This view of creativity involves a purging of mediocrity, the mundane and the everyday. As with Artaud and his Theatre of Cruelty, in an amoral approach to creativity a mode of being is sought that reveals something of the real conditions its target exists in. Cruelty in Artaud's sense does not have to do with viciousness, 'but on the contrary a pure unworldly feeling, a true mental process modelled on the gestures of life itself' (2010 [1938]: 81–82). There is a pathology of purging in this context in that as mass culture incorporates art and the avant-garde, terrorist or cruel acts are necessary to illuminate our irrational selves and what is repressed. It rejects Western art structures of the gallery system, publications (that fact that Artaud's thoughts are published is not mentioned) along with media institutions. Artaud develops an idea of culture as a form of dispute, or 'A protest against the insane constriction imposed on the idea of culture by reducing it to a kind of incredible Pantheon, producing an idolatry of culture and acting in the same way as idolatrous religions, which put their gods in Pantheons' (2010 [1938]: 5). It seeks change, a shift away from totemic art, and a way of life that privileges Eros, the sensual, sexual, anarchic, amoral and passionate. Paradoxically vague because of a belief in the inexpressiveness and insufficiency of language, Artaud pursued a form of theatre of a more primal and physical nature. Essentially, it is theatre of immanence, dynamism, mobility and an affective view of life as a dynamic experience. Redolent of our period, Artaud also articulates that 'contrary to the world slipping into an economic, utilitarian and technological state, it will bring major considerations and fundamental emotions back into style, since modern theatre has overlaid these with the veneer of pseudo-civilized man' (2010 [1938]: 88).

Vivid living

For Bataille, like Marx, Hegel's idealistic dialectic was the wrong way around. We should instead look to nature, dirt and the earth for knowledge as opposed to 'an *a priori* fog of universal conceptions' (2008 [1932]: 107). Humanity is to be found in non-productive expenditure and art, *jouissance*, spectacle, deviancy and perversion. Bataille puts it another way; humanity is to be found in circumstances that have no end beyond themselves, and is that which sits beyond reason, teleonomy and even sense and meaning. Creativity in this sense is far from utility, but is expenditure and the blowing-off of excess. Similarly, life for Nietzsche is the will to power, and also a creative process of excess and expenditure. The crucial characteristic of the living, Nietzsche says, is that it wants to '*vent* its strength' (2003 [1886]: §13, 44, emphasis in original). Why else would life be worth living; surely not for utility and productivity?

Described as an 'excremental philosopher' by André Breton, Bataille (2008) sought to launch an assault on dignity, Hegelian rationality and those who would place reality outside of animality. If folk in advertising like to consider themselves as irreverent, Bataille and his followers wallowed in the profane, displaying utter contempt for divinity. Humanity is animality, and God is a pig. Bataille also, for example, sees the big toe as the most human part of the human body as while we raise our head for lofty visions, it is our big toe that helps keeps us erect and standing. This reflects a division of high/low and for Bataille a bias against that which is cultured and elevated. Reflecting heaven and hell, and principles of evil versus good, the human race is that which distances itself as far as it can from mud and soil, the place where we return on death, and that which is base. Rejecting the sterile and bourgeoisie, life is found in the energy of the obscene. Bataille is not interested in overturning or replacing themes of dignity, godliness, nobility or reason, but his way is that of a terminal subversion of pseudosystems, hierarchies and edifices of order. While Bataille does not provide a cohesive thesis, there is a broader set of politics, loosely drawing on Marxian discourse. Unlike notions of base materialism that pass beyond matter into a theoretical edifice, his is a critique of physicality.

One, like a mole, must literally burrow under various forms of idealisms that underpin discourses ranging between utopian socialism and imperialism. Fascism then is not overcome by competing ideology, but instead through subversion. Such premises today might be seen in a number of sites away from the Spectacle. These tend to be autonomous zones, or liberated zones, whether these are travellers' sites, fetish clubs, perhaps even a good pub, or some similar enclave. These might be positioned in relation to a wide array of contemporary theory, for example Lyotard's *Driftworks* (1984) that seeks to accelerate the obsolescence and transgression of capitalism by means of a renewed interest in our corporeal selves; or Deleuze and Guattari's *Nomadology* (1986) that employs 'psychic nomads', to refer to the seekers and creators of liberated zones. Bey (2003 [1985]) similarly calls for an anarchy of immanence and where the surrealists courted the abstract, Bey proffers a heady mix of élan vital as manifested through sensualism, the body and pre-linguistic understanding. From a Deleuzo-Guattarian (2003 [1980]) point of view, such nomadism upsets the system of the state, of cultivation, of striation, and sedentary modes of being. These represent a vitalist call to arms that serves not politics, idealism, utopianism, nihilism or even art itself. It is instead sabotage, or what Bey designates aesthetic jihad. It is a mode that seeks to damage art establishments or institutions that use art to diminish consciousness or profit through delusion. Importantly, these are all sensational modes of creative being.

Needless to say, the siren-like spells of seduction and advertising are rendered as being along the lines of anthropophagous or cannibalistic incantations that leech vampire-like onto human interiority. In considering the overturning of sterile creativity we might turn back to Bataille, and his destructive drive. This is a form of exercising power, although from below. It is a practice of expenditure seen in ritual destruction, perverse sexuality and is bloody and orgiastic. Contra Nietzsche and his Overman, power emanates from the base. Viewed performatively, there is revelry and a version of creativity that cannot be incorporated into its opposite sterile self. Bataille's notion of heterology is opposed to philosophical systems (Bataille seems to have overlooked the dyadic nature of homogeneity and heterogeneity). To come to an understanding of heterology we should recognise homogeneity as the primary definer of heterogeneity. This means that heterology defines itself through opposition and resistance to the will to homogenise or make the same. Instead it seeks multiplicity and excitation through differences. Heterology then is that which rejects 'the development of a servile human species, fit only for the fabrication, rational consumption, and conservation of products' (Bataille, 2008 [1930]: 97).

Purposefully vague, and pre-empting deconstructive and post-structural tendencies, Bataille highlights that heterology is determined through negation and cannot be associated with common denominators. Heterogeneous elements cannot be placed within objective human domains due to the idea that 'simple objectification of their specific character would lead to their incorporation in a homogenous intellectual system, in other words, to a hypocritical cancellation of their excremental character' (2008 [1930]: 98). Such forms cannot then be assimilated, as they are unpalatable to the homogenous social body. Heterogeneity is that which is unknown, dangerous, taboo, magic and sacred. Like all sacred things, it is unproductive yet powerful and consists of that which is rejected by homogenous being as waste or that which is useless. These are dropouts, vermin, trash, and also dreamers and neurotics. For Bataille the heterogeneous also includes those who do not accept the rule – madmen, aristocracy, leaders, mobs and violent individuals. These are all entities with excess that break the laws of homogeneity.

Heterogeneity in the market

Unsurprisingly, Bataille is scathing of consumerism remarking that, 'The advantages of civilization are offset by the way men profit from them: men today profit in order to become the most degraded beings that have ever existed' (2008 [1936]: 179). However, the critique of the marketplace is not evident in all heterogeneous accounts. Bakhtin (1984 [1965]) in his account of the Renaissance humanist François Rabelais, the Middle Ages, and folk culture, locates heterology as being intimately connected with the market. While this is a different conception of the market from ours today ruled by global companies and abstract financial structures (and breakdowns), there is some applicability to creativity and advertising. This is predicated on Bakhtin's discussion of carnival and folk humour that is not entirely lost on advertising today. For Bakhtin this folk culture was made up of ritual spectacles, such as shows at the marketplace and carnival pageants; comedy, that parodied oral and written Latin; and, the use of obscene language or what Bakhtin designates 'genres of billingsgate' (1984 [1965]: 5).

This irreverence finds echoes today in popular culture and some of its advertising, for example with the use of comedian Peter Kay by TBWA as the award-winning 'No nonsense bloke' for John Smiths beer advertising. A wide-ranging campaign, it sees Kay representing Britain in a diving competition, where he does a dive-bomb into the pool, and another where he tells his daughter that she should be worried about burglars and not monsters. Catchphrases to have caught on in the UK as a result of these include "'ave it' and 'top bombing'. The idea of carnival is that a second world is created outside of the worlds of officialdom, politics and ecclesiastical affairs in which all mediaeval people participated. Being outside of religious affairs, carnival is strongly playful, festive, spectacular and sensuous. It is the same too for Bataille who characterises it as unrestrained consumption, laughter, absence of work and violation of sacred laws, and which temporarily goes against dominant orders. For Bataille laughter is a key dimension and represents 'the whole movement of the festival in a nutshell' (2007 [1976]: 90).

For Bakhtin, it is based on the culture of the marketplace that, 'to a certain extent became one of its components' (1984 [1965]: 7). The popular culture of the marketplace in Bakhtin's account existed outside of the official sphere and acted as a space for carnival and festivity. While few advertisements themselves enter territories of transgression, carnival and excess, unsurprisingly those that do stand out. Interestingly too, they tend to win awards for creativity. This is a highly playful conception of life (and the marketplace), where carnival exists somewhere between art and life. It is predicated on participation and while we might see creative advertising as the creation of spectacles to be consumed by audiences, popular culture is not just something seen, but far more importantly it is something sensuously lived in (by those who work in advertising agencies as well as those who do not). It is laughter-based and there is good reason why the advertising we do find appealing is often humorous. Humour in advertising has been used from the very late eighteenth century onwards and often provides a universalising quality that crosses demography and rank (Gulas and Weinberger, 2006). Symbols of carnival are 'filled with the sense of the gay relativity of prevailing truths and authorities' (Bakhtin, 1984 [1965]: 11) and this irreverence, sense of popular culture and the carnivalesque is another discursive source of creativity in advertising. While this does not account for all creativity in creative advertising, advertising that does not conspicuously take itself and its brand too seriously fits well with this conception. The link to heterology comes from what Bakhtin phrases as grotesque realism. This could not be more different from capitalist realism, usually associated with advertising (Fisher, 2009). Being based on the body, it is an account of folk culture that sees it as more than comfortable with bellies, flesh, drink, defecation and sex.

In grotesque realism these are not hived off to the private sphere, but are seen as universal and standing for all people. It is to disavow any cutting-off of bodily links to the earthy world and reject the private bourgeois ego as exemplified by capitalist realism. While the full excesses of the body may not be seen (although may be witnessed with Peter Kay's belly and bum crack in the John Smiths advertisement mentioned above), bawdiness often seen in advertising represents an echo of this. The point however here is less about the body, but rather the will to represent popular culture, a dose of the obscene and irreverent impulses. Thus, if the transgressive aspects of creative advertising are not carnival itself, they are its sublimation, representation and watered down version that makes for a slightly more acceptable form.

In addition to creativity as coarseness, capitalism itself is deeply excessive. While frequently critique of capitalism and advertising as its outward face points towards instrumentalism, metrics, quantification, accountability and bureaucratic regimes, it would be incorrect to ignore the extravagant dimension of capitalism. Goux (1998) provides an illuminating account that up-ends Bataille's reversal of political economy. In *The Accursed Share* series Bataille (2007 [1967]; 2007 [1976]) develops an economic theory predicated on excess and exuberance rather than scarcity. It reflects on what happens to the excess of a system when all living systems generate more than what they functionally need (be this solar energy or excess energy generated by the smallest chemical reactions).

Seeing his ideas as an 'overturning of the ethics' that grounds dominant economic principles, the innovativeness lay in the reversal of meagre super-structural accounts of expression, art and religion built on the more usual economic infrastructures to one that foregrounds and privileges the surplus and excessive (Bataille, 2007 [1967]: 25). Linking to Weber, Bataille's account of mainstream economic thought, and despising of 'servile man', involves a de-sacralised version of life by dint of the logic of production, labour and exchange where 'time is money'. Bataille's repulsion and rejection of the bourgeois involves the sacred and the profane: where the former centres on unproductive consumption or using-up of what is surplus, the latter belongs to a more utilitarian outlook. This stands in contrast to other civilisations such as the Aztecs (Bataille's example) whose excess was used for useless and profitless ends (as far as we know), as in the building of round pyramids to house bodies, human sacrifices and ostentatious gift-giving behaviour. Bataille's reversal sees a turnaround of emphasis and a privileging of that which is without utility or return and is unrecoverable. Historically this occurs in the arts, architecture and the spectacular, or in catastrophic spending as with war.

However, in the rejection of profane rationalism, Bataille does not disavow capitalism but *affirms* swathes of it – with advertising being a good example of this. As Goux points out, Bataille failed to make the case that capitalism is best characterised as productivist and utilitarian. A fuller account will see bureaucratic impulses, but also comprehends capitalism in terms of gambling, risk-taking, chance and what in Chapter 4 we accounted for as *alea*. This sense of excess also figures well in creative advertising where risk-taking is encouraged, and where the rationale for many creative decisions exists beyond utility so for spectacular event-making to represent both corporate and creative excess.

Conclusion

This chapter began by pointing out that while we tend toward a view of creativity as innately positive there is no particular reason why this should be the case, but rather creativity might better be seen as that disturbing and deconstructive force that prompts us to question dyadic notions. Creativity is neither good nor evil then (although as creativity is impactful it should not be considered blank or neutral either). The chapter also discussed the role of heterogeneous being and while seemingly anti-capital and spectacle (in Debord's sense), a more nuanced look in relation to folk culture and carnival re-orients how we see 'the market', allowing us to position it in somewhat more bawdy terms and away from capitalist realism. An interesting mode of creativity, revelry and celebration of popular culture emerges out of this, one better expressed in terms of a celebration of grotesque realism, excess and that which transgresses.

7 Creativity and the Counter-Enlightenment

In relation to sensation, this chapter surveys the impact of Hamann, Herder, Fichte, Schiller, Schelling and Schopenhauer clustered under the moniker 'Counter-Enlightenment philosophy', along with others such as Vico and Kant whose thinking informed this group. Together, albeit indirectly, they remain influential on what we understand today as creativity. Summed up, this involves the capacity to create and fashion within indeterminate environments, an awareness of the pliability of the real, cultural relativity, and the need to balance intellectual capacities with emotional and sensational understanding.

There are three good reasons to look at the Counter-Enlightenment and its relation to creativity. The first is to better get to grips with that assemblage of thought frequently maligned and too readily connected with lazy discourses of the outsider, the misunderstood artist, and stereotypes involving isolation, alienation, youthful death and suffering for art (Pope, 2005; Runco, 2006); the second is to better understand modes of thinking that permeate not only many contemporary cultural constructions of creativity, but also the humanities and cultural studies itself; the third is to find recognisable antecedents of the arguments presented throughout this book in relation to affect, sensation, intensity, aesthetics and the lived dimension of creative events. The latter two points connect to this book's interest in the 'affective turn' and its renewed interest in the body, feeling and aesthetics, and nowhere are these discourses better expressed than in writing from the Counter-Enlightenment. This chapter, then, depicts the origins of the affective account as it links to what we now know as the humanities.

The Counter-Enlightenment is an expression most commonly connected with Isaiah Berlin (1997 [1979]; 2000), although originated by William Barrett (1949). Typically associated with German Romanticism, it is used to refer to a body of thought that occurred in the late eighteenth and early nineteenth centuries that emerged out of opposition to eighteenth-century Enlightenment doctrine, particularly in relation to the pre-eminence of reason. While on first consideration we might associate Romanticism with gushy discourse on mystery, primal being, terror, the unknown and an over-emphasis on the self, a detailed examination of Romanticist thinkers and philosophers reveals more significant and interesting ideas. Gross mischaracterisations disguise the rigour and sophistication of much output, and the fact that many leading Romantic writers were engaged social and political reformers, and its protagonists were learned in the poetry of numerous languages. As Dewey (2005 [1934]) puts it, we might better think of Romanticism as that which is fresh, spontaneous, individual, strange and unusual. This need not mean overly youthful and frivolous. Other criticisms point to the Counter-Enlightenment and Romanticism as an outright rejection of science and rationalism. This exaggeratedly naïve dyad is also mostly inaccurate, not least because many Romantics followed scientific developments, particularly those that challenged Newtonian worldviews. Opposing mechanical dogma of his time, Schelling, for example, was adamant that nature existed as an organism and was struck by developments in chemistry, electricity and magnetism that indicated forces within living bodies. Similarly, in Britain, Coleridge attended many scientific lectures and counted among his good friends the chemist, Humphrey Davy (they inhaled laughing gas together); and Shelley carried a microscope with him.

Context

Romanticism's origins can be situated between 1760 and 1830, when cracks began to appear in Enlightenment doctrine, particularly in regards to the nature of knowledge and the transparency of what is knowable. Concurrently, a sensibility arose where state of mind and motive mattered more than consequence, and intention took primacy over results. Berlin (2000) relates that many of the original German Romantics and associated, but not necessarily member philosophers, were either humbly born, or of the lower classes. Lessing, Kant, Herder, Fichte, Hegel, Schelling, Schiller and Hölderlin were all devoid of aristocratic connections. In contrast the majority of the key French Enlightenment writers were gentrified and despite a shared hatred of the King of France and the Roman Church, looked with nausea and superiority on the Germans whom they saw as rebels. The Germans looked at the French as soulless, overly self-conscious salon dwellers without an inkling of the inner life of humankind. The problem is not with reason itself, but rather that which seeks to define, deduce and explain in terms of probability. Romanticism then is that:

> ... which looks upon every human activity as a form of individual self-expression, and on art, and indeed every creative activity, as a stamping of unique personality, individual or collective, conscious or unconscious, upon the matter or the medium in and upon which it functions, seeking to realise values which are themselves not given but generated by the process of creation itself.
>
> (Berlin, 1997 [1979]: 17–18)

This is a highly Schillerian (2004 [1795]) conception that privileges self-formation and thought as an active force able to act in a world of passive matter (also note that it differs from the caricature of 'nature' as the primary force). It contributes to the wider understanding of creativity presented in this book involving intervening acts that make a difference, and that which renders and wills new phenomena and events into being. This is predicated on an ontologico-aesthetic conception, and the means by which creative and aesthetic sensibilities can transform 'reality'.

Much of this can be situated against Enlightenment discourses that dictate that we are able to discern what humankind wants, create technical means to satisfy these, and engender wisdom, virtue and happiness. In this account, what is true, right, beautiful and good is demonstrable through the application of replicable and verifiable methods. It is a worldview that sees progress as blocked by unreason, ignorance, fantasy and superstition, and where that which is knowable is recognisable through empirical, replicable and verifiable means.

Typically and historically, reason is predicated on a secular understanding where the nature of reality is permanent, unalterable and subject to immutable and universal laws. Controlled observation is the means of accessing these truths, and mathematics the golden science in which we find perfection of form. Similarly, history represents a data set from which general propositions on how we should live are to be found. The path to knowledge is based on the natural sciences and by extension all claims to truth must be public, testable, communicable, capable of verification or falsification by means of methods open to, and accepted by, any rational investigator. It is comprised of three broad principles: the first is that all genuine questions can be answered; second, all answers are knowable and may be learnt and taught to others; third, all answers must be compatible with another as one truth cannot contradict another (Berlin, 1997 [1979]; 2000).

Centrally for those concerned with creativity and aesthetics, and also politics and ethics, methods used to find certainty and truth in the sciences may also be applied to other fields. Indeed, according to Enlightenment doctrine, if Newton was able to solve the intractable puzzle of cosmology, then topics such as ethics, politics, society, opinion and aesthetics should also be explainable. Nature then is something that may be objectively unravelled before us providing we can free ourselves of that which obscures clarity. If prejudice, dogma and uncritical thought are removed, the full harmony and symmetry of nature may be revealed for inspection, understanding and harnessing. In addition, truth exists in the singular and multiplicity equals error and what is true for one must be true for all (we might recollect here the discussion of convergence in Chapter 4). Berlin (1997 [1979]) observes that this appeal to singular truths goes back at least as far as Plato, who believed that every genuine question had one true answer. If this is not so, the question cannot be real or there is confusion in it. The world in this view becomes a singular system understandable through rational methods.

The language of metaphor, poetry, embellishment and other rhetorical means has no role. In the purging of poetry, metaphysics and mysticism, plain language and precise and literal prose are demanded. Such a worldview sees reason as liberation from error.

There are other formal differences too between the Counter-Enlightenment and the Enlightenment, particularly in regard to the arts. While language, representation and the arts are contingent and in continual processes of transformation, this does not mean that they progress. An artistic tradition or creative period may only be understood through the rules local to that episteme and the conventions that give rise to and inform it. It requires local understanding and not the employing of knowledge schemes from elsewhere. Relativism instead stymies the notion of progress (or regression) in art. In contrast to science that is incremental, structural, and having to do with the Cartesian method whereby, by 'combining the lives and labours of many, we might together make much greater progress that any one man could make on his own' (Descartes, 2006 [1637]: 52), creativity is unique and bounded. Similarly, while experience and knowledge of artistic mediums and treatments may be obtained, recorded and collected, advances in techniques of mediation do not equate to progress in art but rather advancement in media. As explored in later chapters, this involves progress in the capacity of affordances, but not creative progress per se.

The Counter-Enlightenment is the rejection of progressive narratives, and through Hamann and Vico, among others, the establishing of the spirit by which qualitative research would later establish itself. While rational men high on the Enlightenment may count their way to creative understanding, Counter-Enlightenment discourses seek a less positivistic approach to creative understanding. However, to underline the point made earlier, while a number of writers and thinkers are labelled with 'counter', we should not confuse this with being 'opposite'. Much Counter-Enlightenment prose is sweeping in its ambition and more rationalistic than one might expect. The dyad of reason/imagination, or any notion of 'two cultures', does not map onto Enlightenment and Counter-Enlightenment discourses. Indeed, Vico sought to trace 'the *ideal eternal history* through which the history of every nation passes in time' also describing that 'my Science proceeds like geometry' (2001 [1725]: 129, emphasis in original). Similarly in the introduction to Schelling's (2001 [1800]) *System of Transcendental Idealism*, Michael Vater remarks that Schelling is a child of the Enlightenment. This is a useful observation in that it admits of the idea that one may reject and deny principles one has sympathy for. The key similarity between these thinkers and writers is a dissatisfaction with the precepts of the Enlightenment and the surface-nature of its thinking, particularly when it comes to human and cultural affairs. 'Counter-Enlightenment' then is a rudimentary banner for wide-ranging thinking that is at times at odds with itself, as well as with luminaries of the Enlightenment. Hamann for example dissented from Herder as readily as Kant. This said, it serves as a useful catchall for a form of thinking that set the benchmark for hermeneutics and later mainstream qualitative research and its insistence on local understanding. It also functions as a context from which interest in sensation, intensity and the lived dimension of creativity is drawn, both in terms of modes of production and engagement with events and artefacts.

Shallow clarity

Pre-dating Bergson by nearly 200 years, Vico (2001 [1725]) maintained that Descartes was wrong about the primacy of mathematics as a route to knowledge. In *A Discourse on the Method*, Descartes recounts how he attempted to strip bare knowledge and opinions he had acquired so to reconstruct his mind with what he believed to be true. Among other things he considered being real, such as God, he saw in mathematics and geometry incontrovertible truths. He relates that he put aside numerous hours so to deal both with difficulties in mathematics, translate other modes of enquiry into mathematics and that he could 'more or less translate into mathematical terms by removing from them all the principles of the other branches of knowledge which I did not find solid enough' (2006 [1637]: 26).

Positioning his *New Science* in contrast to Descartes and his adherents, Vico (2001 [1725]) argued for the value of the humanities and historical studies. His contribution to knowledge was a new approach to thinking about human history that involved detail, evidence of custom and emotion, and imagination so to reconstruct different values and codes of bygone ages. It is an early form of hermeneutics and one that sees culture as local, and not open to sweeping historical assertions and commonality of fact across the ages. Truths are not eternal, reality is relative, and answers to questions are not always commensurate. This sits in some contrast to a linear and incremental perspective that sees human-controlled aspects of life as subject to development, improvement and refinement.

Unlike many of the Romantics that followed, Vico managed to lay out his relativist precepts systematically. This was no easy task, as he had to fight the self-referential systems of mathematics and the clarity of geometry with the vagaries of historical interpretation. His self-appointed assignment was not to examine the past through the sweeping assertions of philosophy, or the obscurity of philology, but to create an account of history that by definition requires poetic reconstruction. Vico's attack on the primacy of mathematics sees it as a human invention that does not correspond with reality. Instead of providing access to reality it is merely a method, albeit a useful one. This stands in some contrast to conceptions of mathematics that see it as only a short step from divine and sublime designations, perhaps deriving from Greek metaphysical and mathematical abstractions. It is a diversion of abstractions that, although logical, only demonstrates the internal logic of mathematics, not reality itself. As a man-made scheme it is not a system of laws that regulates reality but a system to plot occurrences and regularities on which predictions may be made. For Vico this represents a distinct schism between positive knowledge and that predicated on understanding. This is perhaps best expressed in Vico's criticisms of Descartes who in discussing mathematics remarked that:

> The long chains of reasonings, every one simple and easy, which geometers habitually employ to reach their most difficult proofs had given me cause to suppose that all those things which fall within the domain of human understanding follow on from each other in the same way, and that as long as one stops oneself taking anything to be true that is not true and sticks to the right order so as to deduce one things from another, there can be nothing so remote that one cannot eventually reach it, nor so hidden that one cannot discover it.
>
> (Descartes, 2006 [1637]: 17–18)

For Berlin (1997 [1979]), Vico's most audacious contribution to knowledge stems from the idea that there can be a science of mind that involves the history of its development. This does not involve static truths or principles, but rather understanding that ideas evolve and are a social process, and that this society is synonymous with the signs and symbols that a society makes use of. For understanding to exist, we should know more about context, motive and local matters in contrast to the application of transcending principles. This represents analysis in terms of the object itself and the endeavour to get the inside story. This requires both sympathy for the object of study and a high level of imagination.

Such claims for a new science set the scene for later Germanic hermeneutical insights based on *Verstehen* and *Einfühlung*, and similarly highly qualitative perspectives based on intuition, empathetic understanding, what today we call 'thick description', and the means by which an outside observer of a culture attempts to relate to it and understand others. There is of course significant room for attack and within the humanities itself, Habermas (1988) has taken such intuitionist approaches to task for requiring its practitioners to take themselves out of their lives, traditions, vantage points and all that gives rise to subjectivity so to place oneself in another historical stream of experience. However, as Berlin (1997 [1979]) remarks, while the claims to a new science are extravagant given the likely fallibility of the enterprise and the empirical research required to resurrect a situation, Vico successfully argued for the importance of a mode of perception and enquiry that seeks to understand symbols, outlooks, persons, cultures and the past. This is a different proposition to one that sees geometers as people of good sense best placed to discern rational interrelationships in morality, politics, literature and the wider arts. Vico's gripe is not with the effectiveness of science and mathematics in establishing facts, ordering events, arranging timelines or establishing who did what when. Indeed, Vico suggests that these are indispensable. Beyond history too in the spheres of economics, science, and sociology, Vico has no argument with the boons of statistical methods. His position rather reflects a wish to understand both the past and the present through the eyes of those who lived and are living it. This involves understanding ideals, motivations, wants, needs, desires, aspirations and knowledge outside of logical truths predicated on observation and deduction. For Vico there is a clear schism and divergence of enquiry between the specific, unique and culture-bound versus timeless principles. While such a distinction is nowadays routinely trotted out in research methodology classes it is worth recognising that before the eighteenth century this distinction did not exist, or it was not sharply drawn. While discussion of method occurred in the Renaissance, it was Vico who created or revealed the schism of what we phrase in qualitative and quantitative terms.

Vico also argued that knowledge is not only that laid out by prose. Rather than art, myth and poetry being forms requiring correction from enlightened thinking so to make plain the meaning behind the arts, the arts and creative endeavour embody a vision of the world, represent understanding and are also more than the sum of deconstructed elements. Moreover, Vico's is a pluralistic vision. The notion that there is one reality, available to the enlightened thinker, is anathema. Instead reality emerges by dint of the questions that are asked of it. Likewise, they are bound to the symbols and means by which the question is expressed. It is a highly relativistic view that does not deny knowledge but rather insists on contingency. In arguing against eternal mores, he remarks, 'I have adopted the criterion that *whatever all or most people feel must be the rule of social life*' (2001 [1725]: 131, emphasis in original). For Vico, speech represents or encapsulates a vision of a particular time and place that is only accessible retrospectively through the faculty of imagination.

As Herder (2002 [1774]) tells us, in bridging our culture and another, we should 'feel into' (*Einfühlung*) the outlook or character of an organisation, artistic tradition, people or period of history. As with Vico, the meaning of any given culture is only to be found within that culture and it makes little sense to try to understand the value or meaning of that culture without understanding the gravity of that culture. (Indeed, as Herder notes, even within a given culture people are deeply individual and this should affect how we go about studying them.) Herder is specific, stating that: (1) there is a gulf between the mentality of the interpreter and that which is to be interpreted; (2) research should include not only the text's use of language, but also the historical, social and geographical context; (3) in order to interpret a subject's language, one should be able to imagine conditions of perception and affective sensation; (4) hostility of an interpreter to the culture will mar results, as will excessive identification; and (5) language use, awareness of context and understanding of cognate sensations should be developed so to understand the original context a text was developed in. In this setting, feeling and empathy matter more than cognition. While few would quibble with the notion that cultures differ over time, it is Herder's insistence on the enormity of that difference and worldview from which his critique draws strength. Where Enlightenment doctrine projects and portrays people being much the same throughout history where two moments might be the same, Herder was unique in arguing for difference based on concepts, beliefs, propositions, perceptions, attitudes, affective sensations and language. His critique, although familiar to qualitative researchers now, and those of us attracted to reawakened discourses on affect, is interesting as he takes the dominant paradigm of his time to task. He remarks that future readers may read into his eighteenth century that it is characterised by mechanism, process, order, great progress and first principles that became so commonplace that they 'pass as *playthings* from hand to hand and as *platitudes* from *lip* to *lip*' (2002 [1774]: 321, emphasis in original).

Divorcing thought from sense

Vico's is a cyclical tripartite account of history. The first part involves a poetic nature produced by the powerful illusion of the imagination when reason was most weak; the second involves symbolic language, heroic natures based on heroes' belief in their own divine rights and religion to tame force; the third is the civilised self that is vernacular in orientation, intelligent, moderate, benign, reasonable and for Vico is guided by conscience, reason and duty. However, although characterised by popular democracy, the emphasis on rationality leads to a 'barbarism of reflection', or extreme individualism, he posits that the outcome of this is that civilisation implodes and returns again to the poetic era. In his *New Science* he argues that the 'languages today have divorced our civilized thought from the senses, even among the common people ... and the use of numbers has intellectualized it, so to speak, even among the masses, who know how to count and reckon' (2001 [1725]: 146–47).

For Vico the earliest people did not deal in abstractions, refinement or intellectualisation, and were instead caught up in the senses, passions and bodies. Thus if a common language of all people is sought, the master key is in poetry and the use of poetic symbols and metaphor. We do not get angry, but rather our blood boils! Further, myth becomes the vehicle with which civil history is documented, and poetry the expression of knowledge. Metaphor then is central, so we express rather than tell. For Vico then, 'poets were the *sense* of mankind, and the philosophers its *intellect*' (2001 [1725]: 136, emphasis in original). This has parallels with Herder (2002 [1767–68]) who sees the oldest languages as poetic and formed in response and in accordance with nature, as opposed to categories and dead ideas. These languages would have been more intense than our own, being rich and full of excess. In contrast to philosophers who reason, clarify and categorise, language for Herder was more sensuous, and laden with feeling, metaphor and imagery. Such power is still found in poetry and oratory, although sensuality once common fell away.

'Can the sacred be seized?'

Such sensational discourses that privilege expression over description find daily recognition in advertising. They also find root and manifestation in Hamann, a member of the *Sturm und Drang* (Storm and Stress) movement, who insists that originality and the creative act stem from breaking and violating rules, and that to believe one can imprison nature within rationalist doctrine is folly. Rebelling against the rationalism imposed by Enlightenment, it sought to express subjectivity in light of rationalistic knowledge-formation that fails to adequately capture the human experience. Hamann sought to demonstrate that truth is particular and not generalisable. Moreover, his is a holistic account based on a rejection of the opposition between faith and reason, idealism and realism, objectivity and subjectivity, body and spirit. This is due to a belief that human knowledge is contradictory and piecemeal. In discussion of reason, Hamann (2009 [1784]) notes several problems with how it has been conceptualised. He argues that attempts to make it independent of tradition, custom and belief are untenable and that reason should not be abstracted from experience and everyday induction. He makes a similar attack on the ways in which mathematics and geometry were made to address language. This is done by accounting for the apodictic or clear certainty of mathematics as being based on sensible intuition, synthesis, proof and the construction of formulas in which misunderstanding is excluded of itself. Hamann's critique is less about the value of pure science, but when certainties are brought to bear on language. He comments:

> Through this learned troublemaking it works the honest decency of language into such a meaningless, rutting, unstable, indefinite something = X that nothing is left but a windy sough, a magic shadow play, at most, as the wise Helvétius says, the talisman and rosary of a transcendental superstitious belief in *entia rationis*, their empty sacks and slogans.
>
> (Hamann, 2009 [1784]: 210)

His is a critique of abstraction, or being that has no existence outside of the mind. Ironically, this abstraction stems from the influence of sight and hearing that have become so universal that 'as a result space and time, if not *ideae innatae*, seem to be at least *matrices* of all intuitive knowledge' (2009 [1784]: 212, emphasis in original). That is to say, the language of geometry, extension, points and connection has replaced a more intuitive form of knowledge. Echoing affect-based critique today, he laments the artful text-like stitching together of ideas from the 'academic supply-house' (2009 [1784]: 217). Hamann's is a philosophy of the sensuous where in place of constructions, patterns and abstractions he sought the directly given and unmediated experience. Rather than reality being found in classification and commonality, it is found in multiplicity, diversity and difference. Systems and schemes that seek to map are artifices that turn away from teeming multiplicity, and the task for anyone interested in explaining life is to embrace its contradictions, peculiarities, non-sensical facets, and not to smooth-out or substitute abstractions for reality.

As is now quite clear, at the heart of Counter-Enlightenment critique is an accusation that rationalism and scientism distort reality. It is less a rejection of science itself, than the general worldview of science as it was around the late eighteenth century. This occurs through both its general orientation to singular truth, and the means and tools with which it goes about its work. Such a view is also seen in Schelling (along with Fichte, Hegel, Wordsworth, Coleridge, Goethe, Carlyle and Schopenhauer) who would influence Bergson's conception of the unanalysable flow, at least in terms of schemes of knowledge predicated on mathematics and that which seeks to break up and decontextualise.

In Germany's Schelling we see the culmination of anti-rationalism in which to dissect is to murder.

In England, Wordsworth in *The Tables Turned* expresses the same sentiment whereby our meddling intellect distorts, misshapes and that 'We murder to dissect' (1798: 188).

Schlegel puts it only slightly differently asking 'Can the sacred be seized?' to which he answers 'No, it can never be seized because the mere imposition of form deforms it' (cited in Berlin, 2000: 104). Indeed, in an invective against positive knowledge that in contemporary parlance favours the map over the territory, Herder asks why do his fellows deceive themselves concerning the *'tinsel of their own weighty importance'* and why the 'whole face of the earth becomes a *dungheap* on which we *seek kernals* and *crow*! *Philosophy of the century!'* (cited in Berlin, 2000: 332, emphasis in original). Herder is also highly dismissive of philosophy, or at least those that tend towards universalising theories. His attack is based on those who will apply categorising and universalising precepts to understand the past. Bluntly, and somewhat amusingly, he remarks:

> Strip it, see it with human being's eyes, and it will appear to you a Venus, but not that heavenly Venus, the sister of wisdom etc., but the earthly Venus, the sister of learning etc., the deformed offspring of human beings who fornicate with their fathers.
>
> (Herder, 2002 [1765]: 15)

Predating postmodern methodology, people for Herder are bound by the constitution of the subject, language and its usages, and what they are able to express sets limits for human cognition. However, despite Herder's insistence on language as a vehicle to understanding the orientation to a culture (along with other cultural output), he is critical of words as a means of dealing with distinctive individualities of people, or of huge groups of people inhabiting large regions of the world. Rather, in order to feel into an age, a clime or a history one should 'feel yourself into everything' (2002 [1774]: 292).

While not entirely clear, the emphasis is important, particularly as we understand that creativity is contextual, individual and culturally specific. As a forefather of the hermeneutical tradition, anthropology, cultural relativism, linguistics, interpretivism and anti-positivism, we see in Herder a need to avoid ambitious systemacity and common equivalences so as not to lose what is most valuable. Moreover, systems tend to distort or even exclude that which does not fit. They proceed without deep historical analysis passing over what is individual in favour of what must be made general. This is Herder's great insight that disrupted the efficiency of rationalist doctrine. For Herder this is *mechanical* dogma and in juggling theory 'one dances with his dagger on academic tightropes to the admiration and joy of all who sit around and cheer at the great artist that he may not break his neck and leg – this is his art' (2002 [1774]: 317).

Herder's is a requiem for a life lived immediately, standing in contrast to the French Enlightenment and that mode of exposition that sees itself as master and chief surveyor. It rejects uniformity and revels in the local and the complex. It destabilises the understanding that all questions have true answers that are discoverable and compatible. His attitude towards philosophy and the academy is reminiscent of how practitioners in advertising conceive of theoreticians and academic commentators, particularly if their ideas do not help creatives be more creative, improve their ideas or sell more products. Herder declares that rationalising has spread too carelessly and that it has weakened inclination, drive and activity for living. Instead he calls to 'Dear, weak, annoying, useless free thinking – substitute for everything that they perhaps needed more: heart! warmth! blood! humanity! life!' (2002 [1774]: 319). In some contrast to perspectives based on convergence, unity and analysis, Herder privileges divergence, the local and is suspicious of abstractions. In this he pre-empts the sensuality of Romanticism and its disavowal of what he saw as a cold, philosophical European world incapable of feeling and thus understanding. Herder asks whether 'we have ever taught a child language from the *philosophical grammar?*, taught him to walk from the most abstract *theory of motion?* [...] God precisely be praised! that it was *not required* or *possible!*' (2002 [1774]: 279, emphasis in original).

Life: a project

Underpinning accounts that privilege imagination over reason is the idea of freedom. This finds its best expression in Fichte's (1987 [1800]) *The Vocation of Man*. In accounting for, rejecting and explaining consequences of determinism, humanity is equated with freedom. In arriving at this conclusion, Fichte works through realist and idealist arguments. In the first on realism we begin with the familiar world of things where our knowledge and ideas of the world are derived from our experiences of it. In the second account we begin with minds that produce their own experiences according to the way that they are constituted. Fichte's point is that neither of these is satisfactory, and instead looks towards will and action. This is because we are not simply observers, but rather we are in the world and participants of it. Further, we are not human or anthropogenetic machines working in accordance with 'nature', but rather we are a project or activity with freedom to choose or create. Fichte's argument on freedom and action might not be as durable if he did not presage it with a lucid rendering of determinism. He describes that:

> I enter into an unbroken chain of appearances, since each link is determined by the one preceding it and determines the one following it; I enter into a tight interconnection since from any given moment I could find all possible conditions of the universe by merely thinking abut it. Backward, were I to *explain* that given moment; forward, were I to *infer* others from it.
>
> (Fichte, 1987 [1800]: 7, emphasis in original)

As every condition is prefixed by another, a thing cannot arise out of nothing. So, in addition to being able to potentially chart forward, we also have an eternal deferral of qualification. Thus, 'Whatever I am and become I am and become necessarily, and it is impossible for me to be anything else' (Fichte, 1987 [1800]: 14). In pursuing this, Fichte points out that we cannot resist determinism portraying development in the same manner as we might train a plant to grow one way over another. While we may feel free, there are larger factors at play that render freedom impossible. Accordingly, we do not will or freely create anything but instead we are shaped by nature and whatever we become is an outcome of much larger natural forces. Articulating a division between the body and 'sensuous inclinations' that are bound by deterministic forces and absolute free will, he concludes that neither of these poles can be justified with reason. He recognises the emotionality of these respective poles (that continues to this day) and that the idea of total freedom satisfies the heart, and the opposite mocks and deadens it. Following the deterministic avenue we perversely become alien to ourselves as we monitor affection or good will as an outcome of determining factors we do not control. Indeed, even our interest in freedom may at some point be plainly plotted and mapped. In dialogue with himself, and perhaps emblematic of the dread others have felt in face of deterministic logic, Fichte bemoans:

> It explains everything I bring up against it from my consciousness, and whenever I say that such and such is the case I am always answered in the same cool and self-assured way: I say the same thing [life is determined], and in addition I'll tell you the causes which makes it necessarily so.
>
> (Fichte, 1987 [1800]: 25)

In building his rebuttal, Fichte narrates a dialogue with a presumably fictional visiting spirit who seeks to allay his fears. The argument begins by addressing problems with positivist accounts, and the lack of certainty of the external world and that it is we who produce the *presentation* of the object. This world as we know it is necessarily constructed within human spatial and sensational limitations, and reality is bound by possibilities of experience. To quote, 'consciousness of a thing outside of us is absolutely nothing more than the product of our own presentative capacity' (1987 [1800]: 59).

For Fichte it is not our vocation to know, but rather to act. Pre-empting existentialism (although a believer in God), it is activity that determines worth. Rather than let our intellect schizophrenically flutter, we instead rouse and direct our attention. He observes that 'it is neither blind chance which imposes a certain system of thinking upon me, nor empty chance which plays with my thoughts, but is I who am thinking, and that I can think about what I want to think about' (1987 [1800]: 74). As he moves towards his final conclusion he remarks on the need to listen to our conscience and insists on the necessity of acting on that ethical advice. Arguing for vocation, he describes it as that which recognises the relative nature of reality yet also that we should act ethically and with others in mind who we presume are also free, considerate and beings independent of the mere power of nature. If these were to be renounced, we would sink into absolute nothingness. At the heart of miasma then is will and it is the only thing we can be sure of at any given moment. In terms of what it is that acts there is the spiritual, which consists of pure will and there is also the sensible in which we act through deed.

Volo ergo sum

Some context to will is required. In his *Critique of Pure Reason*, Kant defines freedom as absolute self-activity (1990 [1781]), although qualifying this with the premise that freedom of the self must be consistent with the freedom of others. Although recognising concerns about nature, causality and the influence of preceding states as discussed by Fichte, Kant continues to associate freedom with spontaneity. The question of freedom then for Kant lies in the practical extent to which the will is free of coercion from sensuous impulses and able to engage in self-determination. His account of freedom culminates in the 'noumenal' self that is required to take responsibility for its own character, and not be subject to laws of causality. He makes a division between the phenomenal world of causality, determination and appearances, and what he designates the noumenal world that exists distinctly from the phenomenal experience. Where the former is derived from sense experience, the latter has to do with understanding, reason and that we are quite unique in having imperatives we impose on ourselves. As Kant remarks in regards to things that we ought to do or be, this 'expresses a kind of necessity and of connection with grounds which is found nowhere else in the whole of nature' (1990 [1781]: §B575, 472–73). What ought to be stands in contrast to what is, what has been and what will be. For Kant then, reason, being a mode of autonomy, acts freely. Thought of in positive terms, reason has the power to originate series of events.

To admit to being incapable of resistance is to admit of slavery. Such conceptions influenced Schiller who saw mankind as distinct from nature. Nature for Schiller is amoral, indifferent and destructive. In contrast, man for Schiller 'distinguishes between desire and will, duty and interest, the right and the wrong, and acts accordingly, if need be against nature' (Berlin, 2000: 81). However, there is a twist for Schiller. Whereas Kant tends towards morality and duty as will against nature, Schiller posits that we must be free not only to do our duty but also to follow nature. We must be able to stand above both. This leads to a situation where one is able to be both abominable and superior because choice has been exercised. Those who are bad may be superior to those who follow blindly. The blind and good may be mastered and therefore dominated. We see here another archetype that finds its way into agency life. This is Schiller's (2004 [1795]) figure that acts according to his or her own wishes and wants, serving neither 'nature' nor 'duty'. This derives from a three-stage view of nature where in the first people are consumed by passions, desires and have no ideals; the second involves worshiping idols and principles (including those of a rational form); and the third that has to do with the means by which humans liberate themselves by means of adopting the attitude of games-players.

This latter point involves a 'play-drive' (*Spieltrieb*) that requires people carve a path between the necessities of nature and the commandments laid upon us by everyday and contractual life where we fulfil obligations (Berlin, 2000). In negotiating a route between these two bases we engage in an artistic form of play that allows us to imagine, invent and create. Centrally, it involves freedom of self-definition. Schiller's argument is that rather than mowing each other down we will instead form harmony with one another through artistic self-creation. Ideals in this context are not discovered, but instead invented. It is a transformational conception of being that places our self-determined selves rather than followers at the centre of the universe.

We also see this in Fichte (1982 [1810]) who, along with the pragmatist James and the phenomenologist Bergson discussed elsewhere in this book, sees knowledge as an instrument and not an end in itself. For Fichte life is based on action and knowledge and has to do with knowing how to survive, how to be, how to adapt things, and knowing how best to live and not die. Freedom in this setting has to do with the ways in which we may take the outside world and mould it, as opposed to being moulded by it. Things are as they are because we make them so. Creativity lies at the heart of Fichte (1982 [1810]) and his key premise is that we live in continual action whereby we must go on constantly generating and creating. If we accept what we are given, we may as well be dead. Life then is action with the fundamental point being *volo ergo sum* (I am willing therefore I am) rather than the more familiar Cartesian cogito. In the former we only understand ourselves through action, resistance and opposition.

Schopenhauer (1966 [1918]) addressed the subject of will directly, as a subset of Cartesian, Berkeleyan and Kantian arguments in which the world exists as a representation. Rejecting appeals to the creative power of God, Schopenhauer is more interested in the ways in which will manifests in the world. This world of representation is created and conditioned by the subject and in Kantian terms is made up of transcendental ideality. However, this is not to say the representation is false: instead it is entirely reasonable, intelligible and accessible, but it is created. Schopenhauer's point is that there is more to life than the world as representation – there is that which drives this, which is will.

Schopenhauer's central investigation is to understand the relationship between will and representation (the world). This relationship differs from the representational world and the laws that govern it (having to do with Kantian notions of space, time and causation). Thus, 'we can never get at the inner nature of things *from without*' as we only find images and names (1966 [1918]: 99, emphasis in original). This inner nature is will and Schopenhauer directly links this with the body (although this itself exists as a representation). Thus every act of will involves the body in some way as acts of the body are will objectified, or made manifest in the realm of representations. This is an important point if we are going to ensure that we do not think of will itself as an entity. Further, the body accommodates itself to will as teeth, throat and intestines are objectified hunger; genitals for sexual impulses; and hands and feet being extensions for a variety of will-based activities. It is not an overly large step to see Mumford (1961 [1934]) and McLuhan's (2001 [1964]) technological extensions as extensions of will rather than of sensory faculties. Schopenhauer's point is both abstract and immediate. It is immediate in the sense that will is that which is most immediate to our minds (it is that which motivates the body), yet abstract in the identification of that which governs body and the world. Will is not only to be found with people but in a hierarchy of animals, plants and other forces in the world (for example geological, crystalline, magnetic, gravity and so on). This said, will itself is not a force as with that found in the representational world of cause and effect, but rather it is an essence that for Schopenhauer is not part of this world. Will is a Kantian thing-in-itself or *Ding an sich* and the identification of will in the world according to Schopenhauer grants us an appreciation of the inner motivating nature of the world.

The connection between will and non-humans is not as utterly strange as it might first appear and in a more modern setting we see will expressed at the level of single-celled organisms and their preference to endure and live. Less about a particular faculty or attribute, will is better thought of in neovital terms of that non-conscious dimension that permeates life and impels us to continue. Whitehead also argues that notions of will and desire, as a means of accounting for creation, are not solely to be attributed to humans, or even organic beings, and goes as far as ascribing will to the level of the electron (Shapiro, 2012).

We cannot, then, help but notice that across the biological spectrum creatures have tendencies towards overcoming and prevailing. Without doubt there is potential for a classical vitalist reading here, and Schopenhauer him-self states that 'I shall explain that the vital force certainly avails itself of and uses the forces of inorganic nature' (1966 [1918]: 142). While this book is aligned with a process-based approach, Schopenhauer rejects and mocks what now is assumed knowledge that life emerges out of its parts and the possibility that the transcendental and the immanent might be linked at a fundamental level. He makes a direct correlation between will and Plato's Ideas that are predicated on the objectification of eternal or original forms in the representational world. If we leave to one side this dualism so to allow deeper interconnection, will emerges (in this beyond-human sense) as virtuality, potential, creativity and that which causes things to be. It is protean, and both metaphysical and immanent.

So, for example, as seeds become seedlings and eventually plants, will, virtuality and process is manifested in representational form. As to what we take away from Schopenhauer on will, we understand that the world exists as a mirror or objectification of will and the world is simply a representation. It is the primacy ascribed to will that concerns us here, as it is that active force which initiates all else in and of the world. The world exists as a shadow to that of will.

More recently, Rorty phrases this well when remarking on the contrast between Plato and Nietzsche over questions of 'What is our nature?' vs. 'What can we make of ourselves?' Rorty suggests that 'We are coming to think of ourselves as the flexible, protean, self-shaping, animal rather than as the rational animal or the cruel animal' (2010 [1993]: 353). Broadly speaking, where the former question pertains to eternity, the latter looks to the future. Fervent in belief of self-creation, perhaps the most avowed of non-conformists, Nietzsche (deeply influenced by Herder) waged a personal war against conformity, mechanisation, mediocrity, bureaucracy, homogeneity and all that he saw as stifling men (his well-known views on women are less than charitable) from their higher duties and responsibilities, 'creative full-ness', and the manner in which men will stand alone living by personal initiative (2003 [1886], §212: 144). Unlike other philosophers concerned with truth, Nietzsche's point is that thought is a creative act and the artist is that person who stands alone.

These views are deeply Schillerian and both Schiller's and Nietzsche's figure will turn away from corruption, fortune and everyday needs, and pursue a path guided by his own dignity. Schiller urges the creative self (having Goethe in mind) to live in the century but not be its creature, and to give contemporaries what they need, and not what they want. He comments, 'No doubt the artist is the child of his time; but woe to him if he is also its disciple, or even its favourite' (2004 [1795]: 12). In an expression that will appeal to those in advertising, Schiller defines the creative impulse as the union of the possible with the necessary to produce the ideal. It also involves the play of imagination, and gravity in action of the sensuous and the spiritual (i.e. contemplative).

Although Nietzsche disassociated himself from Romanticism, there are obvious links, particularly in regards to indomitable will, forward motion, the superman, and rejection of the unimaginative existing world. Likewise, Nietzsche's figure or Overman is beyond good and evil, and has a divergent nature that alone through power of will decides what is virtuous and what is not. He is independent of spirit and like Zarathustra, the creative being has little need for comfort and support, and given that he reviles sentimentality and weakness will actively reject them. For Nietzsche such a figure is truly a free spirit who will seek solitude over happiness with the herd. He will have inventive faculties, subtlety, daring, Will to Life, stoicism and something of the serpentine within him. Being neither meek, nor indecisive, those with will do not leave things to chance, but create and control. They order chaos as an instantiation of how life might be.

Creativity has little to do with the good life and is amoral. The creative or free spirit is beyond good and evil, at least as conceived by the herd, and will have little interest in money, position, honours or empty exaltation. He will reject systems of morals as bondage, stultification and a narrowing of perspective. Nietzsche (2003 [1886], §202: 69) in what for him was a transitory age asks, is such greatness possible in an age of herd mentality? Of all Nietzsche's aphorisms perhaps most famous is The Will to Power where all living things will seek to discharge their strength in some way. This is not a characteristic of life but rather an innate instinct like self-preservation. It is not so much a principle, but a modus operandi. It is in combination of will and action, and the capacity to affect, command and receive acquiescence we see the nature of will. It is an active force that forms, delineates, shapes and creates the world. For Nietzsche nobility is to be found in self-determination, lack of need for approval from others and the creation of one's own values. Such self-manufacturing is an outcome of will and the capacity to articulate and render the world.

Aesthetic being

Central for any account of creativity is recognition that creativity does not comprise sensuality alone but requires will that orders the world and subjects it. For Schiller (2004 [1795]) an aesthetic self is composed of the interplay of reason and sensuality. Inspired by Kant, Schiller laid out the composition of what an aesthetic education might consist of. This involves the cultivation of the individual as a being that possesses a totality comprised of sensuality and reason. Where one was singular, local and intense, the other is abstract, diffuse and cool.

In translation and introduction to Schiller, Snell sums up Schiller's letters[1] by observing that:

Man must pass through the aesthetic condition, from the merely physical, in order to reach the rational or moral. The aesthetic condition itself has no significance – all it does is to *restore* Man to himself, so that he can make of himself what he wills.

(in Schiller, 2004 [1795]: 12)

The aesthetic then is personified for Schiller in the humanity of ancient Greece as a unification or harmonisation of matter and form, or sensuousness and reason. One cannot rule alone and these two contradictory tendencies pull in opposite directions. However, in ancient Greece, Schiller idealises that however high reason might soar it never mutilated its object. This was unsustainable as specialisation occurred, and knowledge and means of acquiring insight fragmented. Sensation and contemplation were thus divorced, and truth was pursued on separate paths. Mankind in this context develops as a fragment and the full powers of harmonious being are never established.

The ideal self is that of a sensuous-rational nature able to express form in the world, and to take the world, theorise it and give it shape. By developing both faculties of sensation and rationality, one gains freedom involving a free disposition based on both the sensuous and the physical, and the logical and the moral. For Schiller this is an aesthetic condition. The power to act freely is also the exercising of power and Schiller takes this capacity to act and lets it loose on nature. In Schillerian terms, nature is that which must be subject to will and what once ruled us,

now stands as *object* before the judgement of his glance. In bringing together the two halves of aesthetic education Schiller argues that beauty consists of 'living shape', and this might be thought of as a game. In responding to life and the world conceived of as a universal and immanent game, Schiller even goes as far as to state that '*he is only wholly man when he is playing*'.

(Snell in Schiller, 2004 [1795]: 80, emphasis in original)

Idealism

The background context or miasma for this decentring of human knowing is Kant's (1990 [1781]) self-described Copernican revolution whereby no discussion of what is real can take place without awareness of the role of the human mind in *creating* reality and knowledge. The raising of idealism here is intended as both a diagnostic and a historical note as it has distinct implications for creativity. Indeed, if any one philosopher made the familiar strange, it is Kant. Where hitherto cognition conformed to objects, Kant sought to assess how objects conform to our cognition and the ways in which our faculties create the world through the imposition of *a priori* systems of time, space and causality. Likening the stature of his idea to Copernicus and his positing that perhaps the stars do not revolve around us and that the centre of the Earth is not the centre of the universe, Kant suggests in the

Critique of Pure Reason that we relate to objects through representations that we project into them. Pre-empting more recent constructivist thinking (that deeply influences discursive and semiotically-led thought), the idea then is that our understanding of the world is not a mirror of it, but a creation of our sensory and perceptual manifold (as also broached in Chapter 5).

As noted earlier in this chapter, this gives rise to two dimensions for Kant – the *phenomenal* (the thing as it appears) world versus the *noumenal* (the thing in itself, or famously *das Ding an sich*). Kant's (1990 [1781]) *Ding an sich*, or things as they are in themselves, are unknowable although we are compelled to acknowledge their existence. This is because all things must be processed, structured and mapped by our sensory faculties as we physically interact with an object. This is not to say the subject produces existence outside of the subject (unsurprisingly, life goes on without us), but 'only' that what we perceive is highly contingent on the perceiver/processor in addition to the prompts that the object provides us. This becomes clearer when we appreciate Kant's notion of transcendental idealism and subject-based experiences of the world, as opposed to ones where we comprehend objects in and of themselves. This is predicated on the type of knowledge that comes before the object, or that which allows us to experience those objects as objects. This is *a priori*, and requires that we recognise the 'mind' as contributing features that make it possible for us to experience objects as objects. These features do not derive from experience and are by definition independent of experience. They are that which determine objects found in experience.

For Kant, appearances come about as a dialogue between these categorising and schematising faculties (for example, space, time and causality) and sense data (which we can never know). Consciousness of an object is 'merely' consciousness of the production of a consciousness of an object. For example, when touching an object we do not see or feel *the* object but rather intuit seeing or feeling *as* seeing or feeling a surface. Consciousness then is recognition of this state of awareness where we better understand that consciousness of objects only reflect consciousness of the positing of an object. This view finds radical expression in Berkeley (1988 [1710]) who argues there is no mind-independent reality. This is a step too far and Berkeley's total denial of the world goes to a place where this book cannot follow at all. However his sceptical and immaterialist account is useful so to fracture certainty in the external world and invite in playful (re)creation.

Such scepticism has been a feature of Western philosophy at least since the time of Sextus Empiricus (c. 160–210 CE). It is predicated on the idea that we cannot know the true nature of reality or how things are. Arguing against materialism and objects in the world that have an existence distinct from understanding, Berkeley posits immaterialism where all that we can know are products of our minds. So, for example, on seeing the sun, we see our idea of the sun and not the sun 'itself'. There is a gap between the world and ourselves, and we do not see directly, but through projections and images in our minds. What we call reality thus takes on chimerical properties.

Reality is a local construct made out of ideas where the gap between the perceiving mind and what it engages with is entirely indistinct. Put more plainly, anything we perceive depends on our perceiving it. In depicting the physicality of being sat at his writing table Berkeley remarks on his sensations of touch, smell, sight, sound and being in his study, while at the same time noting that the scene is impossible without the perceiver being there. He comments, 'It is but looking into your own thoughts, and so trying whether you can conceive it possible for a sound, or figure, or motion, or colour, to exist without the mind, or unperceived' (1988 [1710]: 60). So while we may convince ourselves we are handling, weighing up and dealing with the external world, the truth for Berkeley is that we are merely contemplating our ideas. His argument is against the innate existence of 'matter' (being comprised of extension, solidity and weight, among other phenomena), not the reality found in apprehension, sense or reflection. In presenting his anti-materialist argument, Berkeley spiritualises reality by stating that sensible objects are predicated on ideas. This is not to say that the world (and its trees, mountains and rivers) does not exist, but that these do not have continuation without a perceiving mind. Berkeley goes further, making these ideas dependent on God. The latter point also takes us somewhere this book cannot go, but the former point is more interesting in fracturing the notion of reality as a mirror (to borrow from Rorty, 1979) and objective knowledge as benchmark and determinate for the human subject.

This ultra-radical denial of realism is destabilising, discombobulating and exciting as it makes indeterminate that which we thought stable. Creativity is not just manipulating, but potentially about reformulating what is sensible, reconceiving and altering at the most fundamental of levels – experiential ones. As the distinction between ideas and things is removed, the possibility that our ideas are those things emerges. This is different from the Kantian argument as, for Kant, Berkeley's version of idealism is predicated on mysticism whereas Kant saw his own version as compatible with 'empirical realism' (where matter is admitted to exist but that this cannot be known beyond representations made to us beyond our own self-consciousness). Centrally, denying material existence, Berkeley argues that objects we meet in the world have no extra-mental existence. Where we might turn to what we conceive as the material world and point to matter, motion, cause and effect, as independent realities, for Berkeley these are regularities occurring among the ideas in our experience. We do not have to agree with theism or even the full impart of Kantian and Berkeleyan doctrine to recognise that we import much of ourselves into the world and what we might take for objectivity is a projection of subjectivity. We do not create the world as such (life goes on without us), but knowledge of empirical content, orientation, and sense experience is mediated through the productive imagination along with its theories, formulations and intuitions.

Schelling (2001 [1800]) formed part of an arc chronologically ranging across Kant, Fichte, Schelling and Hegel, and in reading him we should keep in mind

Fichtian idealism, freedom and praxis from which Schelling derives much of his gist. In Schelling (as with Fichte) we also see the rejection of certitude in the external world and a need to understand the means by which we self-create this world. This creative capacity constitutes as well as cognises the world through a process Schelling calls *intellectual intuition*. For Schelling, objects and external things must be derived from the process of our intuition itself where thought precedes being. Knowledge for Schelling then has to do with the way in which we conceive of subject/object relations and whether we see reality as consisting of 'stuff out there'. If this is the case, we have to reconcile our subjective experience in a mirror-like fashion with the objective world, thus making the objective world the primary component of reality. Schelling disagrees and remarks that, 'If, then, there is a *transcendental philosophy*, there remains to it only the opposite direction, that of *proceeding from the subjective, as primary and absolute, and having the objective arise from this*' (2001 [1800]: 7, emphasis in original). If we accept that much of what we take for reality exists as projected learned association, such a view destabilises the objective real and opens up wide questions about the nature of objective knowledge, or at least what naïvely appears to us as real. For example, substance-based views of reality are easily attacked. Although when the humanities treads into high-level quantum physics, the result tends not to go well, we might briefly point out that what we think is a solid object is mostly empty space, as the distance between particles is relatively immense (Eddington, 1928). A recent *New Scientist* article also relates that if an atom were scaled up so that its nucleus was the size of the Earth, the distance to its closest electron would be 2.5 times the distance between the Earth and the sun (Jamieson, 2012). The upshot of this is that much of what we take for tangible condensed stuff is actually empty space. Eddington, in making the case for the need for abstraction in physics, highlights that 'reality is a child which cannot survive without its nurse illusion [a substance-based view of reality]' (1928: xiv). Similarly, David Bohm (2004 [1996]) is cited in Chapter 9 making similar points in relation to the premise that things and phenomena are abstractions from a farther-reaching process.

What we experience as reality is a situation where 'the object *as* such vanishes into the act of knowing' (Schelling, 2001 [1800]: 9, emphasis in original). Likewise, Schelling sees 'ordinary thinking' as a mechanism (bearing in mind dominant technologies/metaphors of his time) governed by concepts and rules-based instinctive understanding of how the world works. In this we simply categorise the world without reflecting on the role of the subject. Conceptualising our conceptions of the world via self-consciousness thus makes us more aware of the concepts that we apply unthinkingly about us. Such recognition and awakening allows us to free up the world from convention and begin to see the world of the familiar more strangely. A transcendental view of creativity understands culture (as a set of conventions) to be an article of faith, a void or a consensual hallucination where we are not entirely sure what others see but we place faith that our ontology is not frightfully different. It is a void because we do not know what is beyond subjective projections of understanding.

By means then of scrutinising ourselves, and the ease with which we act in the world, we are able to challenge every assumption and conviction with potential to reframe reality. This does not mean we will penetrate any sort of essence or truth, but rather we understand the conventional nature of reality and that what we take as given is simply a first draft ready for nego-tiation. In Schelling's terms it is a *'constant objectifying-to-itself of the subjective'* (2001 [1800], emphasis in original), or the way in which we can observe ourselves and the ways in which we self-create the world.

This turns life and experience of the external world into an inside without an outside. Such recognition of being involves what Fichte phrases as 'looking out of myself out of myself', as 'living seeing', or 'seeing my seeing' (1987 [1800]: 51). More recently, and as broached in greater depth in the following chapter, Cassirer (1966 [1929]) takes up the transcendental idealist and Kantian project, and that the schema or mental imposition on the world represents creativity *par excellence* by means of symbolism. Cassirer distin-guishes man and animal with the symbolic and interpretive function structur-ing objectivity. Where usually a symbol stands for a known object, here what we consider as objects are simply representations of unknowable objects. Symbolism or creativity in this context is ever-present and all pervading, at all phases, levels of cognition and experience. The point here is that we do not understand symbolism in the abstract, but we breathe and experience it at *all* fundamental levels. Creativity does not involve games of abstraction but is precisely the opposite; it involves the structuring of experience, sense and culture, that itself is understood in terms of sensational schematisation and mapping.

Conclusion

Approaches to creative understanding predicated on affect, intensity, immer-sion, the lived and that which seeks to reintegrate thought and sense find distinct and original antecedents in Counter-Enlightenment discourses, parti-cularly those of a rebellious form that see consciousness as a response to cold, careless and indifferent strains of rationalism. Summarised, these see an emphasis on sensual and poetic expression, along with the requirement that local understanding is not abstractly but qualitatively understood. Indeed, we might even question whether 'Counter-Enlightenment' is the best collective term for what might be better seen as a positive assertion of qualitative knowledge and being that depicts the recognisable origins of contemporary interest in qualia, the lived, affect, unique experiences of phenomenal life and the terrain of creative engagement. While much of the language employed by Herder and Hamann is passionate rather than analytical, the point is made clearly that scientism does not explain the whole of experience. Practically, this cultural construction is lived out in creative departments across the world and via pronouncements by Bill Bernbach on formulae, feeling, stirring people, imagination, talent, disavowal of academics, being provocative, cold arithmetic, the role of science in creative advertising, concern about creative phonies, dangers in playing safe, the energetic displacing the passive, and the centrality of insight (see DDB, 2012).

Out of sensational and aesthetic being, freedom and will emerges *intentionality*. This is a characteristic of consciousness and is that which is able to become objectified representation and made manifest in the world. Consciousness in a creative context is also a condition in which we question what is given around us and recognise the instability of the world. While one might (and probably rightly) seek to tone down some of the Nietzschean excesses, the point remains that will is that which intervenes and transcends the accident of existence and determines whether we destroy, create or make a mark on the world in some way. Creative consciousness then is the capacity to reformulate in light of indeterminacy. This emphasis on the self is not to deny co-creative discourses broached earlier, but to highlight that willing subjects are required to navigate and make sense of the unknown. To continue with cartographic metaphors we might appropriate a line from Lee Nichol's foreword to Bohm's *On Creativity*, where acts of will in indeterminate environments are akin to 'creating a path while walking' (2004 [1996]: xxxiii). It is also to point to an exploratory characteristic and toughness (and perhaps even brutality at least in terms of what one asks of one's self) that is required to fashion and form within indeterminate environments. This is because with schemas and safety scaffolding removed, a sense of nerve is required. Although indeterminacy may be too redolent of Romanticism for some – environments with few familiar reference points require temperaments able to deal with ambiguity so to render what is new and valuable.

Kant's discussion of the subject and transcendental idealism is used functionally here. We need not follow this too rigidly but rather depart with the understanding that the notion of reality as a mirror is untenable, that creativity is deeply linked to possibilities for reformulation, and that processes giving rise to objects are more 'real' than the abstractions we live with. The reason for not aligning with Kant is straightforward. If we go along for a moment with the premise that the noumenal (that which is unknowable to people) is inaccessible because of mediating and *a priori* tendencies, this raises questions about what it would take to know the noumenal – presumably this could not occur without *some* sort of mediating faculty? Meaningful truth then is at best only ever partial, unless we are to entertain the idea of a divine entity. If this is not to be the case then we must begin the road towards pragmatism and its functional truths. Moreover, as discussed in Chapter 5, if we recognise that close relationship between the inquiring mind and the brain, then what of the knowable status of the phenomenal? This takes on noumenal characteristics leaving us in a totally inescapable malaise. More preferable then is to eschew the question of tiers and dual status so to facilitate an ongoing conversation about processes and how things come to be. As Whitehead puts it:

> You cannot cling to the idea that we have two sets of experiences of nature, one of primary qualities which belong to the objects perceived, and one of secondary qualities which are the products of our mental excitements. All we know of nature is in the same boat, to sink or swim together.
>
> (Whitehead, 1964 [1920]: 148)

Note

1 Schiller's *On the Aesthetic Education of Man* is a series of 27 letters written in 1793 to a Danish Prince, Friedrich Christian of Schleswig-Holstein-Augustenburg.

8 Embodying culture

We tend to think of sign-making as an intrinsically human activity, but this is not the case. Quite arguably semiosis, or activities involving signs, is apparent in the most simple of organisms – even those of a single-celled variety. The purpose of this chapter is to place semiosis beyond Saussurean accounts and consider the consequences for creativity and advertising if we frame these in biosemiotic terms, or that which explores codes, signs and meaning in a biological setting that also encompasses non-human sign producers and sign receivers. As to why we should do this, there are a number of reasons, but perhaps foremost is to destabilise the blinkered sovereignty of the human sensorium; to better appreciate the unique virtual dimension of human signifying practices where symbolic practices need not have referents; and ultimately to position advertising as that which wilfully attempts to transform the sense-ratio of an individual or group for the gain of others.

The reason for broadening semiosis beyond the usual human definition is to rescue semiosis from textualism and reinvigorate it with the premise that semiosis occurs at all levels of biological existence. Although the capacity to create and reflect adds a boost to semiotic endeavour, complexifies behaviour, intensifies consciousness, and leads to symbols, stories or narratives without referents – semiosis is at heart biosemiotic, in the Spinozan (1996 [1677]) sense of parallel being as discussed in Chapter 5 (that emphasises and explores connections between mind and body). This has consequences for ideas about affect and allows us to think about advertising in a somewhat less conventional fashion. On destabilising the sovereignty of human ontology yet highlighting the core nature of semiosis to life itself, advertising in this wider biosemiotic context adopts an interesting mantle as the best representation of animal behaviour that playfully and profitably ensnares each other within sensational and semiotic environments. Thus while this book is sceptical about the primacy ascribed to textualism as a highly one-sided phenomenal and projective take on the Kantian coin, it is very much interested in symbolism, particularly as it links to neurological goings-on, mapping, sensation and affect, along with the human feelings and reflections that accompany these.

Insides without an outside

Accounts of semiosis nearly always tend towards human-created sign-based environments. Humans do not have independent claim to sensation or signification as the process of sign-making exists in the most simple of animal structures. A recent *New Scientist* article for example notes that plants are also sensory beings capable of being affected (Chamovitz, 2012). Plants see light throughout their stems and leaves, and see wavelengths we are incapable of perceiving. Plants also feel touch, with the Venus flytrap's hairs radiating a current on being stimulated, although plants do not have a brain with which to transform these sensations into emotions. Uexküll's (2010 [1934]) speculative biology offers a remarkable widening of the semiotic field to encompass animal semiosis. His observations revolve around the premise that we do not have sovereign rights to determine how natural environments are, or what is significant in them. Uexküll seeks to understand the life story of animals by means of their perceptive faculties, organs and the way they act. He recognises that animals of all levels of complexity are capable of making out or generating meaning from environmental cues. Centrally, for Uexküll this occurs *beyond purely instinctual reaction*. While in obvious danger of anthropomorphism, it is a drive to explore the subjective experiences of animals, what exists for them, and what experiences represent or signify. As Buchanan (2008) puts it, the appeal of Uexküll is his endeavour to create ontologies for animals out of the study of animal behaviour (ethology). Uexküll's observations of the life-worlds of animals bring together the humanities and their interest in interiority with the natural sciences and need for generalisability.

His is a post-Kantian insight based on the understanding that we do not perceive things in themselves, but rather our faculties represent the world about us. Reality for Uexküll then is subjective appearance. The way in which Uexküll contributes to disturbed subject/object relations opens up a broader space for semiotic investigation, the role of signs, and how these are produced and understood by creatures other than humans. In the foreword to his book, Uexküll describes an animal's environment as a bubble that contains all features accessible to the creature. Indeed, we might position this alongside the phenomenological observation that sees reality as an inside without an outside (Merleau-Ponty, 2002 [1945]). Uexküll posits that in respective bubbles, 'many qualities of the colorful meadow vanish completely, others lose their coherence with one another, and new connections are created. A new world arises in each bubble' (2010 [1934]: 43). Whereas traditionally for the physiologist, living things are objects in a human world Uexküll points out that each living thing is a subject in its own right in which the creature is the centre of its own world. Organs of perception comprise the qualities we perceive outside the subject and although reception does not create the object, what we know of the world is engendered by local perceptual faculties (potentially augmented by technology). Our perceptual faculties are themselves media whose sensations and nerve excitations come together to form external objects and act as perception marks. Perception is an active process contingent upon our nervous system that, as accounted for in Chapter 5, deciphers signals from nerve endings and involves a process of reacting and learning. Whether these are the blue of the sky, the green of a leaf or the more complex construction of a press advertisement, these external objects (or more accurately, the experience of which) are created subjectively.

As Wheeler (2011) remarks, animals and other organisms also make use of iconic and indexical signs. These are visual, aural, haptic and olfactory/chemical, although it is only human animals that make extensive use of negotiated or convention-based symbolic signs, advanced forms of language, and thereby analysis and criticism. However, it is valuable to recognise that image and meaning-making occurs throughout the wider ecosphere. Damasio remarks that all living organisms – whether these be single-celled or the most complex – are born with the capacity to automatically solve problems, whether this be 'finding sources of energy; incorporating and transforming energy; maintaining a chemical balance of the interior compatible with the life process; maintaining the organism's structure by repairing its wear and tear; and fending off external agents of disease and physical injury' (2003: 30). Although a unicellular creature has no brain and therefore no mind, it can make 'judgements' based upon differences (for example temperature, unwarranted vibrations, being prodded, or the presence of nutrients).

This process of differentiation is important as it quite possibly underpins our own emotional functions that at base indicate preferences for evasion and avoidance, or attraction. This leads Damasio to argue that the common fly undergoes emotion in that it will be angry if swatting attempts occur, happy if fed sugar (movements slow so to 'enjoy' comfort food), and if provided with alcohol will be 'giddily happy' as well as uncoordinated (2003: 41–42). While this may also bring about accusations of anthropomorphism, Damasio might respond that if all other bodily indicators (rises or decreases in viscera) share commonalities, then it is we who overstate our sovereignty and right to emotional life.

On a related point, Boulding (1991 [1961]) observes that a single-celled animal is capable of learning. He tells that if we squirt a harmless dye at a Paramecium (that is between 0.05 to 0.35 mm in length, part of the ciliate group, and found in scums and freshwater environments), it will avoid it to begin with but after repetition of the stimuli it learns that it is harmless and avoidance ceases. Read in human terms, this could mean its universe has been altered by means of a value system in which responses are made. These differences are informational and beyond what is conventionally thought of as natural, yet are immanent enough to affect sense organs. Shapiro (2012) likewise highlights trends in biology that tend towards the observation that information processing occurs at all levels of organisms – even bacteria.

Differences and processes of signification are 'supernatural' in that they are not locatable in x, y, or spaces in-between, although the link between material and immaterial relations is a firm and correct one (Bateson, 2000 [1972]; Harries-Jones, 2010). In this context, meaning does not need to be considered as solely arrived at through the physics of perception and sensation, but rather may be found in relationships and the ways in which organisms create contexts and make connections. This for example might also be found in the relationship between redundancy and meaning and the ways in which we are able to fill in the gaps of a given 'part-for-whole' message so to reconstruct it and guess the missing items. There is then a capacity to learn which moves us beyond a view of biosemiosis predicated on ecosystems defined solely through physicochemical aspects. This is important so to overcome false dualisms of mind/body or nature/culture and reintegrate the fragments back into the whole.

Biosemiosis

Historically in our dealing with signs we have eschewed their biological roots, but we might also see that the purpose of advertising is to be noticed and stand out from wider environmental stimuli. While this much is straightforward, it is the other half of the ethological equation that is perhaps more remarkable – the fact that one set of animals (people) fashion these signs so to ensnare large swathes of its own kind. Where humans and those engaged in advertising take this story further is in their capacity to create non-existent worlds, although still predicated on values and the supernatural. This is achieved through storytelling and narrative, and it is here where animals and humans depart from each other. Advertising sits at an intersection of virtual worlds (symbolic regions without need for real world referents) and biosemiotics (sign-based with referents). Where the latter lets us know of a presence, the former may allow the presence to explain itself through language and for us to imagine the story that is being relayed.

While the author of this book is no biologist, those of us interested in culture would do well to consider the findings of biological studies. Key determinates of culture such as time, duration and wider perceptual events are highly biologically and locally determined. The idea of an all-embracing view of the world is a fiction that helps us get by more easily. Reality as system of signification is much better understood through affective conventions, relations and agreements.

The external world – functionally speaking – exists as an expression of the subject and is fashioned by contingencies of perception. An appreciation of the impact of perceptual faculties on duration grounds the Kantian transcendental experience of the world, shared culture and the relative nature of knowledge. Semiosis is the solidification of biologically local relations, and creativity the wilful transformation of these for given ends. This should be conceived not only in the abstract, but also locally, affectively and immanently too. This, however, is not to return to dumb materialism, and while we might recognise the contingency of human perception and point to particles and waves moving along strange vectors at immeasurable speed in pre-matter form, we do not escape the significatory root of our existence but only deepen it. As sign-making animals we weave the fabric of our own relations (between others and the external world) into reality or what Uexküll calls a 'solid web' (2010 [1934]: 53).

Clearly overlapping with Uexküll, biosemioticians influenced by Thomas Sebeok are somewhat scathing of those who dedicate semiotics solely to the 'parochial' study of television, photography, literary texts, film and similar texts (Petrilli and Ponzio, 2001). Semiosis is not simply 'code', restricted to looking out at the human world and its cultural constructions, but rather it goes to the heart of what constitutes the criteria of life (Petrilli, 2003). Where Saussurean semiology is predicated on verbal language and human signs, Sebeokian semiosis has a much wider field of enquiry ranging from non-human signs to human signs. For biosemioticians there is a bolder aim of semiotics and, inspired by Uexküll, that is to understand more about the universe of signs in animal and human life. In contrast to semiotic perspectives predicated on intentional communication, the biosemiotic position sees signification occurring without need for intentional communication (as with plants and animals). It distinguishes between 'code semiotics', predicated on verbal and linguistic approaches, and 'interpretation semiotics', which tends towards an attempt to understand both cultural and natural signs in the world.

In broadening the semiotic field and addressing Kantian transcendental idealism, biosemiosis critically renders the idea of a singular one-size-fits-all reality as untenable and anthropocentric, but constructively offers routes out of solipsism, life out of connection with each other, and the lack of capacity to share ideas or thoughts. Discussing Sebeok, and questions over biosemiosis and postmodernism, Deely (2003) remarks that modernity is associated with Descartes' *Meditations* (the second in particular) and philosophies that see the mind's machinations as providing objects of experience. This means that the world is only accessed indirectly, as are our own perceptions, images, memories, concepts, beliefs, intentions and so on. In Deely's words: 'what the mind knows the mind makes' (2003: 26). Modernity then, in philosophy, is synonymous with idealism. Although human experience is a mix of nature and culture, the predominant formal patterns are primarily cultural. This has to be the case as nature itself is an abstract and empty term. It is vacuous for two reasons: (1) because it is a sign or vessel leveraged for cultural purposes (ideological); and (2), it is that which sits beyond understanding. Nature, like truth, is a chimera subject to signification. While we will never know the world as 'it' is, we can appreciate that as human individuals we are in this milieu together and approximately speaking we share the same sensory mechanisms (as distinct from animals or plants for example).

Sebeok and biosemioticians argue that signs are fundamental in maintaining and producing biological life. Signification and language are means of differentiation that occurred long before human ancestors implemented it through speech. Language is not so much a device for communication but a faculty for shaping and characterising the world. It is a form of rendering by which a species produces its world. For humans, even before speech, syntax is in operation as we establish interrelationships and ways in which the world works for us. Syntax thus helps us establish Uexküll's *Umwelt*, or our subjectively produced worlds. As Danesi (2003) explains, in biosemiotic accounts the act of structuring and modelling is axiomatic. It is this species-specific process that produces worlds that provide meaning for both individuals and collectives. A key question for biosemioticians who extend their purview beyond anthropocentric interests involves the ways in which human modelling compares and contrasts with other species. The practice of modelling is pre-verbal and occurs in the earliest of years and months as the infant explores a given object with the senses. Examining affordances, one will touch, taste, smell, listen and look at an object's features. The modelling of the world is a sensory process and allows us to build a working scheme of relevance and recurrence. Later the infant will engage in conceptual accounts of the world, dealing with it in more symbolic and abstract terms. It is these meta-symbols unique to anthroposemiosis that allows us to fashion new worlds and posit alternative readings to that which might be given. As humans, most likely in a unique position, we are able to eventually construct an infinite number of worlds.

Imagination and the human bubble

Signification in a human context is a creative act involving the generation of new worlds along with the capacity to construct and deconstruct through the faculty of imagination. In the context of advertising, this involves the creation and fashioning of how things are for us, and how we embrace objects and signs into our schemes of knowledge and perceiving. As accounted for in Chapter 2, this sees emphasis on 'being' and a greater interest how things come to be for us, rather than in what they are. The emphasis on the 'being' part of life involves social institutions, beliefs and representations that need not possess overt connection with what via 'common sense' we consider the physical world. These are not just playful, but 'metaphors that are meant' (Bateson, 2000 [1972]: 183), i.e. our metaphors are not just game-like abstractions but are often emotively charged, important and constitutive for us. Moreover, the proverbial map and the territory are highly indistinct, particularly if we agree with transcendental idealist arguments that result in the territory being a map to begin with.

What comes after the modern is rapprochement and ease with the premise that although the certainty and properties with which we ascribe fixity to objects, relations and conventions are faulty, at least when subject to Cartesian levels of scepticism, this is not to be feared. For those of a more adventurous bent, this is a liberating and exciting notion as we are free to create, re-order and play games. Escaping the solipsism of modernity what comes after the modern is not nihilistic (as is too often claimed), but possibly liberational. The postmodern then is 'simply' acceptance of signification as the modus operandi of our existence. What is called for here is appreciation of how embracing this notion is. While a biosemiotic view of advertising provides little in the way of formal method or granularity of analysis, it does allow us to more deeply understand the significance of the general function of advertising that tends to be missed in more run-of-the-mill accounts. Biosemiotic understanding provides a bridge between the form of advertising; signification in an environment; simulation and symbols where physical refer-ents are not required; and the sensory and sensational ways in which we interact with our environment and things we encounter therein. Advertising in a biosemiotic context is a wilful attempt to transform an environment for the gain of another. It is a means by which the sense-ratio or gestalt of surroundings is altered. The nature and role of advertising become more interesting when we consider that at the fundamental root of our experience of the world is semiosis, which at base is a play of sensational and super-natural differences. While advertising is not the only practice professionally engaged in signification, it is one with enormous reach and this alone gives it a special role, responsibility and requirement for scrutiny. While many of us daily build new worlds in our negotiation with others and perhaps even as we conceive of ourselves, few of us get paid to carry this out on a societal scale.

Conclusion

Culture is the evolutionary emergence of consciousness, language and reflec-tion in the context of a world already loaded with signs experienced through similarity and difference. Humans do not have the monopoly on signification as it permeates even the most basic life forms. This is predicated on the structural coupling of organism and environment. Evolution in this context involves an increase in biosemiotic complexity and depth, breadth, intensity, richness and awareness of a species' Uexküllian *Umwelt*. Understanding semiosis more holistically allows us an ecological viewpoint that embeds our human abstractions in a more immanent, intensive and sensational con-text. The experiential truth of our existence is inescapably located within signification although for this idea to be meaningful, we have had to broaden our conception of semiosis beyond human domains and recognise sign-based environments as common to all life. However, advertising takes on extra layers of consequence when viewed this way and humans are sovereign in the lengths they will go to snare others. More broadly, in relation to creativity, in recognising the relationship between signification and its indeterminate background, we understand that at base of life itself is creativity as to live is a continual act of creation as we render meaning from miasma and fashion the world about us.

9 Concrescence and the unfashionably new

Questions about 'the new' go back at least as far as the fifth century BCE when Parmenides remarked on its impossibility stating that what exists, exists; and what does not exist, does not (Steinitz, 1994). While at the outset straightforward enough, this soon leads us into difficulties because if only 'something' exists, then the existence of 'nothing' cannot be conceived, as 'something cannot come from nothing'. Absolute reality, or what-is, means that change is impossible, and existence is uniform and timeless. Concurrently, in contrast to reason, a creature's sensory faculties lead to premises that are false and deceitful. This cosmology sees reality as eternal and unchanging, and reality as very different from what we suppose ourselves to be living in. This chapter (perhaps thankfully) makes a very different argument – a highly modern virtual opposite. It argues that despite having contributing parts what is new, or that which is uniquely experienced, is definable only in terms of itself. Indeed without the new we have stasis, and much preferred here is a view of life that privileges becoming rather than being.

This point is a crucial one as it reflects a preference for change, plurality and multiplicity rather than an interest in fixity. This is a second-hand argument, although a valuable one, that finds expression in James, Bergson, Whitehead, and Deleuze along with more recent process-based thinkers (for example Shapiro, Massumi and Manning). Although that which is new emerges out of reference to others, creativity is the capacity to go beyond these and bring something new (and valuable) into being. This proposition is predicated on James' (1897) declaration that without the chance that possibility can spill over from actuality, the difference between future and past is wiped out. While it is often the case that what is new emerges because the time is ripe, this chapter argues that what is new must necessarily escape predetermination. In discussion of what is creative and new, this chapter is deeply influenced by Whitehead's (1985 [1929]) notion of concrescence as the coming into being of something new. This is how, out of the many, a new 'one' is added. The way in which this occurs is not entirely determined and chance plays a role, as does will. This chapter then is dedicated to exploring the implications of concrescence for creativity, and how what is new comes to be. Unlike other chapters, this one does not address advertising directly, but the ideas developed here underpin arguments made in the following chapter that deals more directly with media, creativity, transformation, spilling over and excess.

Malleability

Pragmatists are subjectivists who see truth as human opinion, and truth as that which is found in people rather than things or the wider world. With reality being agreed upon opinion, essentialism is eschewed and the 'pretence of finality' is broken (James, 2000 [1907]: 27). As Rorty in reference to Kant puts it, around 200 years ago 'truth was made rather than found' (1989: 3). Nietzsche likewise phrases truth as 'a mobile army of metaphors, metonyms, and anthropomorphisms – in short, a sum of human relations which have been enhanced, transposed, and embellished poetically and rhetorically, and which after long use seem firm, canonical, and obligatory to a people' (2000 [1873]: 56). (Can a better definition of traditional advertising be found?)

Asserting anti-essentialist values, and assaulting others, the pragmatic view is free of absolutes, ahistoricism and transcultural observation points, instead seeing both moral and epistemological truth as human and contingent upon period and context. Championing the new where religion, metaphysics and other past systematic philosophies prescribed human experience, pragmatism seeks for its 'adherents' to determine their own way in a post-metaphysical fashion. Rorty (2010 [1980]) argues that if pragmatism were to be accepted by a culture, this would render us into a post-philosophical condition in that we would not seek to understand 'how things really are' but maintain an ongoing conversation about what and how things are. This is less about keeping philosophers in gainful employment, but rather is preferable to attempts to close off conversation, dissent and points of view that are multiplicitous in character. Seemingly an unashamed relativist, Rorty also points to what is 'true' as an imposition, a force, a ridding of freedom and a means of abdication from responsibility. It is an approach that asks us to make and create, not behave and follow. For Rorty, philosophy has more to do with going forward than looking backward leaving both old and recent rules ripe for negotiation and redescription. It is an instrument for change rather than conservation. Little is sacred, with the possible exception of freedom to define one's own views. In this context the aim is to treat people as subjects and not objects, or 'as generators of new descriptions rather than beings one hopes to be able to describe accurately' (Rorty, 1979: 378).

Where (and when) truth and absolutes are absent, creativity comes to the fore. As James in *Pragmatism* remarks, 'In our cognitive as well as active life we are creative ... The world stands malleable, waiting to receive its final touches at our hands ... Man *engenders* truth upon it' (2000 [1907]: 112). Dewey (1995 [1908]) similarly observes that whereas traditionally knowledge is taken to be a reflection of the world, the subject plays a much greater role in constructing the world. That is to say, our knowing directly participates in the formation of the world giving reality a practical character. Rorty also talks of a 'vocabulary of practise rather than that of theory' (2010 [1980]: 113). This prefers action to contemplation, and truth in this context is defined in terms of use-value over essences and convenience over absolutes. Anti-Platonic (and Parmenides) – it renders absolutes as made rather than found. Such pragmatism is clearly appealing to Deleuze and Guattari (2011 [1994]) who remark that philosophical concepts are not there waiting to be discovered, but are invented and created. Truth is a process of fitting in within a wider matrix of similarly arrived at truths, yet we have a say in how this occurs and happens. It is a status conferred through agreement with a wider relational field. Similarly, that which is designated as creative does not come with a special quality inherently attached, but rather it emerges out of social definition. This lack of absolutes stands in some contrast to conceptions of truth as an agreement between reality and ideas.

Where rationalists and pragmatists depart is at what is meant by reality and agreement. Reality is not a static entity awaiting our description, but we add to reality by dint of our endeavour to fashion. As active participants in the reality that we conceive, reality takes on a more creative character. As has been posited in earlier chapters from multiple perspectives, reality is not a reflection, but at least partly a creation, and we might better understand our own role in the world as active contributors and creators. Truth then, as James tells us, is that which happens to an idea: it is made true. While both rationalists and pragmatists will agree that truth is subject to change and that what we have at any time is our best guess, James pushes further arguing that truth and reality are mutable. Whereas truth for rationalism exists outside human relations, truth for pragmatism is intimately bound to human and changing temporal experience. Truth then is simply that which is more effective than another proposition. Contingent upon human agency, the truth is not 'out there' but is simply a functional and effective idea of how something works. Creativity then involves taking ownership of one's ideas and assumptions, interrogating these, the capacity for redescription so to reformulate, and to rebuild anew if necessary or desirable.

Beyond predetermination

In discussion of concrescence Whitehead provides an influential account that strikes resonance with contemporary views of how habits, truths, institutions, status and conventions over a period of time become seemingly fixed and firm. DeLanda (1997) puts this in geological terms referring to cultural formation and structuration as a thickening, crystallising or a hardening of mineral flow that was once more fluid. Concrescence then is a coming together to form a new thing or entity which provides an addition to the world. If we analyse what is novel, we find that a process of concrescence has occurred. In discussion of relational perspectives on order, Alfred Whitehead remarks that order and disorder go hand-in-hand. If a process or an endeavour towards concrescence is not reached, the endeavour slips back to a miasma of disorder or the constitutive flux. He defines concrescence as being the name for the process in which 'the universe of many things acquires an individual unity in a determinate relegation of each item of the "many" to its subordination in the constitution of the novel "one"' (1985 [1929]: 211).

The privileging of process represents a rejection of Aristotelianism, and the notion that world is made of static substances that carry universal qualities. Preferring and complimenting Bergson's take on time and duration, Whitehead eschews the possibility of moments, instances, stoppages and the unchanging, in favour of process and transition. Indeed, as Shapiro (2012) points out, the Whiteheadian oeuvre is predicated on turning away from a tradition of reminiscence and retrospection (from Plato to Heidegger) to the dynamics of the new and the novel. It is a disavowal of those philosophies that seek changeless order at the expense of delivering only partial pictures of how things are. A less object-oriented and possibly more inquisitive approach sees patterns, relations and further temporary arrangements (even if seemingly firm). Emergence and process is the key to reality rather than things, as a thing is simply an event in an emergent process. An event is a situation, a unity and coming together of elements. Reality in this context is understood though relationships and temporary arrangements, and a process-based approach is preferred to dealing with individual objects (as objects are actually assemblages, arrangements, events and unities).

For Whitehead (1985 [1929]) creativity is the ultimate category by which we can interpret experience. It is the initial phase of a new occasion giving its constituent elements a unity of their own. It can be thought of in terms of the actualisation of potential and the leveraging of elements that on their own may do very little but in conjunction make a difference. This is to 'promote their fusion into a new unity of experience' so for this unity to pass into the future (Whitehead, 1968 [1938]: 151). Put otherwise, but to employ Whiteheadian jargon, out of past concordances and discordances, self-formation and co-ordination, comes novelty and creative advance. Indeed, Whitehead prescribes the word 'creativity' as that which 'expresses the notion that each event is a process issuing in novelty' (1948 [1933]: 274) and in this sense, 'the many become one, and are increased by one' (1985 [1929]: 21). We must, however, divest creativity of purposive links, at least while discussing Whitehead, as the point in a process-based account is that creativity is an accident (Stengers, 2011), and it is 'the highest generality at the base of actuality' (Whitehead, 1985 [1929]: 31). Stengers (2011) likewise comments that Whitehead's technical rendering of creativity is tantamount to the 'plane of immanence' (discussed in Chapter 5). Creativity in Whiteheadian parlance is to point to the constant generation of events in a world that is never the same twice.

Here happenings in the past are continuously synthesised into new and unique events, which become data for future events. Creativity is that process which turns everything into something else. It is the stage between two termini: one of these will be a set of diverse and disjunctive components; the second involves these same components in concrete togetherness (Whitehead, 1948 [1933]). It is, in this view, a metaphysical principle *and* immanent activity that binds appearances (reality) together – a paradox that plagues Whitehead. Whitehead's creativity is without definite character of its own and is instead protean in terms of how it facilitates change. The principle of novelty advances the process of conjoining yet transcends each individual occasion of unification. Whitehead progresses to articulate:

> It is the universal of universals characterizing ultimate matter of fact. It is that ultimate principle by which the many, which are the universe disjunctively, become the one actual occasion, which is the universe conjunctively. It lies in the nature of things that the many enter into complex unity.
>
> (Whitehead, 1948 [1933]: 21)

This conjunction or unity is order. This is specific to a formation and Whitehead highlights that,

> there can only be some definite specific 'order', not merely 'order' in the vague. Thus every definite total phase of 'givenness' involves a reference to that specific 'order' which is its dominant ideal, and involves the specific 'disorder' due to its inclusion of 'given' components.
>
> (Whitehead, 1948 [1933]: 83)

This order may have a self-preservative reaction (or conservative character), which seeks to maintain equilibrium of the existing state of order in face of new fluctuations out of the miasma and possibility of disorder.

As the quantum physicist Bohm (2004 [1996]) puts it, what we take for the new is part of a movement that creates, maintains and dissolves structures. If we follow Bohm we see that 'things' are abstractions and that, ultimately, there are no things but only temporary occasions and events of varying degrees of duration. Creativity is like conceptualization itself in that it singularizes and bridges chaos (Guattari, 1992). In this take on creativity, art is the singular composition of chaos through the elaboration of forms, gestures, and environments assuming a concrete presence in the space of communication, vision, and projection. Chaos is not a void but a virtual in the sense that out of this comes all possible particles and forms and to which these return without history or remembrance. It is that which pre-empts, is the 'genetic' of actuality, or the principle of emergence and creation. It does not refer to 'what is possible' (as what is possible contains what might be actualised), but rather is the condition for a creative event to take place. It is that which allows actualities to appear, but is still not a 'cause' in the fully blown physical sense as it is without extension. Objects, parts, things, galaxies and creations in this context are abstractions from a process, an event or a pattern of movement rather than a solid autonomous structure (Bohm, 2004 [1996]).

Deleuze's (2011 [1969]) quasi-causes are creative and virtual principles that, along with aleatory and stochastic points, bring things into existence. By definition these do not have corporeal dimensions, but remain very real and are that which give form to events, objects and usher in new states of affairs. Deleuze gets around the transcendence question (that is, how are transcendence and immanence reconcilable?) by arguing that quasi-causes are incorporeal and enjoy some independence from corporeal events, yet maintain the capacity to affect and be affected. This means that it is also meta-causal meaning that things exist and occur that cannot be explained in terms of corporeal causes and effects. Likewise, for both Deleuze and Guattari, in a highly Bergson-like fashion, 'every determination is a negation, if determination is not in an immediate relation with the undetermined' (Deleuze and Guattari, 2011 [1994]: 120). This means that any endeavour that privileges fixity and certainty is prone to being misguided. It should be noted too that this is not a tired invocation of the humanities vs. the sciences (particularly given the healthy interest Bergson, Deleuze, Guattari and especially Whitehead had in science and mathematics). On the contrary, this applies equally but differently to the arts, sciences and philosophy. Bohm similarly points to unbroken and undivided movement as that which constitutes the most basic levels of reality. In this account atoms, telephones, galaxies, beer cans, eyebrows and so on are abstractions from this movement of what Bohm designates the 'universal field movement' (2004 [1996]: 94). Thus what passes for the real is actually an abstraction and temporary organisation. To put the same point in Bergson's (1999 [1913]) terms, an attempt to pin down creativity is to seek the meaning of a poem in syntax or the form of the letters by which it is composed.

Bifurcation

This process-based view of creativity sees stages where structures become unstable due to the introduction of new elements or ideas, and we arrive at thresholds of disequilibrium or 'tipping points'. Bifurcation occurs due to external shocks to a system and when a change in the stability of equilibrium is disturbed. This leads to a 'choice' and new patterns or ways of doing things. Creativity, and the balance between order and disorder, involves turbulence, speed and unmanageable intensity, and without doubt its effects are not always desirable – potentially leading to systemic breakdown when equilibrium is lost. As Prigogine and Stengers (1984) remark, the system may disintegrate into chaos or it may evolve into a new level of order, a dissipative structure or towards a state of equilibrium. Such a view recognises that all systems and their subsystems are fluctuating and on occasion a subsystem may undergo a process of positive feedback so to become more powerful and disrupt and destroy the pre-existing organisation. This positive feedback is a creative impetus that culminates in emergence. Capra comments:

> Emergence is one of the hall-marks of life. It has been recognized as the dynamic origin of development, learning and evolution. In other words, creativity – the generation of new forms – is a key property of all living systems. And since emergence is an integral part of the dynamics of open systems, this means that open systems develop and evolve. Life constantly reaches out into novelty.
>
> (Capra, 2005: 37)

By definition a bifurcation point denotes that it is impossible to tell which way change will go. At this moment deterministic description breaks down and we reach the stochastic moment (as with the tossing of a coin) that by definition is a point of unpredictability. Moreover, such instability need not remain local but spread to new macroscopic states. Life then is very much out of equilibrium and new structures, dynamics, modes of understanding and ways of doing things reflect the interaction of a system with its surroundings. A system then is never closed and is forced to deal with change by dint of this interaction causing new modes of being to arise. The point however is that while events may appear determinable after the chance event, this does not take away the existence of bifurcation and which brings about the new. After all, it is untenable to say that the future exists now.

Emergence

The outcomes of emergence are not entirely guided, and chance somehow exists and plays a role. For those interested in creativity, this is something to be nurtured. This is Eddington's (1928) arrow of time view where in contrast to classical perspectives that see the future as contained within the present, the future is open. Other views of time see it as cyclical rather than linear, being predicated on repetition, rebirth and the potential for the future to be the past. This arrow of time view is important for conceptions of creativity as it allows for newness as we confront each stochastically lived moment between 'no longer' and 'not yet'. The idea then is that order is pushed into a state of disequilibrium until a critical or bifurcation point. As disorder reigns there is no determinism or predictability with chance pressing remains of the system into a new mode of being where a new mode of order or creative logic emerges – at least until the next bifurcation point. New constituents that engender novel reactions within a system disrupt the stability of the system. These reactions compete with the system's previous mode of functioning. If a system is stable it will see off these challenges to change and the norm will be re-established. Conversely if the invading forces are quick enough to scale the system then a new mode of being or functioning will occur. The reactions that seek to change the system are characterised by evolution, innovation, creativity, anti-conservatism, transgression, excess and emergence.

DeLanda (2011) locates the conceptual origins of emergence in the middle of the nineteenth century through recognition that causality in physics and chemistry is very different. Whereas classical accounts of causality see molecules as objects that collide and crash into each other, when molecules interact chemically entirely new entities (or events) may emerge. DeLanda gives the example of water as that which possesses properties that do not belong to its constituent parts: oxygen and hydrogen. So whereas the first perspective sees that there can be nothing new, the latter predicated on emergence does. The former classical account gives rise to a deductive mode of enquiry where general laws and principles may be applied. The absence of novelty allows for effects to be explained in reductive and causal terms as one thing knocks onto the next, or that which might be deconstructed back to constituent parts.

Processes of emergence may be linked to immanence. This is the idea that there is no behind or outside but what is, is. Immanence being immanent to itself is that which eschews transcendence or outside causes for mind or matter. Emergent properties of a whole 'can now be explained as an effect of the causal interactions between its component parts' (DeLanda, 2011: 3). The organisational element of DeLanda's matter-energy is the Deleuzo-Guattarian (2003 [1980]) 'Body without Organs' (BwO). Bearing in mind that Deleuze is a realist granting full autonomy to the world (in contrast to transcendental perspectives), this is 'that glacial reality where the alluvions, sedimentations, coagulations, foldings, and recoilings that compose an organism – and also a signification and a subject – occur' (cited in DeLanda, 1997: 260). It is a system of representations diagrammatised and conceived in terms of intensities, born from matter and energy, and the genesis of form and the flow out of which everything stable follows. Crucially, the idea of BwO sees geological, biological and cultural coalescences as 'immanent capabilities to the flow of matter-energy information and not to any *transcendent* factor, whether platonic or divine' (DeLanda, 1997: 263, emphasis in original).

There are a number of links between Deleuze and Whitehead, particularly in relation to coalescences as events, potential and the actual, happenings rather than things, and the emphasis on continual movement, absence of finality, process and becoming rather than being (Deleuze, 1993 [1988]; 2011 [1969]). Also readily linked with Nietzschean discussion broached in Chapter 7, Deleuze's approach is generally excessive, anti-conservative, volatile, dynamic, tending towards multiplicity over normalisation, and that which drives towards disturbance and forcing life out of equilibrium. In Whiteheadian (1985 [1929]) vernacular this is phrased as appetitive, or a principle of unrest that drives towards transformation over preservation (also see Shapiro, 2012). What is prized in Nietzsche, Whitehead and Deleuze is not the creation of form and category, but the processes and movements that give rise to novelty and differences. Indeed, in highlighting appetite and multiplicity we could deny the new, as to recognise what is new means we are able to locate it within an existing and tired scheme. Instead, 'difference – calls forth forces in thought which are not the forces of recognition, today or tomorrow, but the powers of a completely other model, from an unrecognized and unrecognizable *terra incognita*' (Deleuze, 2004 [1968]: 172, emphasis in original).

As discussed, the point for Whitehead is that each act of becoming marks a rupture where something new comes about. What is referred to here as the new, partly for the sake of simplicity, is an event that occurs through discontinuity and a break with the order that has gone before. Importantly, there is a dimension to this that is not predictable or calculable. Becoming is not continuous, but is the ongoing production of novelty and new modes of arrangement or togetherness (concrescence). It is not a tweak or amendment, but a break with what has gone before. Moreover, each act of becoming cannot be given in advance, but may emerge (unforeseen) out of the circumstances provided. Another similarity with Deleuze is Whitehead's equivocation of ideas and objects, mind and matter, and the premise that they emerge out of the same 'stuff'. Solely in discussion of Deleuze, but equally applicable to Whitehead, DeLanda (2011 [2002]) summarises that this is predicated on a rejection of strong transcendence where reality has no existence outside the mind along with weak transcendence that rejects theoretical entities as being 'real' (for example, causation) so to grant reality full autonomy. Things do not receive definition, but rather they are progressively defined within themselves and generate patterns without external intervention or description.

This realism should not be confused with naïve realism that ascribes essences, abstractions and general entities to phenomena in the world, but rather the basis of the Deleuzian enterprise is the way in which he builds an ontology in which character emerges out of dynamic and immanent processes. This is phrased in terms of non-organic life and those events and situations in life that are organisational, but not matter itself. For an idea of life to be encompassing life has to be more than materiality, but must also include organisation, principles of emergence, processes of forming, connections and differences, and that which urges new events into being.

These virtual or forming dimensions should be taken into account as, to put it in Bateson's (2000 [1972]) terms, it is these differences that make the difference. Deleuze and Guattari account for these non-organic but very much real and alive processes by remarking that in dismantling the body we open it to 'connections that presuppose an entire assemblage, circuits, conjunctions, levels and thresholds, passages and distributions of intensity, and territories and deterritorializations' (2003 [1980]: 160). This is predicated in an expanded view of life that does not see it as the preserve of biology and organisms, but where everything is inorganically alive and everything is assembled. Again, this applies to language, ideas, computer code, humans, doorknobs and turnips.

Conclusion

The book perhaps somewhat archaically posits will as a necessary corollary of creativity, particularly of the Schopenhauer (1966 [1918]) variety, and argues that while creativity is highly protean, it is best conceived in terms of a wilful act that makes a difference and shapes within malleable, not-fixed and indeterminate environments. Moreover, it is not a leap too far to link will with notions of appetite for difference, Whiteheadian novelty and the impelling of concrescence. In this sense creativity is deeply pragmatic preferring ongoing renewal, multiplicity and the generation of new descriptions. However, creativity and people are not separate to the world, but very much part of it and are thus quasi-causes or those virtual and incorporeal dimensions to life that steer and initiate processes and affects, but are also affected by the corporeal. Both in relation to itself and to advertising, creativity is best expressed in relation to potential and that which facilitates actualisation out of indeterminate environments. Creativity then is that which mobilizes new formations, organisation and events. It is an excessive drive characterised by being anti-conservative, out of equilibrium, representing an increase in life, or that which disavows stasis. It exists, arises and is most noticeable at each moment between 'no longer' and 'not yet'.

10 Excessive media

On the first introductory page of *Decoding Advertisements* Judith Williamson (1978) remarks that the world of advertising involves separateness from the medium by which an advertisement is carried. For Williamson the significance of advertising, structures of meaning and the ways we might analyse these have little to do with media. From the perspective of 2013, this is no longer as tenable as it once might have been and certainly at the award-winning end of the spectrum, the work that agencies do is sometimes more akin to media engineering. While disinterest in media held well for criticism of advertising from its professionalisation in the 1920s until the 1990s and perhaps into the 2000s, increasingly media do make a difference and this needs to be more deeply factored into consideration of the significance of advertising. This becomes paramount if we agree on the event-based conception of advertising depicted in Chapter 5 that requires we recognise that content cannot be divorced from the means by which it is communicated and co-created.

Media are not simply blank vehicles for content, but represent an inter-action of technical, intellectual, economic, institutional, biological, social, cultural and creative forces. They facilitate certain processes and deny others, and increasingly what is possible is being expanded. Closer attention to media affordances grants new ways of practising and theorising advertising, and this brings about the need for a re-evaluation of both what constitutes advertising and how we might assess its practices. My contention has less to do with the existence and use-value of textual goings-on, and analytical approaches to understanding these, but rather that as a means of accounting for expanding borders of advertising and creative opportunities in advertising, emphasis might be shifted from traditional representational canons to sensationally, affectively and temporally conceived media. Further characteristics include co-production, transmediation, participation, and what in the previous chapter was accounted for in the language of stochasticism, bifurcation, spilling over and that which gives rise to new events and states. As accounted for in Chapter 4, in relation to combinatory, exploratory and transformational conceptions of creativity (Boden, 2004; 2010), there is more to creativity than simply combining elements within a known domain of practice, but rather the very terrain in which the endeavour takes place can be challenged, questioned, refashioned and potentially transformed.

My point is that a textual account of creativity in advertising is inadequate, particularly given technological and media developments that have deeply affected the practice of advertising. Historically media have been overlooked in discussion of advertising and creativity, and advertising campaigns have traditionally followed more or less the same pattern in terms of media choice, which media to privilege and which act as ancillary vehicles. Typically, a creative department within an agency gives form to the strategy for advertising (strategy consisting of the target market, how the advertising should speak to the target market, and the media best suited for reaching that target market). Creativity then tends to be associated with the creation of the message rather than the means by which it is transmitted. Critical analysis tends to focus on this aspect too. Such emphasis is surprising, if not only for the fact that historically much more money is spent on media than on the message (around an 85/15 per cent split in favour of media). Although the careers of media planners are predicated on being sensitive to media, the complexity of the media environment and the ways in which timing, placing, channels, formats, quality of the media space and related factors might impact on the brand, recent expansion of creative media opportunities necessitates a more robust understanding of media.

More recently in advertising, particularly since the 1990s, there exists greater awareness of media, experimentation with media, understanding of the creative potential of respective media affordances, and burgeoning awareness of the value of interaction of mediums. Indeed, increasingly media planners within agencies work with copywriters and art directors, and combine creative thinking with statistical analysis to develop appropriate strategies. However, although awareness of the role of media has grown, agencies and marketers are still trying to make sense of simultaneous media use and get to grips with creative opportunities. *Advertising Age* (an industry newspaper and website for people in advertising, marketing and media) for example cites a report from Time Warner detailing that people in their twenties switch mediums around 27 times per non-working hour (Steinberg, 2012). Rather than committing to a full-length television show, people will 'snack' or graze, moving between television, smartphone, tablet computer and possibly print media. While this might appear as channel-zapping by other means, proliferation of media use presents opportunities for advertisers in terms of longer periods of engagement across multiple media far surpassing the commercial or the few seconds given to print or poster media. Engagement is the key word in this setting and although interruptive advertising will continue to abound, newer forms of media offer distinct opportunities, both for developing ongoing relationships and/or one-off communications programmes that require significant levels of engagement from participants and co-producers of commercial mediated events. Rather than seeing the proliferation of media as an opening to replicate content

across multiple platforms, might media themselves be used in a more interesting fashion? Indeed, to what extent might the premise of media as an
off-the-shelf resource be questioned, particularly as tools hitherto not
considered as advertising media are being harnessed and hacked?

Crafting media

On understanding that creativity need not solely have to do with manipulating
signs that stand for something else, we might consider the role of media
as it links to notions of modification, excess, subversion, affordances and the
ways in which media may be hybridised, interact with each other and become
more than the sum of their parts. We touched upon this latter point in relation to emergence in Chapter 9, and also in Chapter 3 by means of the ways
in which advertising leverages co-creativity and interaction among media
employed in campaigns. Creativity in an advertising context increasingly has
to do with the utilisation of media affordances, exploration of what new (and
longer standing) forms of media are capable of, and experimentation with the
ways in which they might be co-operated or inter-bred.

Given that we are in a period of constant media innovation, creation and
experimentation, there are continually new affordances that facilitate new
local branded ecologies, novel transversal effects and branded intensities
accountable for in terms of strength, duration and specificity of qualia. Grosz
(2008) in her discussion of the arts likewise refers to forms of creative
production as that which generate intensity, sensation or affect. These might
involve music, painting, sculpture, writing, architecture, design, landscaping,
dance and that which harnesses, exercises, expends, shapes, sharpens, harmo-
nises, discords, connects and deals in intensity and sensation. A by-product
of the media-based discussion in this chapter is the proposition that
creative advertising as an applied art straddles the sensational requirements
of Grosz's definition of art, yet manages to fulfil a task of some sort (as
with craft).

This is to switch the focus from content to better account for the role
of media and while textual factors (immanently and affectively understood)
undoubtedly play a role, this chapter adopts a different tack. Instead we
might think of advertising and media by means of affect and expertise in
organising and modulating intensities. This is to explore the ways that new
media might be leveraged, transformed and played with so to help engender
novel experiences that suits an advertiser's particular brand ontology or
outlook. This chapter, then, is interested in the poetics of media, and the
sensitivity with which mediums might be understood, harnessed, reformulated
and used as a means of sensational expression in themselves. Although
advertisers have always used multiple forms of media as a means of reaching
potential consumers, increasingly there has been much greater attention to the
arrangement of media elements. On roll-out of creative media campaigns,
their components in turn modify the values of each other and rather than

having elements working as channels in isolation (as historically has largely been the case) creative media campaigns function as emerging wholes that develop and become something in excess of their planned constituents as they are machinically engaged with by people.

There is nothing especially novel in this as the link between media, materiality and creativity is not new, particularly given that mastery of materials and processes is essential for any trade or art. Painters know their paints and canvases, potters their clays and glazes, clothes designers their fabrics and fasteners, and sculptors their stones, metals, woods, carving tools, and so on. Likewise, programmers should know the material and processes with which they weave, design, debug and maintain code. Similarly, the tangible experiential properties of materials and manufactured artefacts have long provided a source of inspiration. While an architect will pay attention to shaping experiences for the prospective inhabitant of a given space, place or building, media specialists will pay attention to the affordances of media structures and the interaction of media elements that gives rise to experiences of these. They should be both phenomenologist and alchemist of media, potently understanding media affordances, media ecology and what are later accounted for as transversal possibilities of media. This involves an assessment not only of specific mediums, but what happens when standards, protocols and conventions are hacked, distorted, used out of context, played off against other mediums, and what happens when media culture takes on a life of its own, transforms, feeds-back on itself, is amplified, and becomes something new and novel.

It is about creativity understood as emergence and the ways in which media tactics are utilised in the wider field of marketing strategies. That is to say, as new media are created along with concurrent expectations of use, creatives will tactically create new modes of use, new pathways and combinations, and push the technology to new horizons so to facilitate novel branded experiences.

Affordances

In *Media Ecologies*, Fuller (2005) demonstrates an approach to machinic semiotics involving detail, custom, emotion and imagination so to reconstruct different values, codes and contexts of use. Reminiscent of Vico and Herder's insistence on local understanding, as accounted for in Chapter 7, Fuller's account is a thick description and poetic reconstruction of context, characters, use, properties, mutual stimulation and the means by which media technology might be harnessed and transformed beyond their original purpose. In addition to considering discrete media items and their properties, he also points to ways in which media mutually stimulate each other. For us, we might take away from Fuller the emphasis on media, and in regard to advertising and technical affordances, that conventional language-based conceptions of advertising are at the very least temporarily less important when new physical, technical and media affordances have received such little attention.

There are three basic approaches to how things work: affordances, constraints and mappings. While affordances refer to properties, constraints do exactly that: they constrain. Slots and holes for example will only admit certain things to be inserted. Constraints then are those things that restrict behaviour and limit relationships to other objects or operations than can be done with the original object. These may be natural or technical in that certain things can only be turned or pressed a certain way, but they may also be cultural having to do with learned behaviour or combinatory possibilities. Mapping likewise utilises cultural standards and physical analogies. While many of these analogies are cultural, some are pre-linguistic. For example, a rising noise may indicate 'more' and decreasing noise 'less'. Such phenomena sit within wider pre-linguistic experience such as suffocation, heat, ecstasy, pain, fire, redness and hunger that are recognisable without the need for classification or being related to anything else. They are intensities, i.e. those sensations that do not refer beyond themselves for substantiation.

As Guattari (1992) notes, linguistic and narrative aspects of expression have been granted a primacy over all other modes of semiosis, leaving aside machinic production and their affordances. What then is the enunciative use of machines and media? A medium is not simply a lifeless cart for content, but has its own materiality. This latter point is poetically expressed by Fuller who in discussion of pirate radio and drum and bass/jungle/breakbeat techno writes that we might look below the instrument itself

> ... to its substrata, the various means for the extrusion and torture of electrons. It is this – whether it occurs as representation as bits of information, as slider bars on a sequencer interface, as the scraping of a vinyl trench against a needle, in stamping on a fuzzbox, or in the direct construction of circuits and hardware – that calls to mind that semimystical force experienced at the same time of Edison and Tesla.
>
> (Fuller, 2005: 19)

Most valuable here is the attention to the materiality of media that is all too often forgotten in accounts of creativity. Such a view is highly attractive because it returns media studies from its dependency on language and overprivileging of content back to consideration of form and affordances. Such a view helps to free us from combinatorial creativity understood in symbolic and coded terms, towards an intensive and sensational semiotisation of matter and machinic creativity. For a media-based consideration of advertising, creativity represents a bisociation of branding with machinic affordances so to tip advertising beyond language-based textualism and the semiotic-turn defined by deferral, referral and textualism.

We might then see a growing emphasis on medium and craft at all stages of the creative process. Media are not blank vehicles through which content is delivered, but rather each medium has its own mode of potential and being, particularly if combined with other media so to bring about cross-media stimulation. A medium has means, properties, and ways of engaging with us and in examining media closely we see a form of creativity definable in terms of expertise in affect and intra-component relations. There is a primal and poetic dimension to media and while plainly it will never be as articulate as the spoken and written word, media by definition do possess particular means of impact that may be harnessed.

Lessons in media affordances and sensation can be learnt from traditional craft skills that involve enactive technologies and distinct expertise in affordances. Exemplars of craft activities include: jewellery, cutlery, hand weaponry, carpentry, furniture-making, dressmaking, millinery, bookbinding, block- and screen-printing, calligraphy, toy-making, ceramics and textiles. Each of these is affordance-based and while they may be seen as textual, sign-based and aesthetically pleasing, they are also sensory and experiential operating in different realms to linguistic accounts of creativity and experience. Importantly, one does not exclude the other. Craft and media affects then are what Massumi (2002) refers to as being those intensities that exist outside fixed significatory systems and may be outside of conventional understanding of meaning, but not experience.

Affordances then are intuitively, physically, intensively and less consciously processed. Instead, a more instinctual mode of intelligence is harnessed that identifies differences, similarities, equivalences, connections, disconnections, ratio or proportion, and so on. Accounts of affordances are prevalent in the field of design. Norman refers to an affordance as 'the perceived and actual properties of the thing, primarily those fundamental properties that determine just how the thing could possibly be used' (2002 [1988]: 9). Gibson articulates that an affordance of something is 'a specific combination of the properties of its substance and its surfaces taken with reference to an animal' (1977: 67). We should however not get into the business of ascribing innate essences to affordances, but rather see them as being progressively defined by dint of person-object interaction, object-object interaction and in the developments of the object itself, which is a Whiteheadian event or arrangement of other objects to form a given object.

Heidegger's (2011 [1962]) approach to technology offers a useful way of articulating and approaching material affordances. He deviates from Kant in arguing that 'things' in themselves are only *mostly* and not totally inaccessible. This is a key point as much of the phenomenological and textual enterprise is predicated on the Kantian impasse and the turning away from this to self-referential human created text-based systems. For Heidegger, what we experience of the world is not merely a representation but rather the thing itself from a very limited perspective. This is a critical point as he rightly sought to avoid the notion that experiences are made up of *only* representations. In addition to the possibility of knowing something of things or objects themselves, he also sought to avoid Aristotelian realism in which people or subjects do not contribute to the being of an entity (Zimmerman, 1990). This begins to invoke thorny questions over whether Heidegger was a realist or an idealist, but such a discussion would take us off track (for coverage see Hoffman, 2000). Instead we might simply observe that for Heidegger objects encountered exist independently but that, as discussed in Chapter 2, the being of these are a product of human understanding, and can only be human, as it is only humans (for Heidegger) who ask questions about being.

To return to media and technology, a Heideggerean view sees affordances come into being through purposeful action and progression from the background status of object to foreground status of thing. The ways in which an object becomes foregrounded is historical. It comes 'to be' for us because it is disclosed to us. This is initially a slightly strange idea that becomes clearer when we realise that, like language, we are born into technological environments in which items or arrangements of items of technology disclose themselves in particular ways. As our technocultural history both precedes and supersedes us, the arrangement or being of a technological item is disclosed in a particular fashion. As things and tools are disclosed to us we relate to them in terms of how they are categorised, coded and purposed for us. This is established relationally and according to Heidegger we should not understand the world as a totality of entities but as a set of relationships 'constituted by and for human existence, a structure that enables entities to manifest themselves or "be" in various ways' (Zimmerman, 1990: 140). Similarly, we have expectations of our tools and media and we tend to classify these (it would be odd to turn on a TV with a hammer or a spoon).

A medium does not exist in isolation but within a domain or context of media and we can say that a creative act has taken place when a medium is repurposed and used in a fashion other than that dictated by its domain. Following Heidegger's logic through, by repurposing an object, piece of technology or medium, one is concealing one version of being and letting come forth another mode of being. This is not entirely different to Whitehead's (1997 [1925]) notion of misplaced concreteness that has to do with the attribution of fixity, structure and purpose where in reality there is none. It is to destabilise arrangements of being and in being freed from these strictures, one is able to connect to other occasions and form new arrangements. Put otherwise, it is to shift from an ontology of being to an ontogenesis of becoming. Misplaced concreteness repeats well a continuing theme of this book that has highlighted the instability of the real in favour of a dynamic of reality that lets us know that the apparent is merely a draft version, or ongoing work in progress.

While we often treat technology as a utility, Heidegger's point is that we should care for it. Rather than using up and exploiting a given tool (or medium) we might more closely understand the ways in we are able to interact with the thing. Use in this context is much more artistic and poetic, and 'is the summons that something be admitted into its own being and that using not desist from it' (cited in Zimmerman, 1990: 161).

Rather than producing in the sense of making, production in the Heideggerian fashion is the way in which we can let something stand on its own and be. The creative or hacker (taken in the broadest possible sense) is the person who steers (or wills) an object or medium to a new mode of disclosure within a given arrangement. This is not as odd as might first appear with the origins of mass media being based on hacking, and creative and bisociative use of media. Many will know for example that Gutenberg's printing press revolutionised the ways in which ideas are disseminated, but it is noteworthy too that it was his interest in wine-making that allowed him to conceive of the screw press for printing purposes. In engaging and potentially transforming the being of objects we too are worldly and deal in being. This means that we do not perceive from afar and theorise, cognise and negotiate abstractions, but rather we manipulate and put things to use. In dealing with an item of equipment, a tool or medium we first recognise that it has an in-order-to character, thus possessing a purpose and relationship with something else (hammer and nail for example). It is, however, in manipulation and use that we disclose the being of the object and Heidegger is worth quoting at some length on this:

> ... the less we stare at the hammer-Thing, and the more we seize hold of it and use it, the more primordial does our relationship to it become, and the more unveiledly is it encountered as that which it is – as equipment ... No matter how sharply we just *look* [Nur-noch-*hinsehen*] at the 'outward appearance' ['Aussehen'] of Things in whatever form this takes, we cannot discover anything ready-to-hand. If we look at Things just 'theoretically', we can get along without understanding readiness-to-hand. But when we deal with them by using them and manipulating them, this activity is not a blind one; it has its own kind of sight, by which our manipulation is guided and from which it acquires its specific Thingly character.
>
> (Heidegger, 2011 [1962]: §69, 98, emphasis in original)

This is an important kinaesthetic point that most creatives, artists, craftspeople, engineers, mechanics, hackers and so on will probably agree: there is more to knowing than observation and that one may acquire deep, useful, sensational and phenomenal knowledge through doing and not conceptualising from afar. Despite being predicated on differences, connections, proportions and so on, inevitably this form of knowing is not easily verbalised. This is not necessarily due to linguistic inability on behalf of the speaker or writer, but rather that the dynamics of decision-making and choice are subtle, nuanced, shifting and not easily rendered into clunky words.

Action and practice thus has its own way of seeing and discerning that is inaccessible to simply looking. Dewey makes a very similar point remarking that the artist 'does this thinking in the very qualitative media he works in, and the terms lie so close to the object that he is producing that they merge directly into it' (2005 [1934]: 14–15). Put otherwise, this is to return to the sensuous philosophies referred to in Chapter 7 that eschew the academic supply house of theory (to borrow from Hamann) and abstraction in favour of lived, directly given and seemingly unmediated experience. Be this craft, art, code or quality toolwork, this person thus understands the technology or medium's 'thingness' and is able to articulate it to a degree that it can be brought under scrutiny, cognised, possibly dissected and finally manipulated, reformulated or repurposed in a different domain. Importantly too, this disclosure does not happen by chance but through acts of will and endeavour. While links, associations and possibilities may be thought of in wandering moments, this still needs expertise and knowledge so to be fashioned, worked, crafted, formed and made to be.

In repurposing objects there is a balance to be played between Heidegger's notions of 'readiness-to-hand' and 'presence-at-hand'. The former is when we manipulate, engage with, use and work objects, and not pay attention to the identity of the object. Keyboard keys, carburettors and kitchen pans all fall into our daily experiences (or lack of) of 'readiness-to-hand'. For Heidegger the being of the thing withdraws so for the object to become pre-theoretical. Should a key on the keyboard become stuck or should the door handle on a train not work as it should when passengers try to disembark, the thing becomes very much present. More positively, the world is not present but waiting to be discovered and known. To this we might add that it is there to be experimented with and reformulated. Being present-at-hand is to take the object that usually fades into the flow of daily experience and focus on it as an entity in itself and to understand more clearly what it is that is being disclosed.

The capacity to transform requires not only technical understanding but also the capacity to hack the 'in-order-to' dimension that goes with being able to repurpose objects and things. Knowledge in this context is very practical and reflects a combination of awareness of thingliness, possibility and that tools come to be by dint of the task to which they are applied. In Heideggerian terms there is little to be gained by sitting analysing a hammer, but rather one understands the hammer through use. This provides a different form of knowledge than that usually associated with theory and for Heidegger use rather than observation provides understanding otherwise unachievable. This form of knowledge is without circumspection, and sympathy for 'ready-to-hand' is gained only through practice. This blurring of person and thing is deeply sensational (hidden to theorisation), and these types of technical affordances are the means by which we are couched in everyday life. So as we get up in the morning and progress through the day we encounter possibly countless technical artefacts that we are able to interpret and negotiate. Moreover, on finding new artefacts our fore-structure is able to discern and possibly negotiate new objects, door handles, can openers and so forth. For Heidegger this everyday understanding or being-in-the-world is pre-ontological and non-theoretical.

Imagining media

Symbolic and textual approaches do not graft well on to creative media processes, particularly when we realise that the affordances of media are revealed through use, engagement and interaction. Indeed, creativity understood through affordances has to do with the willingness to pay close attention to micro-engagement and what it is to 'be-in-the-world' in relation to a given media or technical experience. It is to understand media intensively and affectively, and then subsequently to either leverage these qualities or transform them. This creative engagement returns us to the notion of will and the capacity to go beyond finding the tool (or medium) conducive and useful, to transforming it for given ends. In addition to considering what we commonly recognise as media and the ways these might be transformed, we might also consider what can act as a medium. Indeed, Fuller's critique of the affordances of media and the ways in which they are taken up by artists and activists draws attention to the way in which creativity and innovation can be seen as a process of realising opportunities in the potential grammar and structures of misplaced concreteness (borrowing from Whitehead) of standard objects found in culture.

Along with artists, people in advertising have been exploring for some time how artefacts of everyday life are able to act as a medium. This has met with mixed success: for example, sometimes 'ambient advertising' is deemed intrusive although on other occasions, particularly when brand values, medium, location and wit coincide, it might make even the most vehement loather of advertising smile. More recently, digital tools have expanded what is possible and we might proceed on the basis that media exist not only as a noun or list of vehicles but also as a verb: to mediate (Parikka, 2011). They are always active, not inert, and the act of mediating is an event in itself with its own sensational and semiotic qualities.

What then is able to act as a medium? This is to ask, what possible materials can be imagined as media, how can they be hacked and repurposed, and how might they engage people and other living beings? In a famous experiment that highlights the nature of hacking Dunker (1945), a Gestalt psychologist, gave participants a candle, a box of matches and a box of tacks briefing them to fix a candle to the wall so wax does not drip on to the table below. The solution is to hack the box of matches. This involves transforming and repurposing the box into a candleholder and tacking it to the wall. For those interested in media, the key here is in eschewing the division between form and content so to remember that a medium, and the wider media system that a given platform sits within, may be creatively transformed and repurposed so to invoke new sensations and experiences. It is to take media back from being delivery mechanisms to being tools – those things that are adaptable for different ends. This draws attention to the potential for manipulating, transforming, hacking, pressurising media beyond their original designation, and for things to be defined in terms of the activities we use them for.

For example, while the agency B-Reel serves advertising clients and wins creative advertising awards, the 'About' section on their website does not refer to the company as an advertising organisation. Rather they position themselves as 'a hybrid production company, specialized in the field of advanced digital production for web, mobile, physical installations and other media' (B-Reel, 2012). *The Wilderness Downtown*, an interactive film produced in 2010, exemplifies this and begins by asking the user for the street address where they grew up. After loading, with Arcade Fire (an indie rock band) playing in the background, the first window opens depicting a young person running along a street in one window. Utilising both Google Street View and Maps other windows open and it becomes clear that the street the youth is running down is the street that we entered. Use of Street View and Maps means both aerial and street-level images are obtained and as the camera zooms and rotates (synchronised with the camera in the other windows), we realise the youth is heading towards our homes. Not only are Google tools opened, but they are also overlaid by flying birds and rapidly growing trees. The premise of the idea was simply to have people download Google's Chrome browser as the site was optimised for Chrome. In addition, its cachet was confirmed by the 'film' not being pushed, but shared via Twitter, Facebook and influential blogs.

The example highlights too the ways in which creative use of media often involves re-packaging applications and tools found elsewhere, and on occasion creating non-standard media objects. Where media for marketing and advertising industries were once blankly understood in terms of 'above-the-line', i.e. paid-for, and then the rest, there is now greater awareness of how outdoor, mobile, locative services, web-based platforms, gaming, digital signage, television and other discovered, repurposed or invented mediums might be pushed far beyond designation and co-ordinated so to intermingle with one another for unique affect, raise the media experience a notch and become more than their constituent parts. It is these new interconnections and meta-levels of media affordances that are of creative interest. Creativity in media then has to do with interpretation, re-organisation, layering, and the hacking of assumptions of how media are employed and used. It also has to do with creating the circumstances for events and successful practitioners will be able to catalyse co-emergent happenings, and manage and modulate stages of the unfolding mediated experience. Whereas analogue media provided breakthroughs in storage, time-shifting and temporality, digital provides greater ecological opportunity for interoperability, manipulation, transformation and the escaping of fixity into branded possibilities of transversal indeterminacy.

Ecological creativity

In his review of literature on media and ecology, Strate (2004) summarises that media ecology taken as a collective noun of theoretical approaches involves the study of the interaction of media, technology, technique, strategy and people. The origins of ecological conceptions of media are frequently associated with Marshall McLuhan, but one should go back to Mumford (1952; 1961 [1934]) who so deeply influenced McLuhan, his discussion of biology and mechanical extension, and the formulation that the content of one medium is another. In a 1977 television interview available on YouTube, McLuhan, in a way that indirectly relates to the media planning efforts on behalf of advertisers, refers to media ecology as 'arranging various media to help each other so they won't cancel each other out, to buttress one medium with another' (2003: 271).

The idea of media ecology refers to environment and the ways in which our media are significant in determining social organisation, means of communication, what we communicate, how we think, feel, sense, our way of life and general worldview. Ecological inclinations were originally taken up and advanced by Walter Ong and Neil Postman. Postman uses the analogy of a Petri dish to account for the nature of a medium. In a highly media deterministic fashion, he argues that a medium is a technology that a culture grows within. By this he argues that 'it gives form to a culture's politics, social organization, and habitual ways of thinking' (2000: 10). Ong (2002) conceives of media ecology differently, noting the increasing intensity of informational interrelationships between people and their environment (conceived of in the most profound universal sense). This ecological view emerges directly from wider ecological discourse on open systems and new modes of consciousness (having to do with the interconnectedness of things). This is exemplified in Kuhns' (1973) *The Postindustrial Prophets* where, in his introduction, he observes that ecologists have provided useful frames of reference with which to conceive new (computational) technologies. He refers to notions of 'organic continuity' and 'harmony' between man and technologies, and also the ways in which emergent and spontaneously organised environments take the place of pre-planned environments. Although the expression 'ecology' implies biology, ethology, physiology and environmental sciences, underpinning ecology is merely an awareness of interconnection and interaction. This gives rise to discussion of conceptions of emergence, open systems, self-renewal, allopoeisis and autopoiesis – all important topics in different ways for networked environments. In relation to creativity, there is value in considering ways in which interconnections between media might be harnessed, the ways that these interact, the role of the user as providing machinic sustenance for media events, and the ways in which these arrangements give rise to novel branded occasions that are excessive in nature.

Feedback, prehending and event management

Consideration of interconnection requires we better understand the role of feedback, resonance and the ways in which media might intermingle. As Bateson (1991) remarks, in addition to theoretical value, there is a deep aesthetic attraction in the patterning, interconnection and modulation in eco-logical conceptions. Indeed, the strengths of ecological perspectives on media are in the tallying of aesthetic ideas with materiality to represent feedback, ecosystems and the ways in which a change in a part will influence the whole and vice versa. As Bateson puts it, 'by *aesthetic*, I mean responsive to *the pattern which connects*' (2002 [1979]: 8, emphasis in original). Although when we think about interactivity, we tend to think in terms of human–machine (without the Deleuzian inflection) or human–human interaction, we might also factor in technological interaction and the ways in which different media interact (machine–machine) so to become a larger machine (with the Deleuzian inflection, as accounted for in Chapter 5). With the addition of the facilitating and connective role of software and code, much digital media take on autonomous and autopoietic characteristics, come alive in our hands, and link to a wide range of actors (for example third-party adver-tisement servers, social networks, applications, hardware and people). In considering these links, cybernetic feedback events and ecological relationships it is useful to trace orders of recursiveness (Bateson, 2000 [1972]). This involves understanding the ways in which elements of an ecology or organi-sation interconnect, the ways in which these reinforce each another, and the nature of the event generated from this system.

This sees the possibility of a play of differentials, exchange and interaction so to aid in generating branded affect. In contrast to the lock-down of com-mand and control of traditional advertising, recent novel advertising tends towards seemingly open systems predicated on permeability and collaboration with its environment. This includes ourselves, along with all other elements linked into the system/machine. By means of biotechnical engagement with such advertising systems, what is exchanged between the system and environ-ment are affect, information and sustenance for the system or arrangement. Put otherwise, we might also turn to Deleuze and Guattari's (2003 [1980]) notion of the 'machinic phylum' and the ways in which previously dis-connected elements might begin to co-operate so to form another level of entity. We see tendencies toward this in advertising already. A campaign by Google (working with Johannes Leonardo and Grow Interactive) in 2012 makes the point well. This was created to show the wider advertising industry that there is significant potential in online and mobile display advertising. Taking Coca-Cola's 1971 *Hilltop* (better known for the lyrics 'I'd Like to Teach the World to Sing … ') sung by a multicultural gathering of teenagers on the top of a hill, Google with their partners contrasted the commercial with new media affordances, feedback, ecology and cross-temporal media experience. This works by means of using rich media advertisements with applications running inside them that allowed engagers to literally buy a stranger a Coke anywhere around the world served via vending machines. Givers were then able to send text messages to personalise their gift with messages translated by Google Translate if need be. The route of the gift and message from the giver's location to the receiver was then relayed via Google Maps, Street View and composite motion graphics. Confirmation of the gift came through email along with a Thank You message sent from the vending machine by the receiver along with a video clip of the receiver's surprised reactions upon getting the free Coke. An online gallery also depicted the best responses.

Another example, less grand than the Coke one but making the point about machinic co-operation well, is for Evian water.[1] This involves a musical application called Melotweet (downloadable for Android or Apple platforms) that turns a person's Twitter feed into a game. Urging us to #Liveyoung, the application connects with a Twitter account and each tweet of a timeline appears as a droplet descending from the top of the screen. On catching the drop (which appears as an avatar adapted into a droplet), users are able to read corresponding tweets, retweet, add to favourites, or open content via the link. Interactive panes allow users to both write tweets and drag and drop objects onto the stage to start playing with Melotweet. Each contact between a tweet droplet and an object produces a small sound and users can place as many as they wish to compose their own melodies. Users can pause and play their compositions as well as change the tempo (Lürzer's Archive, 2012).

Note that this 'advertising' is less about interruption, or restricted representation and transmission, as with the original commercial, but more about the staging of a co-creative event or situation within a given period of time. This entails the generation of a transductive character, or that quality that retrospectively is seen to emerge at different phases, points and levels within the event, and bind all of these together. Indeed Mackenzie (2002), drawing on the work of Gilbert Simondon, remarks that transduction is the knotting together of diverse realities so to comprise technical ensembles or assemblages. For most purposes, this is tantamount to what here has been phrased as 'events' although the philosophical genealogy is a little different (Whitehead wrote very little about technology while Simondon wrote extensively about it). Both accounts however place an emphasis on genesis and becoming and, as detailed in the examples above, technical events are those that come to be via networked relations and systems of relay. A transductive characterisation is useful, however, as it points to an intersection or singularity made up of

> ... corporeal, geographical, economic, conceptual, biopolitical, geopolitical and affective dimensions. They entail a knotting together of commodities, signs, diagrams, stories, practices, concepts, human and non-human bodies, images and places.
>
> (Mackenzie, 2002: 18)

Like the events accounted for throughout this book, the emphasis is on the ways that these give rise to that which is unique by means of bisociating influences culled from far and wide to facilitate the emergence of something novel, metastable and possessing individuality (at least temporarily).

While there are a number of mini-products created by advertising agencies in facilitating these events, the emergent transductive character or event is the creative product. Deeply process-based, the significance of the event, while managed and controlled, unfolds (although is not necessarily recognised) in the present. Indeed, in Whitehead's (1928) terms this involves 'presentational immediacy' and how parts of a sensed event might be relevant to each other, generate character, and yet maintain mutual independence.

It is also playful in that it is bounded, live, immediate, engaging, in part improvised, interactive, intense, discrete and demarcated from wider life experience, although we should not get too hung up on defining borders and boundaries as separating out events is messy business. However, although temporary, the arrangement (or combination) is worthy of consideration in terms of cumulative, compound and machinic effects. It is characterised and stimulated by connective software, feedback, emergence, modulation of communicative stages, catalytic effects, porosity between mediums, corporeal action, the leveraging of sociality, and users' physical and tele-technological contributions to the event. As highlighted in Chapter 5, the generation of such events involves our own imbrication within machinic arrangements and any notion that we might simply spectate and not be involved is nonsense. As media proliferate, interconnect and transduce, they contribute to producing events that in their participative and real-time nature are *less* mediated than that deeply contrived artefact – the commercial.

In 2012, Sony in Japan, along with their advertising agency PARTY, harnessed feedback via machine–machine, human–machine and human–machine–human interactions, and launched a crowd-sourced campaign that encompassed and linked together live television, phones and/or tablet computers, Facebook and Twitter. The idea of this was to advertise Dot Switch, Sony's mobile application that links Sony smartphones, tablets, personal computers and televisions so to be able to share content across all Sony products. This involved enabling TV viewers to take part in the making of a new music video. Participants downloaded the Dot Switch Android application to their phone or tablet, or accessed by means of the Dot Switch website. By means of the application or site they were able to push virtual buttons to trigger 13 different devices on the live TV show. Each of the devices required a certain number of pushes to initiate and the more pushes the show received, the more that happened. Viewers also connected via Facebook and Twitter to see their names appear in Japanese national broadcasts. The content created was eventually edited into an official music video, with every participant included in the credits.

The idea of improvisation broached in Chapter 2 takes on double significance here in that often freely available tools and technologies may be reworked for novel ends, and also that advertising events are more open and fluid than the entirely contrived commercial or poster, particularly if involving social media. Sony have been prolific in joining-up and ecologising media and, as mentioned in McStay (2009), Sony in 2007 commissioned a campaign titled 'Rec You' (Record You) by GT Tokyo/Dentsu for Sony Walkman where visitors to the website uploaded a still image of themselves that was consequently animated to wear a Walkman, sing and bob in time to a section of Verdi's Requiem 'Dies Irae'. The site then sends its users a movie of their singing self who then joins a wider choir of singing heads presented through a range of platforms including banners, blogs and YouTube. To cap this, users appeared in outdoor advertising in sports stadiums and screens in large cities, and were told by text messages when they would appear on national television.

As stressed in earlier chapters on concrescence and emergence, what is cumulatively generated does not pre-date, nor is it found in, the assemblage's constituent parts. In an advertising context this event-based dimension emerges out of multimodal opportunities to interface with an ecologised system that on receiving the user is intended to engender feelings (intensities) tailored to each campaign. While each of the media employed are interesting in their own way and are frequently used alone or as a disparate collection of individual channels through which to deliver traditional advertising messages, what is remarkable is the ecological dimension to the media employed and these ways in which each cross-stimulated the other so for the campaign to transgress and be something in excess of its parts. DeLanda (1991) expresses the principle well by asking us to consider the spin of atoms in a metal that co-operate to make a metal magnetic; the interaction of molecules that chemically react and co-operate and engender the patterns of a chemical clock; or even the interaction of termites in a colony so to assemble a nest.

In Whiteheadian (1985 [1929]) terms this involves 'prehensions' and the ways in which elements might be connected with one another so to form an entity or event. Whitehead (1997 [1925]) admits the expression is a somewhat awkward term, but remarks that prehensions involve ways in which subjects experience other objects, perceive them, feel them or take them into account. His reasoning for being able to apply this to non-conscious beings (or to use proper parlance, 'occasions') is the way that one occasion responds to another.

Underlying this is a rejection of Berkeleyan idealism and subjectivism as Whitehead shifts the event from the individual's mind to the world of things. Together these prehensions combine to form events that possess value. They are not just the sum of their parts, but something more. This is not contingent on consciousness, but rather the ways in which objects form unities by feeling, relating, taking-in and ingressing into their environment and new set of relations. A prehension then is a process of unification, and the emphasis on process and becoming is Whitehead's key point: the universe is characterised by processes and arrangements that come about by parts feeling-out one another so to create a new event. The establishment (or concrescence) of an entity occurs by dint of prehensions that grasp or take account of one another and assess environments in their ongoing relations of transforming and becoming so for some relations to operate as a cohesive and distinct thing, or in Whitehead's parlance, 'actual entity'.

This idea is most clearly expressed in *Science and the Modern World* where Whitehead borrows from Francis Bacon's *Natural History* the idea that although an object (or event or process) may have no ability to sense, it might have a degree of perception. Crudely put, it is a non-conscious feeling-out of sorts and perception in this context means taking into account the character of that perceived. That perceived is a unity as: 'An event is the grasping into unity of a pattern of aspects' (1997 [1925]: 119). Whitehead's key point however is that this does not have to be cognitively processed, but rather that such a thing as 'uncognitive apprehension' might exist (1997 [1925]: 69). For example, we easily recollect happenings in the day that we did not overtly cognise at the time. Prehension is the same idea, but with 'uncognitive' and 'app' dropped, and without memory. The key is not in perceiving the objects, but the way in which they are arranged. It is the understanding of unity as formed by prehension or again, that form of feeling-out. This unity or entity is established through relations, patterns and not the objects themselves. Rather, the objects or events are defined through relations. In discussion of an organism, Whitehead puts it thus:

> Its knowledge of itself arises from its own relevance to the things of which it prehends the aspects. It knows the world as a system of mutual relevance, and thus sees itself mirrored in other things. These other things include more especially the various parts of its own body.
> (Whitehead, 1997 [1925]: 148–49)

The principle of mutual relevance does not require consciousness, but rather that objects mutually engage and modify each another. As Whitehead moves on to reiterate, this relation reigns throughout nature and is not contingent on higher organisms. In thinking about media ecology, feedback, co-creation and excessive media events, we might point to prehensions as the underlying logic that connects, gives rise to concrescence and the emergent event sought by advertisers, and their wish to positively influence the next event and period of engagement with the brand.

Transversal imperatives

Transversal forms of understanding find a route through Vico, the German idealists, the Romanticists, Nietzsche, Bergson, Heidegger, Bateson, Whitehead, Deleuze and Guattari, and others dissatisfied with life understood through abstraction preferring the language of transgression. The word 'transversal' in a cultural context means to take from a number of parts and surpass them so to become something more. In taking parts, mixing together and exceeding a collective sum of parts, there is excess and overflow. It involves interconnectivity and ecology, although not in the sense of trying to maintain a system, but rather to push an arrangement over the precipice so to be actualised into something more interesting or valuable. This 'something more' exists within a disorganised and indeterminate environment as what has transgressed leaves behind safe determinates, parameters or boundaries that give definition to a phenomenon. These parameters are the official way of doing things and a transversal act is that which is deviant and usurps the usual given arrangement. In regards to media technology it has to do with positive feedback, scaling systems, becoming and potential, the chance of the new, passing across thresholds, subsequent transformation through excess, and that which for its life span develops and is in-formation.

The imperative to transversalism increases as media become less isolated and solitary, and more ecological and interconnected. What is sought is a sensational account of emergence expressed through the language of ecology as a means of getting to the mass of prehensions, interactions, differentials, internal struggles and relationships between objects, subjects, patterns and matter that push beyond the form–content dyad. There is a surfacing of a will-based dynamic expressed through materiality, machinic life, physiology, matter, and the ways in which thresholds, disequilibrium and bifurcation are reached.

This tendency towards a transversal account of media as it relates to creativity is to recognise the opportunities for positive feedback and commercial harnessing of this. Transversality and media are usually connected with Guattari's (2000) work on media and ecology. Very different from the somewhat marketised version discussed in this book, Guattari sought to create an account of material politics of media that turned away from immaterial conceptions of media. This focused on the 1970s, free radio and political subjectivity examining Radio Alice, a free station that came into conflict with Italy's apparatus of state control. Departing from the norms of radio, free radio in Italy engaged and was created by new modes of subjectivity in a self-referential relationship of positive feedback. Goddard observes:

> ... it was not just a question of giving space for excluded and marginalised subjects such as the young, homosexuals, women, the unemployed and others to speak but rather of generating a collective assemblage of enunciation allowing for the maximum of transversal connections and subjective transformations between all these emergent subjectivities.
>
> (Goddard, 2011: 10)

Should this feel somewhat distant and unknown, modern cultural history in the form of the Arab Spring of 2011 provides more recent examples in Tunisia, Egypt, Algeria, Yemen, Jordan and Libya (among other countries and states) through the use of the affordances of networked media to co-ordinate, communicate and raise awareness of a bottom-up putsch for political and social change. Interestingly, Radio Alice employs only one form of media but the point remains – a mediated version of positive feedback occurs that results in a form of excess, or perhaps surplus. Importantly, these mediated events were spiralled up and amplified by desire and transformation, resulting in the intensification of subjectivity through technical means. There are lessons to be taken here for activists and advertisers alike, particularly in relation to the study of media through an investigation and inquiry into materials so to discern properties and affordances in terms of communication and how they may positively circulate energy, currents and meaning (also see Parikka, 2011). While the results of these interactions are more than the sum of their parts, or at least of what may be logged, as a material account of the media it is a useful approach.

Attention to media affordances involves examination of the hermeneutics of media systems, and their capacity to affect and be affected (as with the discussion of bodies in Chapter 5). These types of observations where media become more than the affordances immediately facilitated by them and collectively take on emergent dimensions through interaction, mutual stimulation and feedback are best seen in light of DeLanda's (1997) *phase space* (map of all possible combinations of affordances) and Deleuze and Guattari's (2003 [1980]) *machinic phylum* (taxonomy of affordances). With elements going beyond their prescribed remit and being in excess of themselves, they become ecological, self-organised, and a complex milieu of pattern and process in which the sum of parts are exceeded. It is the finding of new links and connections and the general sense of 'becoming' that is all-important here.

New patterns of media experience arise through improvisation, open-endedness, open-source, co-poiesis, and autocatalytic properties. Put otherwise, it is 'to embody creative synthesis *in praxis* while intersubjectively jamming with the autopoietic environment' (Amerika, 2009: 183 [emphasis in original]). The machinic phylum represents awareness not only of the taxonomy of constituents and technical affordances, but also the means by which previously unconnected aspects of this taxonomy may cooperate to form new entities. In contrast to the notion of fixed essences or even affordances, this involves substantiation of virtuality so for potentiality to become actuality.

Conclusion

Media affordances are of great interest to advertising agencies as they seek to solicit all possible means of engaging with potential customers. This largely content-free understanding has less to do with characterless vehicles for delivering content, but the creation of sites of engagement, entanglement, process, transversalism and sensation. Media in this context are made up of properties, materialities, forces and processes that deeply contribute to communications programmes. Assessing the relationship between technics, media, craft and advertising, this chapter has depicted some of the characteristics associated with developments in advertising as it spills over from textual representation into a deeper interest in media itself. The development of the bounded commercial, poster or discrete artefact into process and event-based advertising means that advertising conceived of as representation par excellence becomes problematic. Instead, by means of expertise in media and ecological stimulation, events are generated that in contrast to the pictorial representations of old somewhat paradoxically employ more media to generate a less mediated experience of a more immediate nature.

In addition to arranging known media, creativity and inventiveness in this affordance-based context is the capacity to explore and disclose new potential from what might be appropriated as media. While the division between art and craft is porous and leaky, expertise in media and affordances certainly invokes craft-based skills on behalf of advertisers. This involves awareness of both Heidegger's (2011 [1962]) readiness-at-hand and presence-at-hand, and the ways in which media might be taken up, transformed and employed within an event. Micro-considerations of usability and interaction of media forms brings to mind Whitehead's discussion of the major form of beauty, particularly his remark: 'Beauty is the internal conformation of the various items of experience with each other, for the production of maximum effectiveness' (1948 [1933]: 305). In highlighting transversalism as it applies to media we see that where representational advertising tends towards trying to fix and control, creativity in transversal accounts is about positive feedback, scaling, excess, stimulation and affect.

Note

1 See www.luerzersarchive.com/content/show/id/54746

11 Conclusions

Creativity and Advertising is unlikely to be the final or authoritative account on creativity, and nor does it seek to be. It is hoped however that the new insights generated on creativity and their relationship to advertising might be applied, amended, expanded, overturned or connected to others' analytical and/or practice-based endeavours. Indeed, in the spirit of pragmatism, the point of this book has been to facilitate new ways of looking at advertising and creativity, particularly in relation to thinking of these in terms of events and machines, and that which is locally, sensationally and affectively engaged with. Such a renewal of how we think about advertising has been overdue for some time, not least because co-creative developments and deeper interest in media affordances by practitioners foreground limitations of critical textual endeavours. In summing up and offering final remarks on what has been covered, this final chapter is framed in terms of the two propositions about creativity and advertising made in Chapter 1. These respectively stated that: (1) *creativity in advertising is not just representational but sensational*; (2) *creativity involves acts of will in situations without clear determinates*.

Representation

The sources of my arguments on creativity can indirectly be found in Spinozan, Kantian, Heideggerean, Whiteheadian and Deleuzian principles. While a mixed and sometimes inconsistent line-up, each deeply permeates the arguments made in relation to affect, projection, revealing, process and embodiment. Although the Kantian divide generally goes unremarked upon in textual discussion, this is the root of insistence on projection, life as a series of signs and the tendency to textualise all modes of knowledge. It is also that which analyses constructs of knowledge. Put otherwise, Kant's arguments on the possibility of knowledge through direct observation placed the idea of the subject-as-observer in crisis. As the thing-in-itself receded, we turned inward to our ideas and the ways in which we re-present and construct the world to ourselves by means of sensory and mental faculties. This was to establish a split or dualism absolutely skewed one way, to intellectualise the world, rupture our connection with it, and lose sight of the fact that we are of the world.

This book errs to the view that while we should be careful of lapsing into naïve realism, we should also avoid sustaining a pervasive and all-encompassing textual illusion, a metaphysical construct, or spectacular ontology with ineffable leanings.[1] There are straightforward reasons for questioning the usefulness of textualism in accounting for creativity and advertising, not least that because phenomenal knowledge is dependent on matrices of deferred meaning to provide support for a named object, it cannot understand the simplest questions about what something is and how something makes us feel. While combinatorial, symbolic, narratological, ideological, social constructionist and text-based methods are tidier and more straightforward in application, their clarity is won through limitation, disciplining and the imposition of a one-dimensional representational scheme over the lived and sensational dimensions of experience.

If we are to offer a proper account we cannot simply pick and choose the bits we want to analyse but rather we should attempt to deal with entireties and as Whitehead remarks, 'For us the red glow of the sunset should be as much part of nature as are the molecules and electrical waves by which men of science would explain the phenomenon' (1964 [1920]: 29; see also Stengers, 2011; Shapiro, 2012). Much is missed then in a phenomenal, symbolic and reductionist account of creativity, and certainly in relation to advertising we might pay closer attention to wider processes that give rise to advertising events. Even if critics are not yet that attentive to the fullness of advertising events, without doubt agencies are very interested in wider processes that go into advertising (workings of the brain/mind, media, timing, placing, nature of interaction, optimising symbolic dimensions, recording and processing traces of media and content use, and so on).

An affective and process-based approach prefers to explore the fullness of life than retreat to symbolic deferral. While we might not know things-in-themselves, it does not follow that we should deny the existence of these or their capacities for affect. While affect and the lived have been privileged here, what I do not seek to do is resurrect Descartes' (2008 [1644]) child who is solely bound to the body and entirely lost in sensations and its world of tastes, smells, sounds, heat, cold, light and colours. If we are to take Schiller's (2004 [1795]) aesthetic education seriously we see that creativity involves both a sensuous and rational nature, and in our accounting for affect and advertising we should be mindful of a reactionary swing from intellectualism and representation. What is suggested instead is that semiosis is folded into affect and sensation, as with biosemiotic accounts. Latour (1993) likewise points out that the postmodern emphasis on textualism comes about through a modern but false distinction between nature and culture. Similarly, Dewey (2005 [1934]) remarks that the issue is less about demonstrating the existence of hybrid being, but rather the burden of proof lies on those who insist on a dualism of nature and culture, or noumena and phenomena. The point is that we live a quasi-existence between the transcendent and the immanent, and it is at this border and coming together of things where we are linked with (unknowable) things-in-themselves. Heidegger's (2011 [1962]) observation that things-in-themselves are only mostly and not entirely inaccessible has bearing here. As he suggests, what we experience of the world is not merely a representation but rather reality itself albeit from a very limited perspective. In contrast to the textualist sinkhole where experience is made up of an eternity of deferred representations, Heidegger's revision of Kant provides a narrow way through the representational and textual impasse.

If we reject the absolute distinction between culture and nature or the transcendent and the immanent, the unhealthy obsession with abstract texts lessens and we can admit of wider experience and begin to link expertise in cultural coding with sensation and aesthetics. The border between things-in-themselves and culture will always exist (if we accept that perception requires mediating faculties) but the point is that we might better occupy the meeting place between these. This to me seems like a reasonable proposition and it is at this border and coming together of things where we are linked with (unknowable) things-in-themselves we might concentrate our efforts, rather than taking shelter in entirely phenomenal dimensions.

The problem that textualism has faced in accounting for territory (the world) as a map (a representation), whereby the world exists as a projection, is that it has forgotten that the map *must* emerge from the territory and wider ecology of which we are intimately a part. As Whitehead (1985 [1929]) remarks in discussion of the 'superject', where for Kant the world emerges by dint of the subject, Whitehead's superject involves recognition that the subject emerges from the world. Shapiro (2012) phrases the emergent sense of subject as a remnant that comes about through our engagement with the world, in the same way that a solid is precipitated from a solution in a chemical reaction (the same applies to neurological conceptions of consciousness too). This provides a more ontogenetic view of consciousness, acts of questioning and reflection, along with will. We need not be estranged from ourselves, and on this basis, the Whiteheadian and Deleuzian oeuvre is attractive because it does away with question of the transcendent and the immanent by means of positing of quasi-causes and virtuality. This at the very least represents a workaround to the problem of how to better connect the incorporeal with the corporeal.

Virtuality

Žižek (2004) rightly argues that this is a Deleuzian period for all the wrong reasons and lambasts Deleuze as an ideologist for 'digital capitalism', high-lighting Deleuze's emphasis on intensities and the circulation affect. Žižek takes Deleuze to task because this is precisely Deleuze's method too. In Bergsonism, for example, Deleuze (2006 [1966]) conceives of philosophy as a sort of buggery where he would get onto the back of an author and give him a monstrous child that is both a perversity but true to the philosophy. Žižek generously and accurately delivers the same favour by highlighting the relationship between Deleuzianism, intensities, schizoanalysis and digital capitalism.

He is right too – Deleuze's approach sits too easily with the re-evaluation of advertising as an event, along with discussion of affect, process, multiplicity, machinism, bodies and aesthetics presented here. Regardless of complaints raised in Chapter 1 in relation to perverted accounts of creativity, and Deleuze and Guattari's (2011 [1994]) remonstration of the shameful moment when folk in advertising replaced philosophers as those who deal in ideas, the parallel *is* closer than first thought: both philosophers and advertisers are in the business of creating constellations or ontologies of ideas about being by which we navigate the world. Connections do not stop there either as Deleuzo-Guattarian conceptions of virtuality best articulate what creativity is to advertising, that is, creativity is the 'Body without Organs' of advertising. By this I mean that creativity is the virtual and organizing principle that to some extent determines advertising. It is the fluid, potential-based and determining stratum that underpins the actuality of advertising (i.e. the business and world of advertisements). Advertising defines and holds itself so closely to creativity, that its function is 'miraculated' by it. Like capital, creativity in advertising takes on mystical properties that supersede, yet form the industry itself. As with Deleuze's discussion of the virtual then, creativity occupies a quasi-status and is that which induces emergence although, in itself, this does not herald or foreshadow what comes to exist.

Quality

Creative advertising has been framed here in aesthetic, intensive and sensational terms, and such discourse on affect sees advertising as a figurehead of what Hardt and Negri (2000) account for as the affective economy (also see Massumi, 2002). While the emphasis in this book has been on what we might loosely think of as a formal account of creativity, rather than an overt critical account of affect, clearly there is scope for articulating contemporary neuroscientific interest in affect and commercial communication within a wider biopolitical history of the body (conscious and unconscious), its mapping systems, its role within machinic arrangements, and to explore the self as contributing to advertising events or assemblages, rather than linger on ideology or social structure. To this end, a 2012 edition of the journal *Culture Machine* on the 'attention economy' carries a number of articles that sit alongside the material presented here, particularly in terms of the interrelationship of 'bodies, cognition, economy and culture' (Crogan and Kinsley, 2012: 2). Indeed, while this book is wide open to accusations of being apolitical, the emphasis given to the generation of novelty and the new is readily readable in terms of the generation of critique itself, particularly as historically critical theory has appropriated from a wide range of domains so to fashion new events and assemblages to generate visions of better ways of doing things.

In regard to research in advertising, neuroscience, and its employment by advertisers and marketers, it is all too easy to position this in dystopian terms, the colonisation of the cortex, the continuation of technics and control (as per bureaucratic conceptions of power), biopower, and cartographic power over brains and minds. While plainly advertising has always affected neurologically, techniques have been haphazard and undoubtedly both research and its application will continue to be invested in and employed. Although we should guard against the excesses of criticism – regulatory and ethical awareness should be high.

A key problem with affect, however, is that although we can see its effects, recognise its diagnostic power, understand that theoretically it better fits with the practices of advertising than representational approaches, in itself it currently possesses very little in the way of explanatory and analytical power. It draws attention to something extremely important, but it is not easily studied. Where representational concerns might be approached with linguistically-oriented theoretical tools on the one hand and a clutch of print advertisements on the other, in itself, affect is better thought of in terms of ontological clarification and conceptual housekeeping, and at present is less about building a set of tools for experimental and empirical investigation. Indeed, a taxonomy, structure or periodic table of affect would be very useful, if possible, but while one might seek to provide a tonal map or scheme of sorts, this is to forget the highly individualistic nature of affect that in itself leads to all sorts of questions about problems of accessing the inner lives of others, and the possibility of sharing mental impressions and sensations. Taxonomy leads to stasis, and is contra to the dynamic nature and mental life of affects. This is not to mention that many affect-based strategies in commercial persuasion (particularly in wider marketing efforts) are intentionally non-conscious.

However, the diagnostic power of affect should not be understated and to make an obvious but necessary point: affect's critical importance is highlighted by the simple observation that it is that which advertisers seek. While advertising agencies may be impelled by creativity (however we care to define this), those that fund them seek effects by affect (although as mentioned in Chapter 6, larger clients are not entirely averse to using advertising as a means of posturing and blowing-off excess).

An affective account also helps reintroduce the word quality, by means of qualia, back into the analytical mix. Where symbolic and textual accounts are utterly quiet on the role of quality, by means of qualia, affect, nuance and a sensational account of aesthetics, we are now able to reintroduce quality back into considerations of creativity. The affective account, then, has been built on two fronts: first, by means of discussing affect in relation to interest in emotion, feeling and neuroscience; second, by resurrecting instigators of qualitative traditions and contemporary affective trends, and their insistence on the value of sensation and poetic appreciation as a subject of inquiry, over abstraction and intellectualisation. These have helped highlight sensation in terms of both mind (as a non-visually contingent image-making system) and aesthetics (stripped of taste-based association) as core to advertising and creative practice.

Advertising has provided a useful case study for creativity as it is rapidly changing in light of new media developments and in response to a cluttered media environment. Where advertising was once innately connected to representation so for the paradigm of textualism to appear unchallengeable in its capacity to account for advertising, other cultural, social, affective ways of doing and conceiving advertising have crept in and powerfully destabilised solely textual accounts. Textual approaches have been found lacking as they have had the proverbial rug pulled from under their feet. Predicated on a lack of interest in media and a preference for imagery, as networked media and novel affordances move into the ascendant the limitations of representational techniques are highlighted. A more transductive, technical and event-based approach does not exclude traditional approaches but requires that more factors are considered, particularly in relation to the interaction of machinic bodies, media technologies, situated happenings and possibly also neurological goings-on. Ultimately, it is to recognise that there is no seeing from a distance or spectating from afar, because we are either involved or not. Further, although meaning systems play a role within these milieus, advertising read more broadly is about immersion in technical fields and processes of possible affect.

Sensation

In exploring background discourses of creativity this book has uncovered antecedents of recent interest in affect that aid in delineating its role and status, and possibly even suggest ways forward as to how affect may be better embraced as an analytical tool. Approaches to this have been wide-ranging, and have occurred in discussion of the Counter-Enlightenment and the parallels described there that highlight the role of sensation and the lived in relation to the formation of qualitative traditions. Moreover, by invoking both biosemiosis and neuroscientific innovation we have also been able to see affect in much more physicalist terms, particularly in regard to the ways in which semiosis and sign-making permeate all levels of beings. Whitehead's discussion of prehensions is also illuminating as a micro–macro philosophy of how things, ideas and forces feel each other so to constitute larger objects.

Creativity in advertising emerges as that which organises intensities – understood as that mode of experiencing felt within indeterminate environments that changes our perspective, affects us and alters behaviour. This mode of knowing is certainly relational, but on a romantically conceived creative level there is a sensuous dimension to this untapped by textualism where form, texture and capacity for affect is articulated to the extent that it can be manipulated for specific ends.

Will

The invocation of Kant has been twofold in that, first, he provides the background for semiotic discussion and the phenomenal context of representation. As mentioned, this has been useful as a means of clarifying the nature of semiosis and the ontological dimensions of semiotic techniques that tend to get forgotten or misplaced in textual analysis; second, but related, by thoroughly accounting for Kant and idealism we have a more proper sense of how deep the phenomena/noumena split goes in relation to our mapping and relationship with the world. Putting this in biosemiotic and Uexküllian terms only highlights the fragility of our relationship with 'what is' and our naïve dealings with the world. Thus recognition of Kant's Copernican moment has been useful and right as a means of arguing that creativity involves a destabilisation of fixity so to present the world for renewal by acts of will – or that corollary of bodily action, intervention, aim and the directing towards one outcome over another, even if this is only to open new fields of multiplicity and possibilities. By this we mean to say that will is not an entity as such, but rather is that which motivates and is purposive. This Kantian disturbance emerges out of awareness of the cultural construction of reality, lack of absolutes, uncertainty, and opportunity for playfulness and redrafting the rules. Both ontologically and with the tools at our disposal, we do more than negotiate and accommodate ourselves to a world of fixity and given objects, but embrace indeterminacy. We should however be cautious in our understanding of 'indeterminacy' as although wilful and creative endeavours may point to larger uncharted domains, it is highly churlish to ignore inherited assemblages of ideas that deliver us to situations where we might ask new questions. The idea of the entirely new makes no sense and we should not overly celebrate individual acts or people.

James' pragmatism is refreshing and liberating in underlining that the pretence of finality is over. The real is simply an ongoing draft subject to negotiation and articulation, and in approaching the world, we need not hide away in intellectual and textual domains mournful of never of being able to approach things-in-themselves, but rather get on with living, creating and critiquing within the in-between zone where nature and culture cross and infuse each other. Creativity within this process-based miasma is a transformative act of will and that which we understand as reality is pliable and it is only habit that leads us to think otherwise. This transformative act is imaginative, but not in the symbolic sense of manipulating symbols. Rather, we might follow Dewey's sense of imagination as that which operates at the border of mind and universe, makes new things out of the old and familiar, and occurs when 'varied materials of sense quality, emotion, and meaning come together in a union that marks a new birth in the world' (2005 [1934]: 279). This is to engage with a play of forces, novel event creation, and the laying of potential for the activation of a set of becomings (by means of the event and its singularity, concept, superject or subsequent character for the participant). Put more simply – it is the will or compulsion to affect.

In Whiteheadian (1985 [1929]) terms that which brings about the new is decisive. While deterministic causation should not be overlooked or underprivileged, the final push or reaction in which the many becomes something more than the sum of its parts is a decision freely taken. Put otherwise, self-determination is possible and it is by dint of this that what is new and novel comes to pass. However, while necessarily involving a sense of freedom this blind sense of will and appetite tending towards difference and multiplicity is what Whitehead phrases as a condition of unrest. There is very little to disagree with here, but we might also remember that basic congenital willing force that initiates, instigates, drafts and redrafts and sometimes painfully progresses a project. However, we need not be too serious and from the wide array of investigations in this book play emerges as a key mode of understanding creativity, particularly in relation to link-making, affecting, transgression, irreverence, traversalism, epistemological and ontological indeterminacy, will, and a deep sense of spilling over and being in excess.

Note

1 This is despite the interventionist and political intentions behind Derrida's (1982 [1972]) method. It might be noted too, despite the possibilities of deconstruction as a political tool, Derrida never actually engages in politically motivated deconstructive analysis so to avoid having to take up a position and thus be part of the milieu his subversive analysis seeks to escape.

Bibliography

Adorno, T.W. and Horkheimer, M. (2005 [1944]) *The Culture Industry: Enlightenment as Mass Deception*. London: Verso.

Alexandrian, S. (1995) *Surrealist Art*. London: Thames & Hudson.

Amerika, M. (2009) 'Source Material Everywhere: The Alfred North Whitehead Remix', *Culture Machine*, 10: 157–87.

—— (2011) 'Introduction: What is Creativity?' in M. Amerika (ed.), *Creative Evolution: Natural Selection and the Urge to Remix*, Open Humanities Press, http://livingbooksaboutlife.org/books/Creative_Evolution#A_.27Frozen.27_PDF_Version_of_this_Living_Book, accessed 4 November 2011.

Arden, P. (2003) *It's Not How Good You Are, it's How Good You Want To Be*. London: Phaidon.

—— (2006) *Whatever You Think Think The Opposite*. London: Penguin.

Aristotle (2004 [350 BCE]) *The Poetics*, trans. S.H. Butcher. Whitefish, MT: Kessinger.

Arriaga, P. (1984) 'On Advertising: A Marxist Critique', *Media, Culture and Society*, 6: 53–64.

Artaud, A. (2010 [1938]) *The Theatre and its Double*. New York: Grove Press.

Bachelard, G. (1994 [1958]) *The Poetics of Space*. Boston: Beacon Press Books.

Bakhtin, M. (1984 [1965]) *Rabelais and His World*, trans. H. Iswolsky. Bloomington: Indiana University Press.

—— (1986 [1979]) *Speech Genres & Other Late Essays*, eds C. Emerson and M. Holquist, trans. V.W. McGee. Austin: University of Texas.

Barrett, W. (1949) 'Art, Aristocracy and Reason', *Partisan Review*, 16(6): 663–64.

Barthes, R. (1971) *S/Z*. New York: Hill and Wang.

—— (1972 [1957]) *Mythologies*. London: Paladin.

—— (1981) *Camera Lucida: Reflections on Photography*. New York: Hill and Wang.

Bataille, G. (2007 [1967]) *The Accursed Share: Volume I*. New York: Zone Books.

—— (2007 [1976]) *The Accursed Share: Volumes II and III*. New York: Zone Books.

—— (2008) *Visions of Excess: Selected Writings, 1927–1939*, ed. A. Stoekl. Minneapolis: University of Minnesota Press.

—— (2008 [1930]) 'The Use Value D. A. F. de Sade (An Open Letter to My Current Comrades)' in *Visions of Excess: Selected Writings, 1927–1939*, ed. A. Stoekl. Minneapolis: University of Minnesota Press.

—— (2008 [1932]) 'The Critique of the Foundations of the Hegalian Dialectic' in *Visions of Excess: Selected Writings, 1927–1939*, ed. A. Stoekl. Minneapolis: University of Minnesota Press.

—— (2008 [1936]) 'The Sacred Conspiracy' in *Visions of Excess: Selected Writings, 1927–1939*, ed. A. Stoekl. Minneapolis: University of Minnesota Press.

Bateson, G. (1991) *A Sacred Unity: Further Steps to an Ecology of Mind*. New York: Harper-Collins.

—— (2000 [1972]) *Steps to an Ecology of Mind*. Chicago: University of Chicago.

—— (2002 [1979]) *Mind and Nature: A Necessary Unity*. New Jersey: Hampton Press.

Baudrillard, J. (1988) 'Simulacra and Simulations,' in M. Poster (ed.) *Jean Baudrillard: Selected Writings*. Cambridge: Polity.

—— (1990 [1979]) *Seduction*. Montreal: New World Perspectives.

—— (1996 [1968]) *The System of Objects*. London: Verso.

—— (1998 [1970]) *The Consumer Society*. London: Sage.

Benjamin, W. (1999 [1968]) *Illuminations*. London: Fontana.

Bennett, M., Dennett, D., Hacker, P. and Searle, J. (2007) *Neuroscience and Philosophy: Brain, Mind and Language*. New York: Columbia University Press.

Bennett, M. and Hacker, P. (2007) 'The Introduction to Philosophical Foundations of Neuroscience', in *Neuroscience and Philosophy: Brain, Mind and Language*. New York: Columbia University Press.

Berardi, F. (2009) *The Soul at Work: From Alienation to Autonomy*. Los Angeles, CA: Semiotext(e).

Bergson, H. (1998 [1911]) *Creative Evolution*. New York: Dover.

—— (1999 [1913]) *An Introduction to Metaphysics*. Indianapolis: Hackett.

Berkeley, G. (1988 [1710]) *Principles of Human Knowledge and Three Dialogues Between Hylas and Philonous*. London: Penguin.

Berlin, I. (1997 [1979]) *Against the Current: Essays in the History of Ideas*. London: Pimlico.

—— (2000) *The Roots of Romanticism*. London: Pimlico.

Bey, H. (2003 [1985]) *Temporal Autonomous Zone, Ontological Anarchy, Poetic Terrorism*. New York: Autonomedia.

Bigham, J. (1998) 'Commerce and Communication: Commercial Advertising and the Poster from the 1880s to the Present', in M. Timmers (ed.) *The Power of the Poster*. London: V&A Publications.

Boden, M.A. (2004) *The Creative Mind: Myths and Mechanisms*. London: Routledge.

—— (2010) *Creativity and Art: Three Roads to Surprise*. Oxford: Oxford University Press.

Bogusky, A. and Winsor, J. (2009) *Baked In*. Chicago: B2Books.

Bohm, D. (2004 [1996]) *On Creativity*. Oxon: Routledge.

Boulding, K.E. (1991 [1961]) *The Image: Knowledge in Life and Society*. Ann Arbor: Michigan University Press.

Bourdieu, P. (1984) *Distinction: A Social Critique of the Judgment of Taste*. Cambridge, MA: Harvard University Press.

Bowden, S. (2011) *The Priority of Events: Deleuze's Logic of Sense*. Edinburgh: Edinburgh University Press.

Brecht, B. (1964 [1940]) 'Alienation Effects in Chinese Acting', in *Brecht on Theater*, ed. and trans. J. Willett. New York: Hill and Wang.

B-Reel (2012) *About*, www.b-reel.com/digital/about/, accessed 28 April 2011.

Buchanan, S. (2008) *Onto-Ethnologies*. New York: SUNY.

Bullmore, J. (2003) *More Bull More: Behind the Scenes in Advertising* (Mark III). Henley-on-Thames: Warc.

——— (2006) *Apples, Insights and Mad Inventors*. London: Wiley.

Caillois, R. (2001 [1958]) *Man, Play and Games*. Urbana and Chicago: University of Illinois Press.

Capra, F. (2005) 'Complexity and Life', *Theory, Culture & Society*, 22(5): 33–44.

Cassirer, E. (1966 [1929]) *The Philosophy of Symbolic Forms Volume 3: The Phenomenology of Knowledge*. New Haven, CT: Yale University Press.

Chamovitz, D. (2012) 'Rooted in Sensation', *New Scientist*, 25 August: 35–37.

Clough, P. (2007) *The Affective Turn: Theorizing the Social*. Durham, NC and London: Duke University Press.

Collingwood, R.G. (1979) *Principles of Art*. Oxford: Oxford University Press.

——— (1997 [1938]) 'Art and Craft', in S. Feagin and P. Maynard (eds) *Aesthetics*. Oxford: Oxford University Press.

Cook, G. (1992) *The Discourse of Advertising*. London: Routledge.

Cracknell, A. (2011) *The Real Mad Men*. London: Quercus.

Crary, J. (1992) *Techniques of the Observer: On Vision and Modernity in the Nineteenth Century*. Cambridge, MA: MIT Press.

Creativepool (2012) *Art Director – Job Description, Salaries, Benefits and Useful Links*, http://creativepool.co.uk/articles/jobdescriptions/art-director-job-description, accessed 28 April 2011.

Crogan, P. and Kinsley, S. (2012) 'Paying Attention: Towards a Critique of the Attention Economy', *Culture Machine*, 13(1): 1–29.

Csikszentmihalyi, M. (1997) *Creativity: Flow and the Psychology of Discovery and Invention*. New York: Harper Perennial.

D&AD (2011) *What We Do*, www.dandad.org/dandad/about/what-we-do, accessed 14 March 2011.

——— (2012) *About*, www.dandad.org/dandad/about/what-we-do, accessed 14 August 2012.

——— (2012a) *Judging: An Insight into the Judging Process*, www.dandad.org/awards/professional/2012/judging, accessed 13 March 2012.

Damasio, A. (2003) *Looking for Spinoza: Joy, Sorrow, and the Feeling Brain*. Orlando: Harcourt.

——— (2011) *Self Comes to Mind: Constructing the Conscious Brain*. London: Vintage Books.

Danesi, M. (2003) 'Modeling Systems Theory: A Sebeokian Agenda for Semiotics', *Cybernetics and Human Knowing*, 10(1): 7–24.

Davis, G.A. (1986) *Creativity is Forever*. Iowa: Kendall/Hunt Publishing Company.

DDB (2012) *Bill Bernbach Said ...*, www.ddb.com/pdf/bernbach.pdf, accessed 6 August 2012.

de Bono, E. (1990 [1970]) *Lateral Thinking*. London: Penguin.

——— (2007) *How to Have Creative Ideas*. Chatham: Vermilion.

Deely, J. (2003) 'The Quasi-Error of the External World: An Essay for Thomas A. Sebeok, in memoriam', *Cybernetics and Human Knowing*, 10(1): 7–24.

de Sade, M. (1965 [1795]) *The Marquis de Sade: The Complete Justine, Philosophy in the Bedroom and Other Writings*, trans. R. Seaver and A. Wainhouse. New York: Grove Press.

DeLanda, M. (1991) *War in the Age of Intelligent Machines*. New York: Swerve.

——— (1997) *A Thousand Years of Nonlinear History*. New York: Zone.

——— (2011) *Philosophy and Simulation: The Emergence of Synthetic Reason*. New York: Continuum.

—— (2011 [2002]) *Intensive Science and Virtual Philosophy*. New York: Continuum.

Deleuze, G. (1982 [1972]) *Positions*. Chicago: University of Chicago Press.

—— (1988 [1970]) *Spinoza: Practical Philosophy*. San Francisco: City Lights.

—— (1993 [1988]) *The Fold: Leibniz and the Baroque*. London: Athlone.

—— (2004 [1968]) *Difference and Repetition*. London: Athlone.

—— (2005) *Pure Immanence: Essays on A Life*. Cambridge, MA: MIT Press.

—— (2006 [1966]) *Bergsonism*. New York: Zone Books.

—— (2011 [1969]) *The Logic of Sense*. London: Continuum.

—— (2011 [1981]) *Francis Bacon: The Logic of Sensation*. London: Continuum.

—— (2009 [1983]) *Cinema 1*. London: Continuum.

—— (2012 [1985]) *Cinema 2*. London: Continuum.

Deleuze, G. and Guattari, F. (1986) *Nomadology: The War Machine*. New York: Semiotext(e).

—— (2000 [1972]) *Anti-Oedipus: Capitalism and Schizophrenia*. London: Athlone.

—— (2003 [1980]) *A Thousand Plateaus: Capitalism and Schizophrenia*. London: Continuum.

—— (2011 [1994]) *What is Philosophy?* London: Verso.

Derrida, J. (1982 [1972]) *Positions*. Chicago: University of Chicago.

—— (2001 [1967]) *Writing and Difference*. London: Routledge.

Descartes, R. (2006 [1637]) *A Discourse on the Method*, trans. I. Maclean. Oxford: Oxford University Press.

——(2008 [1644]) *Principles of Philosophy*. Radford, VA: Wilder.

Dewey, J. (1995 [1908]) 'Does Reality Possess Practical Character', in R.B. Goodman (ed.) *Pragmatism: A Contemporary Reader*. New York: Routledge.

—— (2005 [1934]) *Art as Experience*. New York: Perigee Books.

Draycott, R. (2012) '"Marketing is Dead" says Saatchi & Saatchi CEO', *The Drum*, www.thedrum.co.uk/news/2012/04/25/marketing-dead-says-saatchi-saatchi-ceo.

Dunker, K. (1945) 'On Problem Solving', *Psychological Monographs*, 58(5): Whole No. 270.

Du Plessis, E. (2011) *The Branded Mind*. London: Kogan Press.

Dyer, G. (1993 [1982]) *Advertising as Communication*. London: Routledge.

Eddington, A.S. (1928) *The Nature of the Physical World*. New York: MacMillan.

Eliot, T.S. (1999 [1920]) *The Sacred Wood: Essays on Poetry and Criticism*. London: Bartleby.

Emerson, R.W. (1995 [1841]) 'Circles', in R.B. Goodman (ed.) *Pragmatism: A Contemporary Reader*. New York: Routledge.

Ewen, S. (2001 [1977]) *Captains of Consciousness: Advertising and the Social Roots of the Consumer Culture*. New York: Basic Books.

Fichte, J. (1982 [1810]) *The Science of Knowledge*. Cambridge: Cambridge University Press.

—— (1987 [1800]) *The Vocation of Man*, trans. P. Preuss. Indianapolis: Hackett.

Fisher, M. (2009) *Capitalist Realism*. Ropley, Hampshire: Zero Books.

Fiske, J. (1986) 'MTV: Post Structural Post Modern', *Journal of Communication Inquiry*, 10(1): 74–79.

—— (1987) *Television Culture*. London: Routledge.

Fromm, E. (2002 [1956]) *The Sane Society*. Oxon: Routledge.

Fuchs, C. (2011) 'Web 2.0, Prosumption, and Surveillance', *Surveillance & Society*, 8(3): 288–309.

Fuller, M. (2005) *Media Ecologies*. Cambridge, MA: MIT Press.

Galton, F. (1869) *Hereditary Genius*. London: Macmillan.

Games, N. (2008) *Poster Journeys: Abram Games and London Transport*. London: Capital Transport.

Gamman, L. and Raein, M. (2010) 'Reviewing the Art of Crime: What, If Anything, Do Criminals and Artists/Designers Have in Common', in D.H. Cropley, A.J. Cropley, J.C. Kaufman and M.A. Runco (eds) *The Dark Side of Creativity*. New York: Cambridge University Press, 155–76.

Gardner, H. (1997) 'The Key in the Key Slot: Creativity in a Chinese Key', *Journal of Cognitive Education*, 6(1): 15–36.

Gauntlett, D. (2011) *Making is Connecting: The Social Meaning of Creativity, from DIY and Knitting to YouTube and Web 2.0*. Cambridge: Polity Press.

Getzels, J.W. and Jackson, P.W. (1962) *Creativity and Intelligence: Explorations with Gifted Students*. New York: Wiley.

Gibbons, J. (2005) *Art and Advertising*. London: I.B.Tauris.

Gibson, J.J. (1977) 'The Theory of Affordances', in R.E. Shaw and J. Bransford (eds) *Perceiving, Acting, and Knowing: Toward an Ecological Psychology*. Hillsdale, NJ: Lawrence Erlbaum Associates, 67–82.

—— (1979) *The Ecological Approach to Visual Perception*. Hillsdale, NJ: Lawrence Erlbaum Associates.

Glaser, E. (2009) 'Touching up the Grassroots', *The Guardian*, www.guardian.co.uk/commentisfree/2009/jun/24/astroturfing-advertising-twitter-politics, accessed 25 June 2009.

Goddard, A. (2003) *The Language of Advertising*. London: Routledge.

Goddard, M. (2011) 'Towards an Archaeology of Media Ecologies: "Media Ecology", Political Subjectivation and Free Radios', *Fibreculture*, 17: 6–17.

Goldman, R. (1992) *Reading Ads Socially*. London: Routledge.

Goldman, R. and Papson, S. (1996) *Sign Wars: The Cluttered Landscape of Advertising*. New York: Guildford.

Goux, J-J. (1998) 'General Economics and Postmodern Capitalism' in *Bataille: A Critical Reader*. Oxford: Blackwell, 196–213.

Gregg, M. and Seigworth, G.J. (eds) (2010) *The Affect Theory Reader*. Durham, NC and London: Duke University Press.

Gross, M. and Yi-Luen Do, E. (2009) 'Educating the New Makers: Cross-Disciplinary Creativity', *Leonardo*, 42(3): 210–15.

Grossberg, L. (2010) 'Affect's Future' in M. Gregg and G.J Seigworth (eds) *The Affect Theory Reader*. Durham, NC and London: Duke University Press.

Grosz, E. (2008) *Chaos, Territory, Art: Deleuze and the Framing of the Earth*. New York: Columbia University Press.

Guattari, F. (1992) *Chaosmosis: An Ethico-Aesthetic Paradigm*. Bloomington and Indianapolis: Indiana University Press.

—— (2000) *The Three Ecologies*, trans. Ian Pindar and Paul Sutton. London: Continuum.

Gulas, C.S. and Weinberger, M.G. (2006) *Humor in Advertising: A Comprehensive Analysis*. New York: M.E. Sharpe.

Habermas, J. (1988) *On the Logic of the Social Sciences*, trans. S. Nicholsen and J. Stark. Cambridge, MA: MIT Press.

Hamann, J.G. (2009 [1784]) 'Metacritique on the Purism of Reason', in *Hamann: Writings on Philosophy and Language*, ed. and trans. K. Haynes. New York: Cambridge University Press.

—— (2009 [1786]) 'Disrobing and Transfiguration: A Flying Letter to Nobody, the Well Known', in *Hamann: Writings on Philosophy and Language*, ed. and trans. K. Haynes. New York: Cambridge University Press.

Hardt, M. and Negri, A. (2000) *Empire*. Cambridge, MA: Harvard University Press.

Harries-Jones, P. (2010) 'Bioentropy, Aesthetics and Meta-dualism: The Transdisciplinary Ecology of Gregory Bateson', *Entropy*, 12(12): 2359–85.

Hegarty, J. (1998) 'Selling the Product', in M. Timmers (ed.) *The Power of the Poster*. London: V&A Publications.

—— (2011) *Hegarty on Advertising: Turning Intelligence into Magic*. London: Thames & Hudson.

Heidegger, M. (1993 [1954]) 'The Question Concerning Technology', in *Basic Writings*, ed. D.F. Krell. New York: HarperCollins.

—— (2011 [1962]) *Being and Time*, trans. J. Macquarrie and E. Robinson. New York: Harper & Row.

Herder, J.G. (2002 [1765]) 'How Philosophy Can Become More Universal', in *Philosophical Writings*, ed. M.N. Forster. Cambridge: Cambridge University Press.

—— (2002 [1767–68]) 'Treatise on the Origin of Language' in *Philosophical Writings*, ed. M.N. Forster. Cambridge: Cambridge University Press.

—— (2002 [1774]) 'This Too a Philosophy of History for the Formation of Humanity [an early introduction]' in *Philosophical Writings*, ed. M.N. Forster. Cambridge: Cambridge University Press.

Hesmondhalgh, D. (2006) *The Cultural Industries*. London: Sage.

Hoffman, P. (2000) 'Heidegger and the Problem of Idealism', *Inquiry*, 43(1): 403–11.

Honnef, K. (2000) *Warhol*. Cologne: Taschen.

Hopkins, C. (1998 [1923/1927]) *My Life in Advertising & Scientific Advertising*. Chicago: NTC Business Books.

Hudson, L. (1966) *Contrary Imaginations*. London: Methuen.

Huizinga, J. (1955 [1938]) *Homo Ludens*. Boston: Beacon.

Husserl, E. (1970 [1936]) *The Crisis of European Sciences and Transcendental Philosophy*, trans. D. Carr. Evanston: Northwestern University Press.

IPA (2011) *UK and International Awards Ceremonies*, www.ipa.co.uk/Content/UK-and-International-Awards-Ceremonies, accessed 1 December 2011.

Jaeger, W. (1986 [1944]) *Paideia: The Ideals of Greek Culture, Vol III: The Conflict of Cultural Ideals in the Age of Plato*. New York: Oxford University Press.

James, W. (1897) *The Will to Believe and Other Essays in Popular Philosophy*. New York: Longmans Green and Co.

—— (2000 [1907]) *Pragmatism and Other Writings*, ed. G. Gunn. New York: Penguin.

—— (2003 [1912]) *Essays in Radical Empiricism*. New York: Dover.

—— (2011 [1909]) *A Pluralistic Universe*. Amazon: CreateSpace.

Jameson, F. (1991) *Postmodernism or The Cultural Logic of Late Capitalism*. London: Verso.

Jamieson, V. (2012) 'The Bedrock of it All', *New Scientist*, 29 September: 36.

Jarmusch, J. (2004) 'Jim Jarmusch's Golden Rules', *Moviemaker*, www.moviemaker.com/directing/article/jim_jarmusch_2972/, accessed 21 October 2010.

Jhally, S. (1990) *The Codes of Advertising: Fetishism and the Political Economy of Meaning in the Consumer Society*. New York: Routledge.

—— (2006) *Advertising at the Edge of the Apocalypse*, www.sutjhally.com/articles/advertisingattheed/, accessed 21 August 2012.

Jones, J. (1998) *Intensity: An Essay on Whiteheadian Ontology*. Nashville: Vanderbilt University Press.

Jones, J.P. (2004) *Fables, Fashions, and Facts About Advertising: A Study of 28 Enduring Myths*. Thousand Oaks, CA: Sage.

Kant, I. (1952 [1790]) *The Critique of Judgement*, trans. J.C. Meredith. Oxford: Oxford University Press.

—— (1990 [1781]) *The Critique of Pure Reason*, trans. N.K. Smith. London: Macmillan.

Kauffman, S. (1995) *At Home in the Universe*. New York: Oxford University Press.

Kaufman, J. and Sternberg, R. (eds) (2010) *The Cambridge Handbook of Creativity*. New York: Cambridge University Press.

Kaufman, J.C. (2002) 'Dissecting the Golden Goose: Components of Studying Creative Writers', *Creativity Research Journal*, 14(1): 27–40.

Kennedy, B. (2004) *Deleuze and Cinema: The Aesthetics of Sensation*. Edinburgh: Edinburgh University Press.

Kember, S. and Zylinska, J. (2012) *Life after New Media*. Cambridge, MA: MIT Press.

Koestler, A. (1970 [1964]) *The Act of Creation*. London: Pan Piper.

Kuhns, W. (1973) *The Postindustrial Prophets*. New York: Harper Colophon.

Lasn, K. (1999) *Culture Jam: The Uncooling of America*. New York: Eagle Brook.

Latour, B. (1993) *We Have Never Been Modern*. Harlow: Harvester Wheatsheaf.

Lau, S., Hui, A.N.N. and Ng, G.Y.C. (2004) *Creativity: When East Meets West*. Singapore: World Scientific Publishing.

Lévi-Strauss, C. (1974 [1962]) *The Savage Mind*. London: Weidenfeld & Nicolson.

Lindstrom, M. (2005) *Brand Sense: Sensory Secrets Behind The Stuff We Buy*. London: Kogan Page.

—— (2009) *Buy-ology: How Everything We Believe About Why We Buy Is Wrong*. London: Kogan Page.

—— (2011) *Brandwashed: Tricks Companies Use To Manipulate Our Minds And Persuade Us To Buy*. London: Kogan Page.

Lovink, G. and Rossiter, N. (eds) (2007) *MyCreativity Reader: A Critique of Creative Industries*, www.networkcultures.org/_uploads/32.pdf, accessed 4 October 2012.

Lowes, L. (1951 [1927]) *The Road to Xanadu: A Study in the Ways of the Imagination*. London: Constable.

Lubart, T.I. and Georgsdottir, A. (2004) 'Creativity: Development and Cross-Cultural Issues', in S. Lau, A.N.N. Hui and G.Y.C. Ng (eds) *Creativity: When East Meets West*. Singapore: World Scientific Publishing.

Lukács, G. (1971 [1923]) *History and Class Consciousness: Studies in Marxist Dialectics*, trans. R. Livingstone. London: Merlin Press.

Lürzer's Archive (2012) *This Week*, www.luerzersarchive.com/content/show/id/54746, accessed 1 November 2012.

Lyotard, F. (1984) *Driftworks*. New York: Semiotext(e).

Mach, E. (1976) *Knowledge and Error*. Dordrecht: D. Reidel.

Mackenzie, A. (2002) *Transductions: Bodies and Machines at Speed*. New York: Continuum.

MacRury, I. (2012) *Advertising*. Oxon: Routledge.

Malefyt, T. de (2003) 'Models, Metaphors and Client Relations: the Negotiated Meanings of Advertising' in T. de. Malefyt and B. Moeran (eds) *Advertising Cultures*. Oxford: Berg, 139–63.

Malefyt, T. de and Moeran, B. (2003) *Advertising Cultures*. Oxford: Berg.

Manning, E. (2012) *Relationscapes*. Cambridge, MA: MIT Press.

Marcuse, H. (1964) *One-Dimensional Man*. Boston: Beacon Press.

Marx, K. (1973 [1939]) *The Grundrisse: Foundations of the Critique of Political Economy*. New York: Vintage Books.

Massumi, B. (2002) *Parables for the Virtual: Movement, Affect, Sensation*. Durham, NC and London: Duke University Press.

—— (2011) *Semblance and Event*. Cambridge, MA: MIT Press.

Mazzarella, W. (2006) *Shovelling Smoke: Advertising and Globalization in Contemporary India*. Durham, NC and London: Duke University Press.

McCracken, G. (2009) *Chief Culture Officer*. New York: Basic Books.

McFall, L. (2004) *Advertising: A Cultural Economy*. London: Sage.

McLuhan, M. (2001 [1964]) *Understanding Media*. London: Routledge.

—— (2003) *Understanding Media: Lectures and Interviews*, eds S. McLuhan and D. Staines. Cambridge, MA: MIT Press.

McStay, A. (2007) 'Regulating the Suicide Bomber: A Critical Examination of Viral Advertising and Simulations of Self-Broadcasting', *Ethical Space: Journal of Communication*, 4(1/2): 40–48.

—— (2009) *Digital Advertising*. London: Palgrave Macmillan.

—— (2010) 'Understanding Audience's Perceptions of Creativity in Online Advertising: The Benefits of a Qualitative Approach', *The Qualitative Report*, 15(1): 37–58.

—— (2011) *The Mood of Information: A Critique of Online Behavioural Advertising*. New York: Continuum.

—— (2011a) 'Profiling Phorm: An Autopoietic Approach to the Audience-as-Commodity', *Surveillance and Society*, 8(3): 310–22.

—— (2012) 'I Consent: An Analysis of the Cookie Directive and its Implications for UK Behavioural Advertising', *New Media and Society*, http://nms.sagepub.com/content/early/2012/09/24/1461444812458434, accessed 4 November 2012.

Merleau-Ponty, M. (1964) *The Primacy of Perception: And Other Essays on Phenomenological Psychology, the Philosophy of Art, History and Politics*, ed. J.M. Edie. Evanston, IL: Northwestern University Press.

—— (2002 [1945]) *Phenomenology of Perception*. London: Routledge.

Miller, D. (2003) 'Advertising, Production and Consumption as Cultural Economy' in T. de Malefyt and B. Moeran (eds) *Advertising Cultures*. Oxford: Berg, 75–89.

Mort, F. (1996) *Cultures of Consumption*. London: Routledge.

Mumford, L. (1952) *Art and Technics*. New York: Columbia University Press.

—— (1961 [1934]) *Technics and Civilization*. New York: Harcourt, Brace & Co.

Negus, K. and Pickering, M. (2004) *Creativity, Communication and Cultural Value*. London: Sage.

Newton, C. (1998) 'Epilogue', in M. Timmers (ed.) *The Power of the Poster*. London: V&A Publications, 232–42.

Nietzsche, F. (1967 [1886]) *The Birth of Tragedy and the Case of Wagner*, trans. W. Kauffman. New York: Random House.

—— (2000 [1873]) 'On Truth and Lie in an Extra-Moral Sense', in C. Cazeaux (ed.) *The Continental Aesthetics Reader*. London: Routledge.

—— (2003 [1886]) *Beyond Good and Evil*, trans. H. Zimmern. New York: Dover.

Nixon, S. (2003) *Advertising Cultures*. London: Sage.

Norman, D.A. (2002 [1988]) *The Design of Everyday Things*. New York: Basic Books.

Ogilvy, D. (1985) *Ogilvy on Advertising*. New York: Random House.

—— (2004 [1963]) *Confessions of an Advertising Man*. London: Southbank.

Ong, W.J. (2002) 'Ecology and Some of its Future', *Explorations in Media Ecology*, 1(1): 5–11.

Page, G. (2011) 'Increasing our Brainpower – Using Neuroscience Effectively', in E. Du Plessis (ed.), *The Branded Mind*. London: Kogan Press.

Pareto, V. (1935) *The Mind and Society*. New York: Harcourt, Brace & Co.

Parikka, J. (2011) 'Media Ecologies and Imaginary Media: Transversal Expansions, Contractions, and Foldings', *Fibreculture*, 17: 34–50.

—— (2011a) 'Introduction: The Materiality of Media and Waste' in J. Parikka (ed.) *Medianatures: The Materiality of Information Technology and Electronic Waste*. Open Humanities Press, www.livingbooksaboutlife.org/books/Medianatures, accessed 4 November 2011.

Petrilli, S. (2003) 'Sebeok's Semiosic Universe and Global Semiotics', *Cybernetics and Human Knowing*, 10(1): 7–24.

Petrilli, S. and Ponzio, A. (2001) *Thomas Sebeok and the Signs of Life*. Cambridge: Icon Books.

Plato (1988 [360 BCE]) *The Laws of Plato*, trans. T.L. Pangle. Chicago: University of Chicago Press.

Poe, E.A. (1997 [1846]) 'The Philosophy of Composition', in S. Feagin and P. Maynard (eds) *Aesthetics*. Oxford: Oxford University Press.

Pope, R. (2005) *Creativity: Theory, History, Practice*. London: Routledge.

Poster, M. (1995) *The Second Media Age*. Cambridge, MA: Polity Press.

Postman, N. (2000) 'The Humanism of Media Ecology', *Proceedings of the Media Ecology Association*, 1: 10–16, www.media-ecology.org/publications/MEA_proceedings/v1/humanism_of_media_ecology.html, accessed 12 June 2011.

Pricken, M. (2002) *Creative Advertising*. London: Thames & Hudson.

Prigogine, I. and Stengers, I. (1984) *Order Out of Chaos: Man's New Dialogue with Nature*. New York: Bantam Books.

Rancière, J. (2009 [2004]) *The Politics of Aesthetics*. London: Continuum.

Ritterfeld, U., Cody, M. and Vorderer, P. (2009) *Serious Gamers: Mechanisms and Effects*. New York: Routledge.

Ritzer, G. and Jurgenson, N. (2010) 'Production, Consumption, Prosumption', *Journal of Consumer Culture*, 10(1): 13–36.

Rorty, R. (1979) *Philosophy and the Mirror of Nature*. New Jersey: Princeton University Press.

—— (1989) *Contingency, Irony and Solidarity*. Cambridge: Cambridge University Press.

—— (2010 [1980]) 'Pragmatism, Relativism, and Irrationalism', in C.J. Voparil and R.J. Bernstein (eds) *The Rorty Reader*. Chichester: Wiley-Blackwell, 122–37.

—— (2010 [1981]) 'Nineteenth-Century Idealism and Twentieth-Century Textualism', in C.J. Voparil and R.J. Bernstein (eds) *The Rorty Reader*. Chichester: Wiley-Blackwell, 111–21.

—— (2010 [1986]) 'Freud and Moral Reflection', in C.J. Voparil and R.J. Bernstein (eds) *The Rorty Reader*. Chichester: Wiley-Blackwell, 259–78.

—— (2010 [1993]) 'Human Rights, Rationality, and Sentimentality', in C.J. Voparil and R.J. Bernstein (eds) *The Rorty Reader*. Chichester: Wiley-Blackwell, 351–65.

Rudowicz, E. (2004) 'Beyond Western Perspective' in S. Lau, A.N.N. Hui and G.Y.C. Ng (eds) *Creativity: When East Meets West*. Singapore: World Scientific Publishing.

Runco, M. (2006) *Creativity: Theories and Themes: Research, Development, and Practice*. London: Elsevier Academic Press.

—— (2010) 'Creativity Has No Dark Side', in D.H. Cropley, A.J. Cropley, J.C. Kaufman and M.A. Runco (eds) *The Dark Side of Creativity*. New York: Cambridge University Press, 15–32.

Runco, M.A. and Albert, R. S. (2010) 'Creativity Research: A Historical View', in J.C. Kaufman and R.J. Sternberg (eds) *The Cambridge Handbook of Creativity*. Cambridge: Cambridge University Press, 3–19.

Salsi, C. (2007) *Advertising & Art: International Graphics from the Affiche to Pop Art*, ed. C. Salsi. Milano: Skira.

Saussure, F. (1959 [1916]) *Course in General Linguistics*, trans. W. Baskin. New York: Columbia University Press.

Sawyer, R.K. (2010) *Group Creativity: Music, Theater, Collaboration*. London: Routledge.

Schapiro, M. (1994) *Theory and Philosophy of Art: Style, Artist, and Society* (Selected Paper). New York: George Braziller.

Schelling, F.W.J. (2001 [1800]) *System of Transcendental Idealism*, trans. M. Vater. Charlottesville: University of Virginia Press.

Schiller, F. (2004 [1795]) *On the Aesthetic Education of Man*, trans. R. Snell. New York: Dover.

Schopenhauer, A. (1966 [1918]) *The World As Will and Representation*, trans. E.F.J. Payne. New York: Dover.

Searle, J.R. (1996) *The Construction of Social Reality*. London: Penguin.

—— (1997) *The Mystery of Consciousness*. London: Granta Books.

—— (2007) 'Putting Consciousness Back in the Brain: Reply to Bennett and Hacker, *Philosophical Foundations of Neuroscience*', in M. Bennett, D. Dennett, P. Hacker and J. Searle, *Neuroscience and Philosophy: Brain, Mind and Language*. New York: Columbia University Press, 97–126.

Sebeok, T.A. (1981) *The Play of Musement*. Bloomington: Indiana University Press.

—— (1986) *I Think I Am a Verb: More Contributions to the Doctrine of Signs*. New York: Plenum Press

—— (1991) *American Signatures: Semiotic Inquiry and Method*. Norman: University of Oklahoma Press.

—— (2001) *Global Semiotics*. Bloomington: Indiana University Press.

Sebeok, T.A. and Danesi, M. (2000) *The Forms of Meanings. Modeling Systems Theory and Semiotic Analysis*. Berlin: Mouton de Gruyter.

Sedgwick, E.K. and Frank, A. (1995) *Shame in the Cybernetic Fold. In Shame and its Sisters: A Silvan Tomkins Reader*, eds E.K. Sedgwick and A. Frank. Durham, NC: Duke University Press.

Shapiro, S. (2012) *Without Criteria*. Cambridge, MA: MIT Press.

Shklovsky, V. (1917) 'Art as Technique', in *Russian Formalist Criticism: Four Essays*, trans L.T. Lemon and M.J. Reis. Lincoln: University of Nebraska Press.

Simon, J.L. and Arndt, J. (1980) 'The Shape of the Advertising Response Function', *Journal of Advertising Research*, 20(4): 11–28.

Spinoza, B. (1996 [1677]) *Ethics*. London: Penguin.

Steinberg, B. (2012) 'Study: Young Consumers Switch Media 27 Times An Hour', *Advertising Age*, http://adage.com/article/news/study-young-consumers-switch-media-27-times-hour/234008/, accessed 9 April 2012.

Steinitz, Y. (1994) *Invitation to Philosophy: Imagined Dialogues with Great Philosophers*. Indianapolis: Hackett.

Stengers, I. (2008) 'A Constructivist Reading of Process and Reality', *Theory, Culture & Society*, 25(4): 91–110.

—— (2011) *Thinking with Whitehead: A Free and Wild Creation of Concepts.* Cambridge, MA: Harvard University Press.

Sternberg, R.J. (2010) 'The Dark Side of Creativity and How to Combat It', in D.H. Cropley, A.J. Cropley, J.C. Kaufman and M.A. Runco (eds) *The Dark Side of Creativity*. New York: Cambridge University Press, 316–28.

Strate, L. (2004) 'A Media Ecology Review', *Communication Research Trends*, 23(2): 1–48.

Suarez-Villa, L. (2009) *Technocapitalism*. Philadelphia: Temple University Press.

Thorson, E. (1999) 'Emotion and Advertising', in J.P. Jones (ed.) *The Advertising Business: Operations. Creativity, Media Planning, Integrated Communications.* Thousand Oaks, CA: Sage.

Trott, D. (2009) *Creative Mischief*. London: Loaf.

Tungate, M. (2007) *Adland: A Global History of Advertising*. London: Kogan Page.

Uexküll, J.v. (2010 [1934]) *A Foray into the Worlds of Animals and Humans*, trans. J.D. O'Neil. Minneapolis: University of Minnesota Press.

Vernon, P.E. (1970) *Creativity*. Middlesex: Penguin.

Vestergaard, T. and Schroder, K. (1985) *The Language of Advertising*. Oxford: Basil Blackwell.

Vico, G. (2001 [1725]) *The New Science of Giambattista Vico*, trans. D. Marsh. London: Penguin Books.

Wallas, G. (1926) *The Art of Thought*. London: Jonathan Cape.

Weisberg, R.W. (1993) *Creativity: Beyond the Myth of Genius*. New York: Freeman.

Wheeler, W. (2011) 'Introduction' in W. Wheeler (ed.) *Biosemiotics: Nature/Culture/Science/Semiosis*. Open Humanities Press, www.livingbooksaboutlife.org/books/Biosemiotics, accessed 4 November 2011.

Whitehead, A.N. (1928) *Symbolism: Its Meaning and Effect*. Cambridge: Cambridge University Press.

—— (1948 [1933]) *Adventures of Ideas*. New York: Free Press

—— (1964 [1920]) *The Concept of Nature*. Cambridge: Cambridge University Press.

—— (1968 [1938]) *Modes of Thought*. New York: Free Press.

—— (1985 [1929]) *Process and Reality: Corrected Edition*. New York: Free Press.

—— (1997 [1925]) *Science and the Modern World*. New York: Free Press.

Willett, J. (ed. and trans.) (1964) *Brecht on Theatre*. New York: Hill and Wang.

Williams, R. (1976) *Keywords: A Vocabulary of Culture and Society*. New York: Oxford University Press.

—— (1977) *Marxism and Literature*. Oxford: Oxford University Press.

Williams, T. (ed.) (2003) *The Cambridge Companion to Duns Scotus*. Cambridge: Cambridge University Press.

Williamson, J. (1978) *Decoding Advertisements: Ideology and Meaning in Advertising*. London: Boyars.

Wilson, R.C., Guilford, J.P., Christensen, P.R. and Lewis, D.J. (1954) 'A Factor-Analytic Study of Creative-Thinking Abilities', *Psychometrika*, 19: 297–311.

Wissinger, E. (2007) 'Always on Display' in P. Clough (ed.) *The Affective Turn: Theorizing the Social*. Durham, NC and London: Duke University Press.

Wittgenstein, L. (1953) *Philosophical Investigations*. Oxford: Blackwell.

—— (2010 [1921]) *Tractatus Logico-Philosophicus*. Milton Keynes: Lightning Source.

Wordsworth, W. (1798) *Lyrical Ballads with A Few Other Poems*. London: A. Arch, Gracechurch-Street.

Yeshin, T. (2005) *Advertising*. London: Thomson Learning.

Y&R (2012) *Who Are We?* www.yr.com/content/who-we-are.html, accessed 13 March 2011.

Young, J.W. (2003 [1965]) *A Technique for Producing Ideas*. New York: McGraw Hill.

Zimmerman, M.E. (1990) *Heidegger's Confrontation with Modernity: Technology, Politics, Art*. Bloomington and Indianapolis: Indiana University Press.

Žižek, S. (2004) *Organs without Bodies*. New York: Routledge.

Index

Page numbers followed by an *n* indicate notes.

www.routledge.com/media

Related titles from Routledge

The Advertising Handbook

3rd Edition

Edited by **Helen Powell**,
Jonathan Hardy,
Sarah Hawkin and
Iain MacRury

The Advertising Handbook is a critical introduction to the practices and perspectives of advertising. It explores the industry and those who work in it and examines the reasons why companies and organizations advertise; how they research their markets; where they advertise and in which media; the principles and techniques of persuasion and their effectiveness; and how companies measure their success. It challenges conventional wisdom about advertising power and authority to offer a realistic assessment of its role in business and also looks at the industry's future.

This third edition offers new material and a new organising framework, whilst continuing to provide both an introduction and an authoritative guide to advertising theory and practice. It is shaped to meet the requirements, interests and terms of reference of the most recent generation of media and advertising students – as well as taking account of some of the most recent academic work in the field, and, of course, contemporary advertising innovations.

Paperback: 978-0-415-42311-3

Hardback: 978-0-415-42312-0

For more information and to order a copy visit
www.routledge.com/9780415423113

Available from all good bookshops

DATE DUE	RETURNED